Why the Civil War Came

Edited by
GABOR S. BORITT

Essays by

DAVID W. BLIGHT
GABOR S. BORITT
WILLIAM W. FREEHLING
WILLIAM E. GIENAPP
GLENNA MATTHEWS
CHARLES ROYSTER
MARK WAHLGREN SUMMERS

New York Oxford *Oxford University Press*

Oxford University Press

Oxford   New York

Athens   Auckland   Bangkok   Bogota   Bombay   Buenos Aires
Calcutta   Cape Town   Dar es Salaam   Delhi   Florence   Hong Kong
Istanbul   Karachi   Kuala Lumpur   Madras   Madrid   Melbourne
Mexico City   Nairobi   Paris   Singapore   Taipei   Tokyo   Toronto

and associated companies in
Berlin   Ibadan

First published by Oxford University Press, Inc., 1996
First issued as an Oxford University Press paperback, 1997
Oxford is a registered trademark of Oxford University Press

Library of Congress Cataloging-in-Publication Data
Why the Civil War came / edited by Gabor S. Boritt:
essays by David W. Blight . . . [et al.].
p.   cm. Includes bibliographical references.

ISBN 978-0-19-511376-1

1. United States—History—Civil War, 1861–1865—Causes.
I. Boritt, G. S., 1940–   II. Blight, David W.
E459.W48   1996
973.7'11–dc20   95–9474

Printed in the United States of America

FOR MY SONS
NORSE, JAKE, AND DANIEL

By late June it is usually warm,
even hot in Gettysburg.
In the night at our farm,
the fireflies glow in the dark,
fleeting specks illuminating the woods and
turning Marsh Creek into a pageant.
In the daytime along the side of the road,
orange tiger lilies proclaim their eternal message.
My heart overflows;
it is time to see old friends again,
time to make new ones.
It is the time for
the Gettysburg Civil War Institute.

Gabor S. Boritt

Acknowledgments

As year follows year and the Oxford-Gettysburg Civil War volumes grow into a shelf of books, my expressions of gratitude—like a prayer—change not.

It was a pleasure to work with the historians who came to Gettysburg to mingle with and speak to the fine people who attend the Civil War Institute sessions in the summer. I looked for outstanding scholars, and that three of them—William W. Freehling, William E. Gienapp, and Mark W. Summers—turned out to have been chiefly mentored by Kenneth M. Stampp, and a fourth—Charles Royster—had also studied with him, speaks eloquently about the kind of disciples he had attracted over the years and the kind of training he had provided. His students, and others in this book, busy historians all, took their assignments to heart. Their audience, too, young and old, played its part well, with enthusiasm and hard questioning, and so helped create this book.

The CWI staff, Tina Fair, Linda Marshall, and Marti Shaw, continue to create a hard-working, happy place. The carefully selected student assistants at our session where we grappled with the sad and difficult issue of "Why the Civil War Came" included Seamus Clune, Christina Ericson, Jennifer Haase, Richard Hoffman, Jennifer Horner, Robert Sandow, Patricia Taylor, and two of my sons, Jake and Dan Boritt. The skillful and conscientious William Hanna, Ph.D., led our fine group of scholarship students.

Susan Fiedler, able summer intern, checked the accuracy of the printed quotations in the chapters that follow. Another fine student, Deborah R. Huso, my research assistant, performed excellently more chores than I dare list. Professor Michael Perman generously shared before publication the introduction of his book of readings *The Coming of the American Civil War* (D. C. Heath, 1993).

Marti Shaw, my cheerful, competent secretary, saw the manuscript of this book through its many versions. At Oxford, the pleasure of working with Sheldon Meyer continued as ever. Stephanie Sakson served as a good copy editor.

Most important, my family. Liz, my wife, was always there with love. Norse, our oldest, created the dedication page design—an awkward assignment this time. To him, his brothers Jake and Daniel, and by extension to young people always and everywhere, the book is dedicated. May they know not war.

Farm by the Ford   G. S. B.
Gettysburg
Spring 1995

Contents

Introduction

THE BOOM of the guns took on their own rhythm. "Load," came the command again. The number one man of the artillery crew, anonymous as most soldiers ever remain, quickly swabbed the barbette gun to get it ready for the next shot. Another soldier, whose name lives in history, private Daniel Hough, number two of the crew, picked up the cartridge to place it in the muzzle of the gun. Burnt and broken battle refuse trimmed the parapet. All eyes—elated and bitter, Southern and Northern—focused on the guns. Hough inserted the cartridge. In a split second, before the commands "ready" and "fire" could begin to be uttered, the explosion came. It took off Hough's right arm. Within moments he was dead. Probably the number one man had failed to sponge the gun sufficiently, leaving a flame in the barrel. The premature burst followed and with it the first casualty of what would become the American Civil War. Some one and a half million came after.[1]

Fort Sumter, April 14, 1861. The Union's farewell salute that Hough's death interrupted had to be cut short, though the private received his burial with honors on the Sumter parade. Why this moment of history came is surely one of the most important questions students can ask about the Civil War and (together with the examination of the results the war wrought) the most important moral question.

IT WAS ASKED from the first. Participants in the war and the generation after spoke partisan and, with rare exceptions, blamed the other side. Like their publics, historical writers saw "us and them." "We," whether Northern or Southern, were the good guys; "they" caused the war. "They" tended to be evil fire-eaters or abolitionists. "We" either defended freedom against the Slave Power, or states' rights against Northern aggression.

A new generation and a new century brought both detachment and professionalism. Individuals as makers of war came to be eclipsed by the large impersonal forces of history. War seemed the logical, perhaps inescapable result of conflicting economic interests, cultural systems, or social institution.

Then, America went to war again in a large way in 1917, in the words of historian-politician Woodrow Wilson, to make the world "safe for democracy."[2] What Americans got was Stalin, Hitler, Mussolini, Tojo, lesser monsters of the same ilk, and the Great Depression. Disillusion set in. Among historians of the Civil War, the disillusioned were called "Revisionists." Slavery had reached its natural limits by 1860, some of them claimed, and so a war over it was needless. Yet war came because extremists on both sides triumphed over the majority of more sensible but incompetent politicians. The individual returned to play a large role, all too large a role, in the coming of the war, albeit he turned out to be a blunderer.

Then Americans fought an even greater war, the Second World War, and few were left with doubts about its justice. In its wake the civil rights movement came to the fore. Among historians of the Civil War, "Revisionism" died. The fundamental forces and structures of history eclipsed to insignificance human agency. The justice of fighting a war that led to freedom for black people grew so self-evident that agony about the war's coming lost its gravity.

Topics also exhaust themselves. In part because in the 1940s and 1950s "Civil War causation was the most intensively discussed problem in American historiography," to quote Don E. Fehrenbacher,[3] from the 1960s it has ceased to be a burning issue. The results of the war, specifically the role black people played in American society, came to be intimately tied to our contemporary problems and captured a large share of the professional historians' attention. Reconstruction studies flowered.

Other factors entered, too. We have grown so morally anesthetized by the horrors of the twentieth century–and our ever more ready visual access to them–from world war to world war, from gas chamber to masses of bodies floating down the rivers of Africa and a thousand other places, that the horrors of the American Civil War grew muted. Perhaps for this reason, too, "why the war came" grew to be a less compelling question. And as the moral bearings of the culture changed for good and for ill, dwindled toward less certainty, the "moralizing" of earlier generations often appeared quaint.

The historians in this book are the children of their own times, too. Like previous students, they, too, bring their individual outlooks to bear on the past. Readers may sense the influence of the Vietnam War, Watergate, the civil rights movement, the women's movement, the conservatism of the Reagan years and the present moment, multiculturalism, the fall of the Soviet Union, and more. But delineating with any reasonable certainty the cultural influences on the scholars of our time is a task for the future.

CHAPTER ONE tries to put morality and the question of individual responsibility back into the center stage of history. It follows one man's road to war, raises questions rather than offers solution. Professional historians today like to explain the past through large impersonal forces and structures. This book, too, looks at the coming of the war in such terms. Chapter One, however, also suggests that to see the individual as a mere victim is unbearably pessimistic. And so it asks, can Lincoln be held responsible to a measurable degree for the coming of the war? Its answer, my answer, is yes.

In the 1850s Lincoln rose to be Illinois's great antislavery champion, and in the process his political career took off. His antislavery convictions, however, were genuine and had deep roots. To deny them is to turn him into America's greatest war criminal. But, like so many of his generation, in order to stand

firm in opposing slavery as the decade wore to its end, he had to
hold to an increasingly untenable belief. He told himself, and
the country, that on the road to freedom no violence, much less a
great war, would be waiting. He marched "against slavery knowingly and toward war unknowingly. This is his achievement and
his failure." Had he allowed himself to see the price of freedom,
most likely he would have been paralyzed. He made a much less
than understanding choice between accepting a terrible killing
slavery and accepting a terrible killing war.

If the difficulty for the historian writing on Lincoln stems
from the vastness of the literature, the dilemma for Glenna
Matthews, who in Chapter Two looks at the role of women in the
coming of the war, is the paucity of serious scrutiny of the
subject. She makes a good start by focusing attention on the
public women of antebellum, people who took active roles in
civic life. They were specially important in the North where they
formed "*one* of the first, if not *the* first" such a group in history.
They created an infrastructure of voluntary associations and
lecturing venues, staged antislavery fairs, circulated petitions,
and exposed the cruelties of the peculiar institution. To illustrate, by 1856 writer Lydia Maria Child publicly condoned
violence. When in one of her stories a women showed physical
courage while attacked by proslavery ruffians, her husband ex-
claimed: "How manfully you stood by me!" She replied: "How
womanfully, you mean."

More extraordinary than the Northerners were the public
women of the South because they were so much less welcome.
Some ventured forth all the same. They defended slavery but
with limited impact because fewer forums and a much smaller
educated public awaited them among women. Of course dissent
from the consensus continued. But the majorities of Southern
and Northern women, pulling in opposite directions but head-
ing the country toward the same point, helped bring on "that
most male of undertakings," war.

Matthews mentions the activities of black women, too, but
the African-American role in the coming of the war receives
focused attention in Chapter Three. David Blight looks at the

black perspectives on the fate of the nation, both in the free North and the slave South. Black abolitionists showed both unity and diversity, and many of them struggled with great ambivalence about their sense of belonging and security in America. The leaders faced a double burden: they had to create strategies for racial uplift and slave liberation. But for practical purposes, traditional political sanction supported them not.

Most important, Blight shows that among the black peoples of antebellum, a "culture of expectation," political and religious, emerged. Even as the existence of the Union seemed to hang in the balance, African-Americans conjured up a tragically violent test of whether they had a future in this land. In the words of an escaped slave, black people "knew what time it was." Although most of them could not foresee its magnitude, by 1861 they had spent lifetimes working and waiting for the war that came.

In Chapter Four, William Gienapp moves on to analyze the relationship between the origins of the war and antebellum political processes. He does not say that the political system caused the war, but he shows that it fell to the parties to attempt to resolve sectional disputes to preserve the peace. Their inability to do so in "the single greatest failure" in the history of the American political system.

In surveying the road to war, Gienapp provides uniquely American mileposts. The Constitution contained dangerous ambiguities. The evolution of the presidency, the two-party system, and third parties all held elements that moved the country on the same tack. So did the replacement of the republicanism of the American Revolution with the democracy of the nineteenth century.

"Then abruptly and without warning," parties realigned themselves. The creation of the Republican party formed "one of the most crucial links, if not *the* most crucial link" on the war road. The events of the next few years strengthened the new party by feeding popular fears on all sides. Gienapp looks at ideology, voters and leaders, political blunderings, and concludes that "both sides went to war to save democracy as they

understood it." Secessionists would fight for white self-government. As for Northerners, irony would taint their stand, too.

Gienapp sees the Civil War "as an understandable product"
of the American system, and so does William Freehling in
Chapter Five. He compares the United States' way to black
freedom with that of other nineteenth-century slaveholding
societies on the continent. Violence, or its threat, shrouded
every emancipation. However, bloody civil war sired freedom
only in one case. This happened, Freehling argues, because only
in the United States had republicanism progressed far.

Here, under the Constitution, a highly developed republican system of government threatened slavery. That same system
also gave the slaveholders the confidence to secede and to accept
trial by fire. Various crises preceded the war, tending to center
on the border South, where black slavery's future held the least
certainty. Indeed, Freehling concludes, by the 1850s "America
had become an ugly City Upon a Hill, demonstrating that the
world's most advanced republic could end slavery only by one of
the bloodiest fratricides in human history."

Now at the end of the twentieth century, "Democracy has
become the most coveted American export." But Freehling feels
the obligation to point out that universal panaceas do not exist.
After all, "the coming of the American Civil War is a case study
in democracy's limitations."

From this comparative perspective on the Southern white
revolt, Chapter Six takes the reader to the Northern response to
that revolt. Scrutinizing the language of the North 1861, Mark
Summers finds "national mission, sectional pride, paranoid fears,
and just plain cussedness," all leading to an eagerness to fight.
Undergirding all, beneath "the near-obsession" with the flag,
however, was a "profoundly political, profoundly conservative"
commitment to the status quo, tradition, existing institutions,
and above all to the Constitution. This was the price exacted by
the need to fuse behind the war as much of the old Union as
possible. Summers speculates that this, the way the North went
into the war, may have influenced what the bloodletting in the
end wrought: a conservative society wedded to law and order,

mistrustful of radical movements. He concludes that had the Founders of the Republic, so often invoked in 1861, returned to see the land in 1865, they would have found it "so well preserved, that they very well might not have recognized her."

In the concluding Chapter Seven, Charles Royster turns to what British military writer B. H. Liddell Hart described as "that vast sigh of relief" with which people appear to have often greeted the dawn of war over the ages. Americans did let out such a collective sigh after Sumter. Long years of sectional wrangling had failed to resolve their problems through the political system. War promised to end the endless discord. Relieved Northerners and Southerners, like primitive tribes of old, hoped that bloodshed would cleanse them, make them better people.

So it happened. The American Civil War was an unmatched moment of cleansing, an immense and ultimately beneficial event for this country—with great consequences for the world, too. Yet, however much a war accomplishes, since time immemorial, to quote Lincoln's antebellum words about the American Revolution, war "breathed forth famine, swam in blood and rode on fire; and long, long after, the orphan's cry and the widow's wail continued to break the sad silence . . ."; or as he spoke about the war of his own days: "It has carried mourning to almost every home, until it can be almost said that the 'heavens are hung in black.' "[4] These words only make a beginning of the inescapable accounting. Since time immemorial, the question of "Why" has hovered over the bloodstained fields of the world. And so it is fitting to end this introduction where it began. One of the most important questions we can ask about this era and (together with the examination of the results the war wrought), the most important moral question is: *Why the Civil War Came.*

Fort Sumter and Gettysburg   G.S.B.
Spring 1995

Why the Civil War Came

1

"And the War Came"?

Abraham Lincoln and the Question of Individual Responsibility

GABOR S. BORITT

I am the man behind it all;
I am the one responsible.
> *—Peter Appleton, "The Responsibility," 1968*

I shall be telling this with a sigh
Somewhere ages and ages hence:
Two roads diverged in a wood, and I—
I took the one less traveled by,
And that has made all the difference.
> *—Robert Frost, "The Path Not Taken," 1915*

"STRIKE A BLOW!" Roger Pryor, the Virginia fire-eater, had preached the spirit for years. On April 10, 1861, in Charleston he said it again from the balcony of the local hotel. But now, in the early morning hours of the 12th, this night of no rest, when Captain George S. James offered him the "honor" of firing a ten-inch mortar to signal the start of the general bombardment, he quailed. Fighting to control his voice he said No: "I could not fire the first gun of the war." At times the distance between words and deeds can be an eternity.

At 4:30 a.m. Captain James himself sent the signal shot. Its fuse spit stars, and like a doomed comet the shell flew in a high arc, bursting over Sumter. At a nearby battery, another fire-eater was ready. Edmund Ruffin, with his long flowing white hair, another momentary exile from a still reluctant Virginia, sixty-seven-year-old honorary Palmetto Guard, was ready. Staring into the dark, knowing where the enemy was, he sent the first shot from a columbiad into the fort flying the unseen flag of the United States.

The booming guns woke the town of Charleston. Their long echo would wake Americans, and re-make Americans, as they never had been before and, God willing, never would be again. Mary Boykin Chesnut, the brilliant wife of South Carolina's junior senator, bounded out of bed and, as she wrote in her now famous diary, "on my knees–prostrate–I prayed as I never prayed before."[1]

THE POPULAR UPRISING, North and South, that followed the fight over Sumter, combined with willing leadership on both sides, made the Civil War inevitable. It was not that before. The probability of war kept growing in the 1850s, but the country's fate was not sealed until the ides of April, 1861. The first axiom of the present essay suggests the usefulness of looking at Lincoln's part in the coming of the war right to the actual moment when the *New York Times* could announce: "The ball has opened. War is inaugurated."[2]

Historians long debated the question of whether the Civil War was inevitable, and the proponents of the "irrepressible conflict" have won. After all, they had what actually happened on their side. The war did come. With slavery as the focus, the point of origin for the war could be placed in the colonial period when African slavery was first introduced into America. The point of no return perhaps could go to the establishment of the United States under the Constitution that led to a country half-free, half-slave. Someone else might see the fatal turn in the drawing of the Missouri line to mark that divide in 1820—Jefferson's "fire bell in the night." Or the rise of abolitionism in the 1830s might be highlighted. The possibilities go on. To use an example from recent scholarship, Kenneth Stampp, the distinguished Berkeley scholar, argued in a fine 1990 narrative that "1857 was probably the year when the North and the South reached the political point of no return—when it became well nigh impossible to head off a violent resolution of the differences between them." A year later, Stampp's University of Illinois counterpart, Robert Johannsen, suggested that such a state of affairs was reached sometime in 1860. And so it goes.[3]

It is too easy for historians to merely ratify the past and suggest what happened had to happen. Going in the opposite direction, however, can lead to endless possibilities, and make the weave of history incomprehensibly complex. Dogmatism therefore is not in order. Yet what Raymond Aron, the French thinker, called an *"illusion of fatality"*[4] is specially difficult to accept in the face of a great tragedy such as the American Civil War. If in our time war had broken out between the Soviet Union and the United States, scholars, and others too, would surely have argued that such conflict grew unavoidable in 1917 or 1945 or at the moment of the Cuban missle crisis in 1962—or whenever. So in the American antebellum, some hope for peace, and with it moral responsibility for the coming of war, remained until the fire erupted at Sumter.

The second axiom of this essay—and perhaps a prejudice about history and life—emphasizes the importance of the individual. This view makes Lincoln a central figure not merely of American mythology but—so far as historians can admit to such—of American history. The same can be said of the Civil War, a central event of both American history and mythology. One might be tempted to be apologetic about making such broad statements in an age of scholarship which is inhospitable to "kings and queens and great men," and tends to minimize the importance of particular events, seeing the story of humanity in terms of long-range processes and dominant structures. Yet apologies are not in order, for scholarship can accommodate many approaches to illuminating the past. In any case, written history is ultimately an act of faith—whatever road one takes to the past. Without saying (somewhat like Lord Keynes is supposed to have) that the *longue durée* be dammed, it may be declared with confidence that a giant in the earth, or a crucial moment, weighs more in the scales of history than dreary ages.

With these axioms in mind, Lincoln's role in the coming of the Civil War may be divided into four increasingly important stages. First, in the 1850s as tensions grew, Lincoln was one of many political leaders, familiar mostly in and around Illinois, though as the decade progressed so did his reputation in the North. Second, in 1860 he won the presidential nomination of the Republican party and became a nationally known figure. Third, from his election in early November to his inauguration on March 4, 1861, he was the president-elect. Fourth, in the White House he presided over events that led to Sumter. As one stage followed another, Lincoln's stand changed only gradually, but his voice grew ever more weighty until the end when, together with the voice of President Jefferson Davis, it proved to be decisive.

LINCOLN IS ALSO a mythological figure, his legend ever changing. In part the myths grow because Lincoln, unlike most characters of history, belongs to everyman, and she/he contributes to the common fount. Most recently Ken Burns's remarkable PBS epic, "The Civil War," ended its Prologue with the words of the twenty-nine-year-old Illinois politician to suggest how he presaged the American tragedy to come. "At what point then is the approach of danger to be expected?" he asked. "I answer, if it ever reach us, it must spring up amongst us. It cannot come from abroad. If destruction be our lot, we must ourselves be its author and finisher. As a nation of freemen, we must live through all time, or die by suicide."[5] The Civil War approached being national suicide and, as these words appeared to announce, Lincoln saw it loom in 1838 already.

But he saw it not at twenty-nine, nor at forty-nine as he debated Stephen Douglas in part over that very issue. At the Springfield Lyceum of 1838 Lincoln directed his words against lawlessness, especially mob violence, including its interracial variety. As a cure simple for a danger which he conservatively exaggerated, Lincoln recommended "reverence for the laws" as "the *political religion*" of the nation. If he ever had any early intimations of the Civil War, he left no records of them.[6]

Not that others failed to issue Cassandra-like warnings. Visions of fratricide, such as Lincoln would preside over, had cropped up aplenty from the founding of the United States under the Constitution, as historian Robert Bruce has shown in a sparkling essay. And to invoke his colleague Charles Royster's Lincoln Prize-winning portrait of America: as war approached, some visions grew apocalyptic.[7] However, like so many in the country, Lincoln paid little attention to alarms even when they had come from his two principal political teachers, Henry Clay and Daniel Webster. Indeed, as the years went by and both Lincoln's conscience and his partisan political interests came to demand it, his deafness, if anything, deepened. Thus during the antebellum decade he could march against slavery knowingly and toward war unknowingly. This is his achievement and his failure.

Much of the debate over slavery in the 1850s with its focus on the territories partook of subterfuge. People argued about an institution where it did not exist, out West, instead of where it did, down South. Americans tried thus to compromise, to soften the sectional confrontation.[8] Yet when Northerners demanded the containment of the "peculiar institution" to states where it already existed, they set up a policy not unlike the containment of Communism in the twentieth century. Over the long run, the Republicans of the 1850s, consciously or otherwise, meant to bring on the death of slavery just as a later generation of Americans intended to bring on the death of Communism by isolating it.

By 1858 Lincoln was crystal clear about where he stood:

> "A house divided against itself cannot stand."
> I believe this government cannot endure, permanently half
> *slave* and half *free*.
> I do not expect the Union to be *dissolved*—I do not expect the
> house to *fall*—but I *do* expect it will cease to be divided.
> It will become *all* one thing or *all* the other.[9]

Lincoln's words, with their Biblical intonation, are some of the best-known in American history. In 1858, however, when he first uttered them, people in both the North and the South came to know the basic idea through the words of the much better known William Seward of New York, who soon after spoke of an "irrepressible conflict." The words were harsh and implied war to some, especially to Democrats and white Southerners, but not to Lincoln, Seward, or most Republicans. They had in mind politics, not war, though their typically male language at times borrowed military parlance. Even when Lincoln despaired in 1855, saying that "there is no peaceful extinction of slavery in prospect for us," a tumultuous political war and not a military one was on his mind.[10]

Nonetheless, the likelihood that the crusade to contain slavery would lead to actual secession and war occurred to many with increasing frequency in the 1850s. Responding to the rise of Republicans, one old Whig, for example, shuddered that should the new party capture the government, it would appear to be "an alien government . . . a hostile government" to the South. "Then and thus is the beginning of the end." Douglas believed that the "House Divided" speech pointed to war. In a remarkable augury he charged, or so Lincoln understood, that the Republican's message meant that "unless he shall be successful in firing his batteries until he shall have extinguished slavery in all the States, the Union shall be dissolved." In reply Lincoln elicited "Roars of laughter." Yet as late as 1856 he himself admitted that the charge that Republican "*sectionalism*, endanger[ed] the National Union" was "the most difficult objection we have to meet."[11] But in meeting it he showed almost no signs of taking the possibility of war seriously.

All around Lincoln, Republicans dismissed threats of secession and Civil War as a political ploy to extort concessions from the North. Had not Southerners blustered about secession from the days of John C. Calhoun and South Carolina nullification until reasonable men were left either shamefaced or in laughter? Maine's Senator William Fessenden, Lincoln's future Secretary of the Treasury, dismissed secession talk thus in 1854: "We have heard that threat until we are fatigued with the sound. We consider it now, let me say, as mere *brutum fulcrum* [brute influence], noise and nothing else." In 1856 Ohio's Ben Wade complained: "We have had the Union saved five or six different times within my day, and is the only thing I ever knew to suffer by salvation." Not to be outdone, Pennsylvania's old Thad Stevens added that Southerners "have tried fifty times, and fifty times" they had succeeded in intimidating the North. Even as secession was upon the country, he growled: "We have saved this Union so often that I am afraid we will save it to death." It needed no saving. Massachusett's Henry Wilson quite exploded about the "DISUNION FARCE." And Abraham Lincoln in Illinois went along with the best of them, cheering them on.[12]

It is true that at moments he admitted some potential for small-scale violence. For such an unhappy eventuality the experiences of Andrew Jackson, John Brown, and the people of Kansas appeared to have been his points of reference. Over the years Lincoln had spoken repeatedly of Jackson, and the country knew how he had faced down the South Carolina nullifiers in 1832. It had become American legend that Old Hickory had threatened to hang John Calhoun, his ex-vice president, and later expressed regret that he had not done so. But the nullification crisis came to an end without resort to violence.

As for John Brown—he was executed in 1859. Lincoln did not object, though, as he explained, "Old John Brown . . . agreed with us in thinking slavery wrong." Lincoln went on: "That cannot excuse violence, bloodshed, and treason. It could avail him nothing that he might think himself right." He also added, however, for the benefit of would-be Southern rebels: "if constitutionally we elect a President, and therefore you undertake to destroy the Union, it will be our duty to deal with you as old John Brown has been dealt with." The incident at Harper's Ferry had lasted less than two days. Violence cost seventeen lives. "We hope and believe that in no section will a majority so act as to render such extreme measures [again] necessary." In short, when Lincoln seemed to think of matters reaching an "extreme" state, what came to mind was John Brown and not a horrendous Civil War.[13]

Later that war taught Lincoln to "think anew, and act anew." But until then his knowledge of history and his own experience taught him to expect little or no violence. He believed his epoch to be "less inclined to wars" than earlier ages. Even when actual war, albeit the guerrilla variety with atrocities, had come to Kansas in 1856, the casualties amounted to no more than two hundred men. Again, however awful that was, it would hardly compare to the coming Civil War. In 1854, Congress had paved the way for what happened in Kansas by repealing the compromise prohibiting slavery above the Missouri line in that territory. Lincoln described the legislation "not as a *law*, but as *violence* from the beginning. It was conceived in violence, passed in violence, is maintained in violence, and is being executed in violence." He used hyperbole (metaphorical language if one wishes to be generous) in the hope of plugging up the new opening for slavery in the West. And he worried that actual physical violence may result from the Kansas-Nebraska Act. He even asked: "Will not the first drop of blood so shed, be the real knell of the Union?" Though it was unusual for Lincoln to speak in such dramatic terms about the subject, in predicting violence over Kansas, like others, Lincoln had been prophetic. But in the end violence was contained, peace restored. Kansas did not come to an end, much less the entire United States.[14]

It could have even occurred to Lincoln that his own fears about the danger of violence to a democracy had been exaggerated. Faced with the rise of mobs in the 1830s, he had warned that such lawlessness was the road to tyranny and national suicide. Though he never learned to love mobs, he did live to see mob violence subside. Should worse come to worse, the United States was strong enough to survive a little violence in 1860 or 1861 as it had in Kansas in 1856 and in Virginia in 1859. But history, as Lincoln understood it, turned out to be a poor guide.

And so, like others, he spoke with contempt about Southern threats of violence. "Through all this, bowie-knives and six-shooters are seen plainly enough; but never a glimpse of the ballot-box," he thundered in 1854. In 1860 he still mixed outrage with contempt when faced with what he took to be Southern extortion, the demand that the North reject a Republican presidential candidate to avoid secession. "This is cool. A highwayman holds a pistol to my ear, with 'stand and deliver, or I shall kill you, and then you will be a murderer.'. . . the threat of death to extort my money, and the threat of destruction to the Union to extort my vote, can scarcely be distinguished in principle."[15]

From contempt Lincoln could move on to ridicule. Even in 1860 secession threats reminded him of the joke about "the man who had a poor old lean, bony, spavined horse, with swelled legs. He was asked what he was going to do with such a miserable beast—the poor creature would die. 'Do?' said he. 'I'm going to fat him up; *don't you see that I have got him seal fat as high as the knees?*'" Now this was an age when the horse was the automobile, and the crowd rewarded Lincoln with roars of laughter. So he concluded: "Well, they've got the Union dissolved up to the ankle, but no farther!" and received more applause and laughter.[16] Those with psychological bents might note that though the point of the joke was to make secession threats seem empty, in Lincoln's formulation the Union was the "poor old lean, bony spavined horse, with swelled legs," "the poor creature that would die." Did Lincoln fear somewhere deep inside something he would not admit openly even to himself?

However that may have been, in the year secession came he continued to stand strong as a rock for the right, as he understood it, blind to the consequences. He ended his great address at Cooper Union with barely a hint of danger of *any* sort: "Neither let us be slandered from our duty by false accusations against us, nor frightened from it by menaces of destruction to the Government nor of dungeons to ourselves. LET US HAVE FAITH THAT RIGHT MAKES MIGHT, AND IN THAT FAITH, LET US, TO THE END, DARE TO DO OUR DUTY AS WE UNDERSTAND IT." But again, the duty was political, not military. America's "republican robe" had been "soiled," he said in 1854; it needed to be purified. "Let us turn and wash it white, in the spirit, if [but] not the blood, of the Revolution." In 1855 Joshua Speed of Kentucky, once his most intimate friend, wrote in private of his preference for disunion over giving up his right to slaves. Lincoln did not take his friend seriously. In 1856 Lincoln announced that "All this talk about the dissolution of the Union is humbug—nothing but folly." In 1857: "To give the victory to the right; not *bloody bullets*, but *peaceful ballots* only, are necessary." And in the closing statement of the debate with Douglas in 1858, he had assured all that "this controversy will soon be settled, and it will be done peaceably too. There will be no war, no violence."[17]

History tells us that Lincoln was dead wrong. Six hundred and twenty thousand dead wrong. This is Lincoln's cardinal sin.

Such a statement, of course, can easily be seen as a scholar's conceit. The French philosopher Mailtand's thought is to the point: "It is very difficult to remember that events now in the past were once in the future."[18] Or to use the vernacular, Monday morning quarterbacking is easy. And yet we must ask why did a man of pre-eminent common sense like Lincoln not see the coming of the War? Why did he not listen to the somber warning voices? Why did he not pause at all? Answering such queries should shed some light on an entire generation. The fits and starts, the changes in his stance during the fifties are so marginal as to make their careful delineation unnecessary. Why and why? One and a half million casualties in a nation of thirty-one and a half million demand that we ask the question.

Lincoln never did. He was a sensitive and moral man, and the agony of the Civil War transformed him physically and morally. He changed from a vigorous middle-aged man into an old one, and he grew into America's greatest prophet of democracy. He thus attested his good faith, and in the end it was "morally and dramatically" fitting, to use Edmund Wilson's words, that Lincoln's life, too, was taken.[19] Had he had time to reminisce, he might have asked the question about his antebellum blindness—and that of so many of his generation. Or he might not have. As it is, we need to do it for him.

Lincoln was part of a generation, sharing many of its characteristics, but he had his own peculiarities, too. As early as 1838, Robert Bruce has noticed, Lincoln showed a curious "personal reluctance" to face the possibility of war between the North and the South.[20] It rather seems that his personal history may have stood in the way. He was born in Kentucky. So was his wife. Three of his brothers-in-law would die for the Confederacy. At Christmas, 1863, the guest in the White House would be the widow of a rebel general—Lincoln's sister-in-law, perhaps his wife's favorite relative. What would they talk about at the dinner table? Of course Lincoln knew none of this grim stuff *before* the war, but his heritage instinctively made the contemplation of a war of brothers all too painful. It was better left alone.

Lincoln disliked violence and war in a way that went well beyond the common. On the floor of Congress in the midst of the War with Mexico he defined "military glory" as "that attractive rainbow, that rises in the showers of blood—that serpent's eye, that charms to destroy." He combined anti-violence feelings with an excessively optimistic belief that a democracy would invariably find peaceful solutions to all problems. His liberal faith held that, as a rule, war provided few or no solutions. In the spring of 1861 he still pleaded with his countrymen: "Suppose you go to war, you cannot fight always; and when, after much loss on both sides, and no gain on either, you cease fighting, the identical old questions . . . are again upon you." Sensible people like Americans would not have a gigantic blood bath among themselves.[21]

The kind of war Americans would have itself clouded Lincoln's vision. The conflict would be a civil war–the most terrible kind of them all. Lincoln most likely thought of civil war in terms of the English experience–Roundheads fighting Cavaliers year after year with King Charles eventually losing his head. Lincoln also knew something about the French Revolution and its terror. Americans would never degenerate to such horrifying levels. Even after war came, at first he tried to head off what he called a "remorseless revolutionary struggle."[22]

Most Northerners did not want such a war, and he knew most Southerners did not either. In any case, in a war the odds, he thought, would be so much on one side that it would be utterly foolish for the other to start it. The romance about how one Southerner could beat ten damned Yankees was damned nonsense. Lincoln himself got cocky on the subject, showing how light he made of it. Said he in 1856: "But the Union, in any event, won't be dissolved. We don't want to dissolve it, and if you attempt it, *we won't let you.*" More than three years later his tone had changed not. Speaking in Cincinnati, and facing his birthplace in Kentucky, he said: "Will you make war upon us and kill us all? Why, gentlemen, I think you are as gallant and as brave men as live; that you can fight as bravely in a good cause, man for man, as any other people living; that you have shown yourselves capable of this on various occasions; but, man for man, you are not better than we are, and there are not so many of you as there are of us. [Loud cheering.] You will never make much of a hand at whipping us. If we were fewer in numbers than you, I think that you could whip us; if we were equal, it would likely be a drawn battle; but being inferior in numbers, you will make nothing by attempting to master us." Later some took this to be another prophetic statement from Lincoln, showing exactly what he would do in the presidency. But the net effect of his words in the 1850s was to dismiss the likelihood of war. It was in the above-quoted 1856 speech that he said: "All this talk about the dissolution of the Union is humbug–nothing but folly."[23]

We even know how he was likely to have accentuated the word "humbug" from one of his letters. Just before his election to the presidency, with tempers boiling, Lincoln was warned that should he win, some officers at a fort intended to go South with their arms and resist. Lincoln asked a friend to keep an eye on the matter but added, "I think there are many chances to one that this is a hum-bug."[24]

With his Kentucky origins, with the twang that stayed on his tongue for life, at times he may have thought of himself as a Southerner and, in any case, thought he understood Southerners. He wasn't and he didn't. Though he associated with former Southerners, he did not travel in that part of the country and was ignorant of its people's passions as were Republicans in general who could not campaign in the South. For someone for whom personal contacts were crucial, who would throw the doors of the White House open to all comers to have "public opinion baths," here was a grievous flaw. And Lincoln did not know he suffered from it. During the campaign of 1860 he wrote: "The people of the South have too much of good sense, and good temper, to attempt the ruin of the government. . . ." He permitted a shadow of doubt, for he added: "At least, so I hope and believe." Even after the war began in earnest, he kept expecting common sense to return. In the fall of 1861, for example, he predicted that "the people of Missouri will be in no favorable mood to renew, for next year, the troubles which have so much afflicted, and impoverished them during this." As it turned out, Missouri came to experience the war at some of its ugliest. In 1863 Lincoln could still maintain to his secretary that Jefferson Davis's only hope was his army: "If that were crushed the people would be ready to swing back to their old bearings."[25]

Lincoln overestimated Southern unionism to the end of his life. He misread the people below the Mason-Dixon line in part because his own devotion to the Union was so deep. He had difficulty fathoming the disenchantment of others. This, too, in part was personal. After all, the American Union permitted this son of an illiterate father and perhaps illegitimate mother to become one of the most important people in the state of Illinois by the 1850s. Nor would it end there. In 1864 he would tell the soldiers of the 166th Ohio: "I happen temporarily to occupy this big White House. I am a living witness that any one of your children may look to come here as my father's child has." Would many common people want to destroy such a Union? And did they not determine events in a democracy? After secession came he admitted: "The political horizon looks dark and lowering; but," he added, "the People, under Providence, will set all right."[26]

His unionism had various facets, including one quite akin to "religious mysticism," to borrow Alexander Stephens's words, though Lincoln would not have owned up to it. Mysticism, in turn, is not open to the messages of everyday reality. Nor was Lincoln—on the question of Union. It is possible that his religious training in the predestination of Calvinism (his family were Baptists), and a degree of life-long fatalism it engendered in him, also helped him travel the road to Civil War. Before horrifying bloodshed taught him better, he could proclaim "God is with us" meaning the North, the Republicans, and the best of what they stood for. But even in more sober, more broadminded moments, could he admit that God might desert "this, his almost chosen people"?[27]

Lincoln's faith in the inviolability of the United States, the physical impossibility of dividing it up, also made a war for secession pointless and therefore almost inconceivable. "Physically speaking, we cannot separate," he would say in his first inaugural address. The Mississippi River, for example, could not be divided up as it ran from North to South. But he went beyond the brute uniting of force of nature to emphasize the economic system based upon it. The prosperity desired by all would ensure that no secession came.[28]

Lincoln turned out to be wrong in part because he misunderstood history. Specifically, he failed to grasp that revolutions can be made by minorities. The legend of the American Revolution pictured a large majority of the colonists as patriots united—democracy ruled. So it would in the South. It rather seems that when Lincoln claimed that Southern majorities would not want to break up the Union, he was for a long time right. He failed to see, however, that a relatively small minority on the coast of South Carolina might get secession going—that is how revolutions are often made—and there would be no stopping it. And enough unhappiness existed in much of the white South to embrace revolution in the end.

How much of Lincoln's blindness was unique to him—how much was shared by a good part of his generation? The question awaits the exploration of the subject individual by individual in place of generalizations. Still it is clear that they shared much. Unlike Lincoln, later many would claim they had long seen the war coming, but the observation of Charles Francis Adams, Jr., from as late a time as mid-1860, contained much truth: "We all dwelt in a fool's Paradise."[29]

Republicans did so, in part, because they stood to benefit politically from the antislavery crusade. Lincoln himself, though always antislavery, did not make this the centerpiece of his political action until 1854—when that became practical within the mainstream. Then he rose from being one of the leaders of the minority Whigs of Illinois (many said a moribund party) to be *the* champion of the majority Republicans in the state and, in time, in the country. The cynical view that this was all to the rise of the Republicans, or even that this was at the heart of the movement, is unfair. So is de-emphasizing the political benefits obtained from believing that at the end civil war could not be waiting, that Southern threats of secession were gasconade at best, blackmail at worst. Lincoln's stance changed so little from the 1850s into 1860, when he became a presidential nominee, as to deserve no notice except that as the Republican candidate, his views came to have a nationwide impact. He fully understood that the health of his party depended on standing firm on its commitment to the containment of slavery. And he continued to believe that the risk of war was practically nonexistent. As his influence grew, so did his moral responsibility, making his blindness ever more damnable.

But Lincoln or the Republicans were not alone in living in "a fool's Paradise." It is true that in the middle of the political spectrum John Bell of Tennessee led the Constitutional Union party with the avowed aim of saving the Union. The candidate of the Northern faction of the Democratic party, Stephen Douglas, also strove to occupy the center and made "titanic efforts to focus the campaign upon the danger to the Union," to quote the words of those fine historians of the period, David Potter and Don Fehrenbacher.[30] But such a course had no more attraction to the Southern Democratic candidate, John Breckinridge of Kentucky, and his followers, than it did to Lincoln and his party. They had nothing to gain from it politically. Therefore, Breckinridge and company, too, emphasized their love of the Union rather than the likelihood of secession and war. Southerners, like Northerners, would rather vote for peace than war.

Interestingly enough, and consistent with the Illinoisan's overall approach, he defended the authenticity of Breckinridge's unionism (if only to attack Douglas). In the fall of 1860, Lincoln created an imaginary dialogue between the Northern and Southern Democratic candidates. The chief characteristic of this brief venture into political playwriting was its lightheartedness. It concluded thus:

> DOUG . . . and you, and your friends, are a set of disunionists.
> BRECK Bah! You have known us long, and intimately; why did you never denounce us as disunionists, till since our refusal to support *you* for the Presidency? Why have you never warned the North against our disunion schemes, till since the Charleston and Baltimore sessions of the National convention? Will you answer, Senator Douglas?
> DOUG The condition of my throat will not permit me to carry this conversation any further.[31]

What Lincoln failed to notice was that many of the Dixie unionists of the Breckinridge stripe, who ignored the potential for a horrible war, used a rationale different from that touted in the North. Above all, they seemed to say that the Yankees would never fight and therefore danger there was none. And, in the words of Robert Bruce, "those who denied the possibility of war invited it."[32] By 1860 Lincoln was chief among them.

In the end, the search for the source of Lincoln's blindness to the coming war leads to the psychoanalytic concept of avoidance. Though a man of proverbial good sense, he was able to fool himself in other cases, too. He could refuse to face dangerous realities and indulge in wishful thinking and behavior. Anna Freud gave the classic modern statement about the subject of avoidance, but common sense suggests her truth, too. Said Shakespeare in King Lear, a drama Lincoln loved well: "I have no way, and therefore want no eyes."[33]

Lincoln did not permit himself to see that a bloody war might come, misled himself and his people, in short lied the way honest people lie, because he felt politically and morally impelled to fight slavery. The political benefits that he obtained have been noted. His moral commitment must be, too. "If slavery is not wrong, nothing is wrong," he said in 1864. "I can not remember when I did not so think, and feel." Or as he put it in 1837: "The institution of slavery is founded on both injustice and bad policy." At the bottom, as he explained in the Great Debates of 1858, was "the eternal struggle between . . . right and wrong." Therefore and ultimately the United States *had* to put an end to the abomination of slavery. Had Lincoln admitted to himself that a colossal war would be the price of freedom, he might have been paralyzed. Could he have squarely faced in the 1850s a future that would require, in the calculations of David Potter, "the life of one soldier, either Rebel or Yank, for every six slaves who were freed . . ."? As it was, Lincoln ignored the potential consequences of the antislavery crusade and so could lead Americans to emancipation, the Thirteenth Amendment, and "a new birth of freedom."[34]

We may speculate about what might have occurred had he permitted himself in the 1850s to face the stark alternatives of freedom or war. We will never know, but I think he could not have accepted the war he actually got between 1861 and 1865 and so would have opted for peace in the hope, vain or otherwise, of merely postponing freedom further. With that choice, he would have disappeared from public life. The Republican party would have continued toward war. Lincoln alone was not going to stop the march to war. For that, the Republicans as a whole—and/or many white Southerners—would have had to stop avoiding reality and face the likely truth.

Where does that leave us if we look upon history with moral eyes from the end of the second millennium? If our focus is on slavery, Lincoln comes out beautifully right. If our focus is on war, he comes out dead wrong. And if the two parts are combined, as they must be? You, the reader, decide.

What we do know is that, for good or for ill, Lincoln cast his lot with liberty.

IN MORAL TERMS nothing changed on November 6, 1860, when he became president-elect of the United States. His avoidance continued, his responsibility for it increased, and his hands were tied ever more by his party. South Carolina called a secession convention and Lincoln wrote, among others, to Republican Senator Lyman Trumbull of Illinois: "Stand firm. The tug has to come, and better now, than any time hereafter." What kind of "tug" did Lincoln have in mind? He did not say. But he refused to mention the possibility of war. Surely he wished not to escalate the crisis through wild talk, but it is also true he still did not see a bloody war on the horizon. Andrew Jackson, however, was certainly on his mind. And when a reporter came to visit in Springfield, Lincoln managed to be found reading Old Hickory's "celebrated proclamation" against the nullifiers of 1832.[35]

Before another newspaperman, more trusted and less used, Lincoln "laughed" about the notion that "the Southern people were in dead earnest, meant war." Donn Piatt of Ohio later wrote: "Mr. Lincoln did not believe, could not be made to believe, that the South meant secession and war." While Piatt had visions of the land "whitened with tents," Lincoln joked that the fall of the price of "pork at Cincinnati" had affected the man.

At another time, the president, who would so skillfully use the patronage from the White House, explained cheerfully that Southerners would not give up the largesse from Washington. Working perhaps from old notes, Piatt quoted Lincoln saying: "Were it believed that vacant places could be had at the North Pole, the road there would be lined with dead Virginians."[36]

Dead Virginians and Pennsylvanians and people from every state would line the roads and the fields—but not to the North Pole. Lincoln's words make us shiver today, for we know what happened.

Thanks to earlier, careful investigations by historians, we also know full well what Lincoln did from the time of his election to the time of Sumter's fire. A summary suffices here.

Northern reaction to secession can be divided into three principal positions. Some, especially the strongest antislavery people, seemed ready to let the "erring sisters" go, though how serious they were is open to question. Still, even Horace Greeley, the editor of the most influential Northern newspaper, the *New York Tribune*, and Salmon P. Chase, Lincoln's future Secretary of the Treasury, toyed with the idea. So did Frederick Douglass, fearing concessions to the South. Lincoln rejected this approach.[37]

On the other extreme, demands could be heard from the first for the use of massive force against the rebels. A relative moderate such as Indiana governor-elect Oliver Morton could declare as early as November 1860: "If it was worth a bloody struggle to establish this nation, it is worth one to preserve it." Lincoln refused to speak in such harsh terms and for long rejected the option of "coercion," too, as he understood it. "Marching of an army into South Carolina," he said in mid-February, 1861, had no appeal to him.[38]

Between these pole positions, perhaps a majority of Northerners wanted some kind of compromise to avoid secession and war. Lincoln gave them little encouragement. For compromise meant backing off from the containment of slavery, the principle his party, too, stood for. He also saw at stake the principle of democratic elections under government of laws. Yet the largely (and to some strangely) silent president-elect did go along with some concessions. One, perhaps permitting New Mexico to enter the Union without restrictions on slavery; two, a proposed amendment to the Constitution that would guarantee slavery in perpetuity where it already existed. If one shudders at this second concession—as one does at the prospect of an awful war—it is worth remembering that Lincoln believed that slavery locked up would eventually die. And so this proposed thirteenth amendment did not contradict his view that the Union could not endure "permanently half *slave* and half *free*." Amendment or not, in time the United States would be free.

Yet even as Lincoln could no longer ignore the growing depth of the crisis, he had a difficult time letting go entirely of the view that Southern extremists were merely engaging in a political game. On January 11, 1861, he wrote about the secessionists in a private letter: "They are either attempting to play upon us, or they are in dead earnest."[39] If the former, he had already conceded too much. If the latter, Lincoln would play for time until the Southern Unionists regained power. So he would hold on firmly to symbols of the Union, most importantly some federal forts in the South.

At the same time, he could still make light of the crisis, as he so often did throughout the fifties. On his way to Washington on February 15, 1861, he told the people of Pittsburgh, for example: "Notwithstanding the troubles across the river, [the speaker pointing southwardly, and smiling] there is really no crisis . . . except an *artificial one*! . . . *there is no crisis*, excepting such a one as may be gotten up at any time by designing politicians." In speaking thus, of course he also hoped to keep matters "cool." "If the great American people will only keep their temper, on both sides of the line, the troubles will come to an end . . . just as other clouds have cleared away in due time, so will this. . . ."[40]

As if in reply, Tennessee historian A. Waldo Putnam wrote to his senator, and Lincoln's future vice president, Andrew Johnson, one Unionist speaking to another: "But, my dear Sir, it will not do to allow the impression to remain on the minds of the Northern people that [the crisis] 'is only *artificial*,' as the President elect has so often recently said,—and that it 'will soon pass away,'–'and nobody be harmed.' " Though the upper South then experienced a strong anti-secession wave, the historian feared "a war of desolation, the extent and duration of which no human Ken can limit. . . ."[41]

Lincoln himself began to face the enormity of the situation in some moments. His former mentor and ally in harshly opposing the War with Mexico, Congressman Thomas Corwin of Ohio barely hedged his words when he wrote him in the second part of January that "a long and bloody Civil War *must* follow." Some weeks later, leaving his hometown of Springfield, Illinois, "not knowing when, or whether ever, I may return," Lincoln spoke of the task before him as "greater than that which rested upon Washington." Was the task war? On the day Jefferson Davis was inaugurated, Lincoln admitted that the time may come "when war is inevitable." On the same day at Independence Hall in Philadelphia, he said, "I would rather be assassinated" than surrender what America stood for. Yet in the same speech he added: "Now, in my view of the present aspect of affairs, there is no need of bloodshed and war. There is no necessity for it." And he made a pledge: "there will be no blood shed unless it be forced upon the Government. The Government will not use force unless force is used against it."[42]

What did Lincoln *expect* now? If we take his cabinet building as a test, the answer is peace. Ordinary politics and not the possibility, much less the probability of war, governed his selections. William Seward, the most important compromiser among leading Republicans, became Secretary of State. The post of Secretary of War went to a shady Pennsylvania politician, Simon Cameron, who would have preferred the Treasury. Until a week before the inauguration, the job of Navy Secretary had been reserved for John Gilmer of North Carolina. Then it went to Gideon Welles, Republican politico and ex-Jacksonian newspaper editor from Connecticut. Lincoln created a peace, not a war cabinet.

If he expected peace, keeping it Lincoln also believed, required a willingness to accept something of a war. In his inaugural address, on March 4, in what James McPherson called "the most important such speech in American history," Lincoln repeated his pledge that he would not start a war and pleaded for peace. "We are not enemies, but friends. We must not be enemies." He also made clear that to save the government he would fight "a civil war." Was this brinkmanship? Or somewhere hidden inside him had he always carried an inkling that it may come to war? Had his use of avoidance not ever been complete? Even as he laughed at Donn Piatt, joked about how the fall of the price of "pork at Cincinnati" had brought on the newspaperman's visions of war, Lincoln added: "we won't jump that ditch until we come to it."[43]

Then the time came to jump the ditch. The strong words and the soft words and the laughing words were mostly done with. Lincoln was president. A day after his inauguration he learned that the Sumter garrison had no more than six weeks of supplies left. Buffeted by various pressures, conflicting advice, and changing public opinion, Lincoln leaned toward abandoning the fort, then moved to reinforce it but only with non-military provisions. There was hope that food, at least, would be allowed in. If not, the first shot would be fired by the other side.

JUMPING THE DITCH to possible war put Lincoln through hell. If from late February he began to say that "it may be necessary to put the foot down firmly," that foot, light or heavy, was all too theoretical. To quote Navy Secretary Welles, Lincoln "indulged a hope, longer than most of his friends, that a reconciliation could be effected." The end of March brought the moment of painful transformation: a decision had to be made on Sumter. On the 28th, General Winfield Scott recommended abandoning that fort, and the one at Pickens, too. The president informed the cabinet that evening, pulling the members away from the pleasantries of the first state dinner at the White House. The emergency gathering rejected the general's advice. "That night," to quote the history of Lincoln's secretaries, "Lincoln's eyes did not close in sleep."[44]

On the following morning, Good Friday, a deep depression shrouded the president. The day after a migraine savaged him.

Mary Todd told a visitor that "her husband had keeled over with sick headache for the first time in years." Easter Sunday, 1861, came and Lincoln's temper exploded. But through it all he kept on working. Sumter would be relieved, the attempt would be made. On Tuesday, April 2, he took his family to the Navy Yard and received a twenty-one-gun salute. That afternoon he visited military barracks. At last Lincoln knew that the time may have come for those *"bloody bullets"* which, for so long, he had promised would not be "necessary." The *"peaceful ballots"* had not been strong enough.[45]

Historians have offered three sets of views concerning Lincoln's role in the start of war at Sumter. One argued that Lincoln deliberately provoked the first shot to unite the North behind him. Reaffirming with poor scholarship contemporary Southern partisan charges (later dignified by Jefferson Davis and Alexander Stephens), this view has few adherents among historians. It can be readily dismissed.

Another approach, most clearly delineated by a penetrating David Potter, pictured a somewhat bungling Lincoln desiring peace and believing to the last that he might be able to avoid war. A third view sees the president more firmly in charge, expecting the peaceful provisioning of the Sumter garrison *"possible,"* but the starting of hostilities *"probable."* Two excellent scholars, Kenneth Stampp and Richard Current, are the leading proponents of this position.[46]

Professors Current and Stampp focused on too narrow a span of time, and thus did not take fully into account Lincoln's genuine, deep devotion to peace and how badly and for how long he misunderstood the reality of the Southern movement toward war. Conversely, Professor Potter failed to appreciate fully that sometime during the secession crisis Lincoln clearly recognized that war may indeed come. "It is not with any pleasure that I contemplate the possibility that a necessity may arise in this country for the use of the military arm," he said to applause in Harrisburg, Pennsylvania, as early as Washington's birthday, 1861. But he did "contemplate" the possible "necessity." He also added, however, to louder applause, his "most" sincere hope that it will never be the people's "duty to shed blood, and most especially never to shed fraternal blood."[47]

A day earlier in New Jersey, Lincoln promised, "The man does not live who is more devoted to peace than I am. [Cheers.] None who would do more to preserve it." In fact, others might have done more for peace; Secretary of State William Seward, for one, tried to do exactly that. Like General Scott, he wanted to abandon Sumter. Seward wished to wait for what he saw as the secession craze to subside and work toward that goal. Much earlier and much more vividly than Lincoln, Seward saw in the secession crisis the great likelihood of war. During the March of 1861, to quote historian Daniel W. Crofts, "a truly momentous debate" took place inside the government. Lincoln, too, considered abandoning Sumter, hoping thus to keep the loyalty of Virginia and other border states, and perhaps making the Confederacy of the Deep South less than viable. Of course, it was one thing to speak as a cabinet member, and another to act as president, open to enormous pressures. Still, Stampp, Current, and Crofts are accurate in saying that on the Northern side Lincoln's was the "decisive voice" in turning America toward war.[48] On the Confederate side Jefferson Davis, with his cabinet, made the choice to fire on Sumter four years to the day before Robert E. Lee would surrender at Appomattox. History turned at Sumter. Could it have turned in another direction?

Sumter served the cause of war-making on both sides. Lincoln got a North united as never before, ready for some fighting after the fire on the flag and the fort. (A large number of other forts had been taken by rebels without bullets or much public attention.) Davis, in turn, got a South; if not as united as the North, more united than ever before, including Virginia, North Carolina, Tennessee, and Arkansas. It, too, was ready for some fighting.

Davis is not our focus here, however large a personal burden he carried for the war's coming, as did so many in the South. But should Lincoln have done more to avoid war? Perhaps if he had done so, war would still have come. Most historians think so. But when Lincoln accepted war, he still practiced avoidance, like multitudes of the people he led and opposed. He remained part of the larger American culture. In the spring of 1865 he would remember that "Neither party expected for the war, the magnitude, or the duration, which it has already attained." However much truth that statement may have contained, Lincoln certainly underestimated tragically the magnitude of the horror that was to come. Indeed he could defend the road to war in the name of peace and saving lives. In 1861, three days before his fifty-second birthday, he agreed with future Senator Orville Browning of Illinois that "far less evil & bloodshed" would come from upholding the Union than permitting the formation of two hostile countries side by side. By then, many saw the horsemen of apocalypse advancing on America. The future general William Tecumseh Sherman, after meeting with Lincoln in the White House, angrily damned all politicians for failing to fathom that "the country was sleeping on a volcano." Jefferson Davis feared "a war . . . the like of which men have not seen." His vice president, Alexander Stephens, predicted as early as the spring of 1860 "the bloodiest civil wars that history has recorded" and added, "What is to become of us then, God only knows." Did Sherman, Davis, Stephens, and those like them, really understand what was about to happen, or had rhetoric carried them away? In any event, Lincoln called for 75,000 militia, men whose term of service was fixed by law at a mere three months. Perhaps he was still trying to limit what was to come. But calling 75,000 men for three months was also a fitting conclusion to the road he had taken since 1854. At Gettysburg, in three days the casualties would be more than 50,000.[49]

"I had no thought in the world that I was doing anything to bring about a war between the free and slave States," Lincoln had said during his debates with Douglas. "But I must say, in all fairness to him, if . . . I am doing something which leads to these bad results, it is none the better that I did not mean it. It is just as fatal to the country. . . ." So it turned out to be—in part. How would Lincoln have reacted to such words had he the time after Gettysburg to reread the text of the Great Debates which he had so carefully and proudly prepared for publication as a book?

In 1858 he had gone on to ridicule the accusation that he was helping to set North and South "at war with one another." There was no more likelihood of that than for the people of Vermont to "raise sugar cane" or "the people of Illinois to cut pine logs" on the treeless prairie. As the press reported, Lincoln's words reaped the reward of "Laughter."[50]

Then the laughter ended. Lincoln had no time to read old debates. But somewhere deep inside he knew what was in this, his popular book of the 1860 election. And perhaps because his sin was so stupendous, for long he could not face up to it.

Lincoln came from a humble background, and to the end of his days in many ways humility remained a deep part of him. He also knew full well how to accept responsibility. But for long he did not do so for any part in making the war–like so many others who had a part, North and South. "In *your* hands, my dissatisfied fellow countrymen, and not in *mine*, is the momentous issue of civil war," he announced in his inaugural address in the March winds of 1861. "If I had had my way, this war would never have been commenced," he continued in 1862. "I hope you do not feel . . . that I am in any way responsible for all this sorrow," he was remembered to have told in 1863 his sister-in-law, the new widow of a Confederate general. He added in 1864, "I claim not to have controlled events, but confess plainly that events have controlled me." Sometime after that he wrote about "this mighty convulsion which no mortal could make, and no mortal could stay." And he concluded in 1865, in the second inaugural, "The Almighty has His own purposes." In the pain of war Lincoln shifted responsibility from his own shoulders to those of the people, and finally to God. And so he could finish the work he was in.[51]

In the spring of 1865, looking back at the origins of the war, Lincoln felt impelled to focus on the weeks before Sumter. By then he distanced himself sufficiently from the bitterness of the conflict to be able to say that "All" had "dreaded it–all sought to avert it." Northerners *and* Southerners. The sentiment was generous, even if less than entirely accurate. After four years of bloodshed, he could find little blame in his heart for others, no more than he would accept for himself. One side wished to save the Union, Lincoln remembered, the other to dissolve it. Both hoped to succeed "without war." "Both parties deprecated war; but one of them would *make* war rather than let the nation survive; and the other would *accept* war rather than let it perish. And the war came."[52] Of course this, too, was less than good history. After all "one of them would *make* war," not merely to destroy the old Union but to create a new Confederacy. And the "other" "would *make* war," too, to save the old—and its bright future. Yet at least, and at last, Lincoln accepted a share of responsibility for the start of the war.

By focusing on the outbreak of hostilities, on a time when at last he himself faced up to the possibility of a war, the president could largely ignore the longer run, the 1850s and 1860, too. He did, however, make one fundamental generalization that also fit the long coming of the war. "All knew" that "somehow" slavery was "the cause of the war." If Lincoln would cast blame, like many modern historians, he would cast it at the feet of society. After all, he was in many ways a modern person. But he also reached out to God. "If we shall suppose that American Slavery is one of those offenses which, in the providence of God, must needs come, but which, having continued through His appointed time, He now wills to remove, and that He gives to both North and South, this terrible war, as the woe due to those by whom the offence came, shall we discern therein any departure from those divine attributes which the believers in a Living God always ascribe to Him? Fondly do we hope—fervently do we pray—that this mighty scourge of war may speedily pass away. Yet, if God wills that it continue, until all the wealth piled by the bond-man's two hundred and fifty years of unrequited toil shall be sunk, and until every drop of blood drawn with the lash, shall be paid by another drawn with the sword, as was said three thousand years ago, so still it must be said 'the judgments of the Lord, are true and righteous altogether.' "[53] In the face of such judgments, those of individual human beings paled to insignificance. Lincoln could thus forgive others. Perhaps he could forgive himself.

2

"Little Women" Who Helped Make This Great War

GLENNA MATTHEWS

MEETING HARRIET BEECHER STOWE, author of *Uncle Tom's Cabin*, during the Civil War, Abraham Lincoln is said to have remarked, "So you are the little woman who wrote the book that made this great war." This was a striking testament to the power of the pen wielded by a famous and beloved woman. Yet Lincoln's acknowledgment of a certain level of female agency where the onset of the war was concerned has been seen as nothing more than an historical curiosity by most twentieth-century historians of that conflict. This essay will argue, conversely, that while Lincoln may have been engaging in slight hyperbole, he was also demonstrating an awareness of an important development in world history: a female public in the North—*one* of the first, if not *the* first, ever—had played a role in precipitating that most male of undertakings, an outbreak of armed hostilities. What is more, in the ongoing tension between the pragmatic Northern war aims that sought to keep the border states loyal to the Union and those of a moralistic nature, most importantly, emancipation, that female public was making itself heard in the crusade for freedom—as Lincoln was surely well aware when he made his remark to Stowe.

To comprehend the emergence of a female public in the antebellum years and then to assess its impact, four interrelated and largely simultaneous developments must be understood. In the first place, the years between 1830 and 1860 saw a remarkable Northern flowering of what the German social theorist Jürgen

Habermas has called civil society, that is to say, a public sphere independent of the state. Spurred on by public investment in education and by democratic ferment, people in towns and cities in the free states formed voluntary associations, read a plethora of newspapers, attended lectures on a wide variety of subjects, staged civic rituals and parades, devoured overtly political novels, and listened to stump oratory. (People did many of these things in the South, too, but to a lesser extent because of that region's more hierarchical social structure, its lack of public education, and a lessened respect for free speech after abolitionism had begun to pose a terrifying threat to the Southern way of life).[1] As a consequence, Northern public opinion was broadly based and could be expressed in a number of different ways.

In the second place, Northern women had begun to participate in civil society, albeit not on the same terms as men. Lacking the vote and still suffering from other effects of the old common law tradition of coverture whereby women were civilly dead, they nonetheless were finding ways to express their views publicly. From the earliest decades of the colonial experience, "public woman" had been an invidious term, one which easily equated with "Jezebel" and connoted illicit sexuality.[2] Yet by 1800 women in several denominations had legitimated the right to be heard about their religious convictions, and women authors North and South would shortly thereafter achieve the power of the word, writing novels and even best-sellers by the antebellum period. Indeed, thanks in large part to substantial investment in the education of girls in the North, women authors had an increasingly sizable and literate audience by that period. By 1850 they were also editing and writing for periodicals such as the immensely popular *Godey's Lady's Book*.[3] From the 1790s on both black and white women had been organizing voluntary associations, at first religious and charitable, but some with more overtly political intent by the antebellum period.

Most hard-won was the right to give public lectures, still a controversial act when performed by a woman in the antebellum United States. The first woman to breach this barrier had been the British-born reformer Frances Wright, who in 1828 began to give fiery political speeches on a variety of topics and in a number of states. Not much later, in 1832, the African-American abolitionist Maria Stewart gave three antislavery lectures in Boston. Next came the Southern-born abolitionists Sarah and Angelina Grimké, who began to speak out against slavery in New England in the late 1830s. All of these women faced harsh criticism and even ostracism for their temerity. (In the case of Fanny Wright her problem was compounded by the fact that she had the courage to tackle the subject of sexual mores in addition to attacking slavery.) Nonetheless, by the outbreak of the war, Northern audiences in many locales might well have had the opportunity to listen to a woman reformer hold forth on the need to abolish slavery, on women's rights, or on both. There are even a few recorded instances of women speaking in the South, spurred on by devotion to temperance or by political affiliation.[4]

Third, during this period when civil society was growing and developing and women were finding ways to participate in it, home and motherhood were enjoying an unprecedented societal respect. Indeed, in the North the loving Christian home provided a touchstone of values for reforming the entire society, and the competent, diligent housewife became a cultural ideal as well as a linchpin of the moral order.[5] Women could then use their domestically based cultural authority—reinforced by messages from the pulpit and by prominent writers of both sexes—to justify their activities in the public sphere. The outstanding example of this phenomenon is Stowe's invocation of maternal authority in her great antislavery novel.

And finally, slavery touched the family life and sexual being of millions of slave women in the South who had little ability to protect themselves from unwelcome advances by white men. This terrible vulnerability to sexual predation provided women in the North with a cause about which some felt a strong call to speak out. Put another way, slavery gained in salience for Northern women because assessing its morality involved matters on which they could claim as much or more expertise as their menfolk. Conversely, the tariff or the fate of the Bank of the United States, for example, also important issues in the 1830s, might affect women's lives throughout the country. Yet women had no special basis for claiming expertise about these economic issues–unlike the fate of slave mothers and children.

All four of these developments–the growth of civil society, public women's participation in it, public women employing the cultural authority of home and motherhood to justify that participation, and the special way slavery intersected with woman's sphere of influence–culminated in the breathtaking success of *Uncle Tom's Cabin*. By the time that the first install-ment of "Uncle Tom" appeared in the June 5, 1851, issue of *The National Era*, the American publishing industry had begun to experience unprecedented prosperity, thanks in part to the bur-geoning success of the domestic novel written by women.[6] In effect this meant that women writers had a new means for disseminating their ideas. Hence when Stowe was incensed by Congress's passing the Fugitive Slave Act in 1850–and despite lacking both the vote and the capacity to run for office–she could pick up her pen. She subsequently explained to a British admirer that she had been motivated to do so because, ". . . as a woman, as a mother, I was oppressed and broken hearted with the sorrows and injustice I saw."[7]

At first serialized, the novel she wrote eventually sold some three million copies–in a country with a population of approx-imately 25 million inhabitants–and it changed the nature of the discourse about slavery by imbuing the crusade against it with all the sacredness attached to purity of family life in the American society of the mid-nineteenth century. Stowe achieved this end by vividly dramatizing the many ways in which the "peculiar institution" threatened the slave family. Of numerous episodes embodying this theme, the most poignant, perhaps, is the young slave mother Eliza Harris's harrowing passage across the frozen Ohio River to free territory while carrying her four-year-old son, a flight necessitated by his rumored sale away from her. Arriving at the home of a senator who has recently voted for the Fugitive Slave Act, Eliza asks for refuge (and what amounts to civil disobedience, because the new law will have to be flouted). She appeals to the senator's wife, Mrs. Bird, for help by saying,

"Ma'am, have you ever lost a child?" It so happens that Mrs. Bird had buried a beloved child shortly before—as had Stowe herself and, doubtless, many of her readers. Mrs. Bird then uses the moral authority of a bereaved mother to talk her husband into helping Eliza. Throughout the book Stowe depicts women using their housewifely competence to achieve large political and social ends. In effect, she is preaching a gospel of female efficacy. She also depicts the crusade against slavery as having a specifically Christian character.

In February 1854, in the midst of congressional debates about the proposed Kansas-Nebraska Act, Stowe published an "Appeal to the Women of the Free States," in which she enumerated a number of means by which voteless women could influence public opinion. First of all, they must thoroughly master the intricacies of the debate for themselves. She went on to suggest:

> In the second place, women can make exertions to get up petitions, in their particular districts, to our national legislature. They can take measures to communicate information in their vicinity. They can employ lecturers to spread the subject before the people of their town or village. They can circulate the speeches of our members in Congress, and in many other ways secure a full understanding of the present position of our country.[8]

Stowe was merely the best-known of many public women who helped mobilize a female public in the North in these years. Even earlier had been the efforts of the New England writer Lydia Maria Child. Her publication of *An Appeal in Favor of That Class of Americans Called Africans* in 1833 constituted the first important abolitionist manifesto by a woman as well as the first book to advocate immediate abolition written by any American, and it launched her career as an antislavery activist. The author of a popular book of domestic advice, *The American Frugal Housewife*, Child found herself labeled as a radical after she published her *Appeal*. Indeed, she was turned out of the Boston Athenaeum as an undesirable. Undaunted, she devoted much of her effort over the next several decades to such abolitionist activities as attending the first Anti-slavery Convention of American Women in New York in 1837, editing an antislavery newspaper in the same city in the early 1840s, and working on behalf of Kansas antislavery settlers in the 1850s.

"The Kansas Emigrants," a short story she published in the *New York Tribune* in 1856, reveals the evolution of her thought. Outraged by the caning of Charles Sumner on the floor of Congress one day after he had delivered a fiery speech about events in "Bleeding Kansas," Child turned to fiction to convey her own reaction to these events. In her story she made the case for armed struggle against the "Slave Power," eschewing the non-resistance that had been her approach up to 1856. Indeed, one of her female protagonists, Kate Bradford, begins to practice with rifle and pistol as she comes face to face with the brutality of the proslavery "Missouri ruffians" on the other side. Earlier in the narrative, after Kate has displayed courage during an attack, her husband exclaims " 'How manfully you stood by me!' 'How womanfully, you mean,' she replied, smiling."[9] Here Child is not only calling for women to display physical courage but also using her domestic credentials to give this trait the imprimatur of being womanly.

The Child biographer Carolyn Karcher, pointing out that the story was serialized in a newspaper with a circulation of 175,000, concludes: "The prominent place Child's narrative occupied in a major newspaper testified to the stature she had achieved by the 1850s, not only as a woman of letters, but as a political analyst."[10] Even more remarkable was the public circulation of her correspondence with and about John Brown after his raid on Harper's Ferry in October 1859. Having begun to come to terms with the need for a militant response to the Slave Power after the caning of Sumner, she found herself moved by Brown's self-sacrifice while ambivalent about the violent means he had chosen to adopt. Drawing on substantial experience in tending the ill and failing, she wrote to Governor Henry Wise of Virginia for permission to travel to his state to nurse the wounded Brown. Governor Wise chose to make his reply public, and Child responded in kind. The correspondence eventually included Child, Brown himself, Wise, and Margaretta Mason, the wife of Virginia Senator James M. Mason—with Child emerging as a formidable spokesperson for freedom. The American Anti-slavery Society issued a tract consisting of the entire body of letters, a tract which enjoyed a circulation of 300,000 copies. In addition, that year Child produced three other tracts and personally mailed them "by the hundreds to key opinion-makers." Karcher argues that with all of this activity Child was "revolutionizing public opinion" in the North.[11]

In the late 1850s Child also showed the character of her commitment to justice for African-Americans by editing a narrative written by a former slave, Harriet Jacobs. Jacobs had earlier approached Harriet Beecher Stowe for help but had encountered a noteworthy lack of respect from the famed author, who proposed to appropriate Jacobs's dramatic story for her own uses.[12] Child, on the other hand, donated her editorial services to Jacobs without imposing her own agenda on the novice author and then wrote an introduction to *Incidents in the Life of a Slave Girl* in which she testified to Jacobs's good character, despite the "indelicate" nature of some material in the book. Sadly, after all the effort by both women, the book failed to attract much of an audience, because its publication coincided with the outbreak of war. The book is still remarkable, however, among other reasons because of the bravery they both displayed in making public Jacobs's choice, while enslaved, of an extramarital liaison with one white man in order to obtain protection against the unwanted advances of another.

CHILD DISPLAYED enormous courage by writing and publishing what was, at first, so controversial that it made her suspect in Boston literary circles. Abby Kelley, another of the prominent women abolitionists and one who adhered to the most radical wing of the movement, repeatedly had to display courage in an even more immediate way as she traveled throughout the North giving speeches which caused her to be labeled a Jezebel by conservatives. Said Kelley's fellow abolitionist Theodore Parker:

Here is a woman who has traveled all over the North, laboring for [the slave and] woman's cause. She bore the burden and heat of the day. She was an outcast from society. Other women hated her; men insulted her. Every vulgar editor threw a stone at her, which he picked up from the mire of the street. Many a minister laid sorry stripes on her. . . . The noble woman bore it with no complaint; only now and then, in private, the great heart of Abby Kelley would fill her eyes with tears at the thought of this injustice; but she never allowed her tears to blind her eyes, or quench the light which was shedding its radiance down her steep and rugged path.[13]

In 1839 Kelley left a teaching job to lecture against slavery. In the ensuing decades she "dodged rotten eggs, rum bottles, and the contents of outhouses" while hearing herself called "Jezebel" and "nigger bitch." During that period, according to a recent biography, she "probably logged more miles in farm wagons, stage coaches, and trains, spent more hours on the platform than any other antislavery speaker."[14] Despite this record of extraordinary travel, her "greatest contribution was as an organizer," because everywhere she went she took soundings of her audiences, learning the most effective arguments for reaching people in far-flung locales. She also helped launch a network of regional antislavery newspapers. A spellbinding orator, she especially captivated audiences with her tales of the wrongs visited upon slave women and children.

White women like the Grimkés, Child, Stowe, and Kelley had their counterparts in black women like Frances Watkins Harper and Sojourner Truth, both forceful antislavery advocates in the antebellum years. Born to a free black family in Baltimore in 1825, Harper made contact with abolitionists working for the Underground Railroad in the early 1850s. They helped her launch a lecturing career in 1854. She then spoke to antislavery societies in Ohio, Pennsylvania, New Jersey, New York, Massachusetts, and Maine in the ensuing years. Truth, born a slave in upstate New York in the late eighteenth century, was unlettered but developed a powerful and eloquent platform presence when she became first an itinerant preacher and then a lecturer during the 1840s and 1850s. Six feet tall and possessing a sonorous voice, she made a lasting impression on her audiences.

A number of Southern women, too, were spokespeople for their region—hence, public women—during these years. Their careers were extraordinary, because they were "living in a society that for the most part discouraged their intellectual growth."[15] Indeed, recent scholarship suggests that the gender hierarchy was much more rigid in the South, with its aristocratic ethos, than in the North. Moreover, for Southern women, honor and prowess were linked most closely to chastity, at best a passive virtue. (In the North, conversely, female prowess was linked to an active ideal, that of the accomplished or "notable" housewife, an ideal replete with substantial cultural authority.) But the rise of abolitionism—and the impact of abolitionist women writers—created the need for a proslavery response, including one from women.

MOST IMPORTANT, perhaps, were Louisa McCord and Caroline Lee Hentz, the first a proslavery and anti-feminist polemicist, and the latter a proslavery novelist. The brilliant author of poetry and drama as well as of articles on political economy, McCord, according to Elizabeth Fox-Genovese, adopted "the voice of a latter-day Roman matron who measured personal feelings against their social consequences."[16] For her part, Hentz wrote the best-known Southern response to *Uncle Tom's Cabin*, the novel *The Planter's Northern Bride*.

In fact, Hentz was one of a constellation of Southern literary domestics who were well-known writers in the antebellum period and who enjoyed a widespread national audience. For example, Hentz's most popular novel, *Linda*, published in 1850, went into thirteen editions in two years. Needless to say, what such a woman wrote had an impact on public opinion.

Where many of the Northern domestic novelists attacked social injustice either openly, as, for example, Stowe in *Uncle Tom's Cabin*, or covertly, Hentz and the other well-known Southerners, Maria McIntosh, Caroline Gilman, Augusta Jane Evans, and Mary Virginia Terhune (Marian Harland), were deeply conservative defenders of their region's mores, including its gender norms.

Their works display tension between their professed desire to mediate between the two sections—perhaps at least in part because they wanted to attract readers throughout the country—and their profound loyalty to the South, which they saw as morally superior to the money-grubbing North. Contends Elizabeth Moss, a student of the five writers: "But while the South was championed in a variety of forums by a broad cross-section of its sons and daughters, the most consistent and convincing effort came from the handful of southern domestic novelists."[17] This was because they softened their proslavery arguments with the trappings of the domestic genre, thus employing "a vocabulary and a set of images designed to affect the heart."

In an important work of revisionist scholarship Elizabeth Varon contends that a certain component of Virginia women played significant political roles in the antebellum period. First in the movement of colonizing black people in Africa—before abolitionists made this stance unpopular in the South—and then on behalf of political parties, most especially the Whigs, women attended public meetings, wrote letters, and circulated petitions. Varon writes, for example, of an occasion in 1840 when Daniel Webster addressed 1200 Richmond women on the nature of woman's political role. Not surprisingly, he defined woman's role as that of upholding public virtue.[18] The rise of feminism in the North then precipitated a concomitant decline in this activity in the South by way of reaction.

Yet while the South had public women of some accomplishment, they were fewer in number than in the North. Moreover, deprived of the extraordinarily high rate of literacy and the ideological justification for public activism possessed by women in the North and, in addition, lacking the infrastructure of reform clubs and lecturing venues taking shape there, Southern women never evolved into a public with the same efficacy and visibility as the female public in the free states. The current scholarly consensus is that, to the extent that it is possible to fathom female public opinion in the region, that opinion seems to have been proslavery. Elizabeth Varon's research has uncovered private papers suggesting that on the eve of the war in

Virginia, "many women disagreed with their men about the prospect of secession."[19] We do not know how many secession debates may have taken place between husbands and wives in the privacy of the home. However, once war came, women and men forged an ideal of Confederate womanhood, even if adherence to the ideal was far from universal.

As for the North, how did the female public affect the coming of the war itself? The answer to this question must necessarily be inferential, because no one took opinion polls at the time, and women were unable to register their opinions at the ballot box. Nonetheless, despite this difficulty, there are certain indications that women imparted greater moral urgency and more religious fervor to Northern public opinion than it might otherwise have had, especially after more than two decades of agitating by the likes of Child, Stowe, Sojourner Truth, and the rest. In other words, the Northern public opinion that sustained the coming of war and then held steadfast despite the sacrifices during the war included and was shaped by both men and women.

One piece of evidence revealing the opinions of "ordinary," as opposed to public, women and the means by which such women may have been able, subtly, to influence the opinions of others is contained in the quilts they made, some of which still survive. From the 1830s on abolitionist women, white and black alike, quilted to raise money for the cause and then sold their quilts at Anti-slavery Fairs. Certain well-known quilt patterns were re-named to reflect the new purposes to which they were being put; "Job's Tears" became "Slave Chain," for example, and "Jacob's Ladder" became "Underground Railroad." One still extant cradle quilt displays this refrain:

> Mother! when around your child
>   You clasp your arms in love,
> And when with grateful joy you raise
>   Your eyes to God above,
> Think of the negro mother, when
>   Her child is torn away,
> Sold for a little slave—oh then
>   For that poor mother pray!

In fact, many women used textiles as political texts in the spirit of a remark by Sarah Grimké, "May the point of our needles prick the slave owner's conscience."[20]

Public women were lecturing and publishing and other women were stitching, reading, talking among themselves, staging Anti-slavery Fairs, attending lectures, and singing abolitionist songs. Between 1834 and 1843 women were also circulating antislavery petitions, many of which—with their hundreds of thousands of signatures by both men and women—are now reposing in the vaults of the National Archives. These petitions reveal an important dimension of the female public in the North and the way in which it could influence public opinion.

The abolitionist women's willingness to attend notorious trials involving the status of African-Americans attempting to attain their freedom in Northern courts provided another means for shaping public opinion. In effect, such women risked their reputations for respectability in order to dramatize their support of oppressed people. Says the legal historian Paul Finkelman: "As spectators women abolitionists unnerved proslavery jurists and lawyers. In this role they were effective because their very presence in the courtroom challenged the prevailing role of women." But the women went further. Finkelman describes how "the Boston Female Anti-slavery Society initiated litigation on behalf of the cause." For example, in 1836 they were "sparkplugs" in bringing to the courts the case of Med, a six-year-old slave girl who had come to Boston with her owner.[21]

By means both dramatic and subtle, then, abolitionist women undertook to shape public opinion in the years preceding the war. But the full extent to which they had succeeded in mobilizing a female public capable of playing an important role is also revealed by the events that followed the firing on Fort Sumter. That is to say, lacking the same kind of direct data bearing on women's opinions that we possess about men's—voting statistics—the true female impact on the coming of war must, at least in part, be inferred from an examination of what transpired during the war.

The most important points to be made are that many thousands of women throughout the North contributed to the war

effort, that they mobilized both with swiftness and with remarkable generosity of spirit, and that they did so without being
drafted. Surely there would not have been an estimated ten
thousand soldiers' aid societies in the North during the war,
for example, had not large numbers of Northern women become fully engaged well before that time. In a sense the war
gave women the opportunity to act out the widely circulating
"scripts" provided by Stowe and Child, scripts in which female
efficacy and female valor were brought to bear against the
Slave Power.

The United States Sanitary Commission is the best example of
a crucial wartime institution that came out of a women's initia-
tive, taken, in fact, very soon after Sumter. Less than two weeks
after that epochal event about fifty women and a few men met at
the New York Infirmary for Women to discuss what they could
do to ensure the health of the men in arms. (At that point the
Union army employed a mere 26 doctors.) Among the notables
present was Dr. Elizabeth Blackwell, the first American woman
to become a physician. The Unitarian minister Henry Bellows,
also present, would become the president of the relief organization that was born at this meeting. He sold the idea to a skeptical
Abraham Lincoln and a more than skeptical Army medical
establishment by referring to an "uprising of the women of the
land" and convincing these men that it was better to organize
the women than to let them go off in all directions to make,
potentially, nuisances of themselves.

Several weeks elapsed before the Army would accept what
became the Sanitary Commission. The men around Bellows
were put off by the military resistance, but the women were
undeterred. Then on June 9, 1861, Secretary of War Simon
Cameron issued an order setting up the Commission and putting Bellows and his distinguished male colleagues—several doctors, several clergymen, and one reformer—in charge. If the
women were undeterred by military opposition to their plans,
they were also undeterred by having men assigned to head the
operation. By the time the war had ended, these women and
thousands of others had shown their mettle.

Women were urged to form soldiers' aid societies under the ultimate direction of the Sanitary Commission so as to provide a variety of supplies. They responded so enthusiastically that "[t]he estimated value of the stores distributed to the army during the war was about fifteen millions of dollars," about four-fifths of which was the value of contributions in kind from American homes. Women conceived of the idea of staging sanitary fairs as fund-raisers–and made the needlework to sell at the fairs–by which the sum of three million dollars was raised for the Commission. Women were employed as agents, and women ran regional offices.[22]

Powerful evidence for the role played by women in shaping Northern public opinion about slavery before the war and for their "comfort level" in participating in political discourse is the way in which certain of them mobilized during the war to push Lincoln and the Republican party in a more radical direction. The pioneering suffragists Elizabeth Cady Stanton and Susan B. Anthony, for example, organized what they called the Woman's National Loyal League in order to collect signatures on a petition in favor of emancipation. As of early 1865 when the Thirteenth Amendment, ending slavery, passed both houses of Congress, the League had gathered nearly 400,000 signatures, making this petition drive the most successful in American history up to this time.[23]

That women quite visibly participated in political discourse during the war is demonstrated with particular force by the career of Anna Dickinson, who became a major orator for the Republican party. A Quaker from Philadelphia, Dickinson was only seventeen when she gave her first public address shortly before the war broke out. Before long Radical Republicans were enlisting her services on the speaker's platform, because they knew her to be a powerful advocate of emancipation as well as of public funding to help the freed slaves. On one occasion she addressed an audience of five thousand people at Cooper Union in New York. The pinnacle of her career came on January 16, 1864, when she spoke to the House of Representatives on the subject of the Freedmen's Bureau–with Abraham Lincoln in attendance.

The President of the United States, who as a young Illinois politician came out in support of women's suffrage, came to hear a twenty-one-year-old woman speak in a public setting, but he listened to many women in private as well. When one reads the memoirs of those involved in the war work, it is striking to note how many times they bring up a visit to the White House. They also mention contact with other prominent politicians such as Massachusetts Senator Charles Sumner. It is highly unlikely that these busy men would have given a hearing to women during wartime had politicians not learned in the period leading up to the war that they were, in some sense, accountable to women. And these men may well have understood how important women were to the maintenance of civilian morale. Above all, in corresponding with soldier husbands, women could–and did–stimulate their loved ones to continue to see their sacrifices for the Union as worth making.[24]

In the Confederacy, on the other hand, politicians seem not to have made these connections. Women made many sacrifices during the war, and they echoed the achievements of their Northern counterparts in nursing and in fundraising, albeit on a more limited scale. But they lacked access to the civil society that had been built in the North, hence they lacked the means to gain similar attention from politicians or to express their views in a public forum, except in most unusual cases.[25] In consequence, women were largely ignored, other than in terms of rhetorical gestures. Says the distinguished historian of the South, Drew Gilpin Faust:

> Historians have wondered in recent years why the Confederacy did not endure longer. In considerable measure, I would suggest, it was because so many women did not want it to. The way in which their interests in the war were publicly defined–in a very real sense denied–gave women little reason to sustain the commitment modern war required. It may well have been because of its women that the South lost the Civil War.[26]

Historians of the American Revolution have taught us in recent years that women became involved in the political discourse in the years leading up to that conflict because a consumer boycott required cooperation from wives and mothers. But the decisions were made—the public opinion took shape—informally in all-male venues such as taverns as well as formally in congresses or legislatures. By contrast, the public opinion that supported Northern entry into the Civil War took shape in a vast array of locales, many of which were accessible to women. One can imagine, for example, a quilting bee at which women discussed the Kansas-Nebraska Act, in accordance with Stowe's injunction to them. In fact, Henry Bellows used the quilting metaphor in a letter to two of his women colleagues in the Sanitary Commission work:

> The women have constituted themselves as a great national quilting party; the States so many patches, each of its own color or stuff, the boundaries of the nation the frame of the work; and *at it* they have gone, with needles and busy fingers, and their very heart-strings for thread, and sewed and sewed away, adding square to square, and row to row; allowing no piece or part to escape their plan of Union; until the territorial area of the loyal states is all of a piece, first tacked and basted, then sewed and stitched by women's hands wet often with women's tears, and woven in with women's prayers; and now at length you might truly say the National Quilt—all striped and starred—will tear anywhere sooner than in the seams, which they have joined in a blessed and inseparable unity![27]

What is especially noteworthy about this heartfelt testimonial to the engagement of women and to their effectiveness is that it came from a man who, in the period after Sumter, had seen women as good-hearted pests.

Beginning in the 1830s a few brave female pioneers had begun to teach other women—and men, too—that slavery violated every moral standard they held dear, and that women should become publicly active in the crusade to end it. These pioneers faced opprobrium from conservatives and opposition from other abolitionists who thought that women should remain silent. Nonetheless, by the 1850s hundreds of thousands of women had absorbed at least part of the lesson about the necessity for action.

During the war itself these women "voted" to support the cause with their loving involvement in humanitarian aid for soldiers and for the freed people—as the contrabands voted with their feet by running away from slavery. A true democracy could not permanently deny citizenship to groups whose members were acting on the basis of belief in their own democratic efficacy—although this citizenship would not come easily. For their part, historians must acknowledge the multiple ways in which those who live in a democracy can exert influence on it.

3

They Knew What Time It Was

African-Americans and the Coming of the Civil War

David W. Blight

*One-eighth of the whole population were colored
slaves, not distributed generally over the Union,
but localized in the Southern part of it. These
slaves constituted a peculiar and powerful
interest. All knew that this interest was,
somehow, the cause of the war.*

—Abraham Lincoln, "Second Inaugural Address,"
March 1865

*However much they who marched South and
North in 1861 may have fixed on the technical
points of union and local autonomy as a
shibboleth, all nevertheless knew, as we know,
that the question of Negro slavery was the real
cause of the conflict.*

—W. E. B. Du Bois, The Souls of Black Folk, *1903*

*F*ROM DIFFERENT EXPERIENCES and perspectives nearly forty years apart, Abraham Lincoln and W. E. B. Du Bois expressed the same truths about American history: that the Civil War would never have occurred without sectional conflict over slavery, and that the fate of four and a half million African-Americans, slave and free, was inextricably tied to the fate of the nation in the 1860s. Exactly when and how "all . . . knew" that slavery was the cause of the war, and just how Americans came to understand, or deny, emancipation and the promise of black equality as central legacies of the war remain questions open to debate. Indeed, just how much we "all know" or understand today of the active role of blacks themselves in the coming of the Civil War—what sectional strife, the lived experience of slavery, the war, and emancipation meant to black people—remains a rich field of inquiry.

These questions are at the center of an ongoing exploration of the place of the black experience within the fabric of American history. The opening lines of Benjamin Quarles's *The Negro in the Civil War* (1953) are as good a starting point now as when he wrote them forty years ago. "What is America?" asked Quarles. His answer reflected his own era's search for an identifiable national character, and yet, after four decades of remarkable development in historiography, especially in African-American history, Quarles draws us back to the challenge of generalization amidst our rich, new particularism. "A clue to a nation's character is revealed when a crisis comes," wrote Quarles, "in a time of troubles, a nation's culture crops out. Certainly during that fateful span of the Civil War–the only great war in the hundred-year period in world history from Waterloo to Sarajevo–this query received an illuminating answer."[1] For blacks, the coming of the Civil War would be more than the nation's culture crop-ping out; the test of America's national existence would deter-mine whether African-Americans had a future at all, with human rights and secure social identities, on the North Ameri-can continent.

Blacks were both direct participants in, as well as historical recipients of, what many historians now refer to as the "Second American Revolution." In its fundamental causes, its scale, and certainly its results, the Civil War era was a revolutionary turn in the course of American history. As much recent scholarship has demonstrated, emancipation was something both seized as well as given. By probing the meaning of the coming of the war to blacks, in free black communities, among fugitive slaves, and on southern plantations, we might yet harvest new fruit in these old vineyards. Moreover, as long as the question of whether the Civil War was "irrepressible" persists as an integral part of pedagogical and scholarly considerations of the coming of the conflict, then we can still learn much by examining both the meaning of America and the war's inevitability, through the eyes of ante-bellum black leaders and from the experience of slaves. To most blacks, slavery was self-evidently a world of brutal contradiction, a system of human and inhuman relationships that operated daily on an assumption of irrepressible conflict. Neither slaves nor black abolitionists were any more prescient than their white fellow Americans about just how and when a war would result from conflict over slavery. But that, as Kenneth Stampp put it, "the issues dividing North and South were genuine and substan-tial and that conflict between them was natural . . ." were assumptions about which most blacks harbored no doubts.[2]

Although African-Americans could not know the course of the revolution they were about to experience when secession and war came in 1861, it may safely be said that among their leaders, "all knew" in their own ways what had caused the conflict. Their greatest leader, Frederick Douglass, spoke for the vast majority of blacks in the summer of 1861 when he declared slavery the "primal cause" of the war. Earlier, during the emotion and confusion of the secession winter, Douglass wrote worried editorials in which he feared "peaceful disunion," but resolved to make the best of it. Writing at least a month before Fort Sumter, Douglass envisioned a future where abolitionists might become guerrilla agitators attacking slavery in a separate country. "Hereafter, opposition to slavery will naturally take a new form," announced Douglass. "The fire is kindled, and cannot be extinguished. The 'irrepressible conflict' can never cease on this continent." Abolition might be postponed and its methods could change, reasoned Douglass. "But it cannot be prevented. If it comes not from enlightenment, moral conviction and civilization, it will come from the fears of tyrants no longer able to hold down their rising slaves."[3] Faith in an inexorable logic of conflict born of the inherent injustices of slavery in the South and racial caste in the North, and of a disinherited people's essential belief in permanent struggle, sustained most black leaders both before and after the outbreak of the war. The process by which emancipation would, in time, emerge out of total war was something black abolitionists could only begin to imagine in the crisis of 1860–61. But as Douglass and many others had already surmised, the course of the war, like its causes, would be driven by a combination of fear, ideology, and the force of events, by human will and military necessities. The logic and the expectation of such a conflict, if not its inevitability, was something blacks had contemplated and analyzed for at least two generations.

As EARLY AS the late 1820s and early 1830s, black abolitionists organized, both with their white counterparts and separate from them, to improve their lives and attack slavery. They founded their own churches, newspapers, and moral reform societies, and forged their own protest and self-improvement strategies through black conventions at the state and national levels. Although militant, even revolutionary, stances emerged before the 1840s, especially in such writings as David Walker's *Appeal to the Colored Citizens of the World* (1829), most black leaders devoted themselves to a self-improvement formula based on the guiding assumption that "condition and not color" was the principal dilemma blacks faced. If they could socially elevate themselves through education and employment, and by embracing middle-class values, then racial prejudices among white Americans would erode. By 1840, northern free blacks had founded hundreds of mutual aid societies, schools, orphanages, lyceums, library companies, and the like. In 1832, in one of the first public lectures by an American woman, Bostonian Maria Stewart called her fellow blacks to self-reliance. "O do not say, you cannot make anything of your children," said Stewart, "but say, with the help and assistance of God, we will try . . . lay the cornerstone for the building of a high school . . . unite and build a store of your own." In a society where slavery rapidly expanded westward, however, where the peculiar institution's philosophical and political defenders became ever more intransigent, and where racism became an increasingly rigid barrier to even the most highly talented blacks, the self-improvement doctrine lost viability.[4]

Changing contexts forced new strategies upon black abolitionists. In the discriminatory world of antebellum northern cities, where they enjoyed no civil or political rights, scrambled for decent housing and schooling, and where their children were discouraged from high aspirations, black leaders could ill afford adherence to abstract principles of antislavery reform. Given the emergencies of their lives, black abolitionists became increasingly pragmatic activists; no single strategy characterized their work by mid-century. Moreover, during the 1840s a new generation of black abolitionists came on the scene. Many of them, like Henry Highland Garnet, William Wells Brown, James W. C. Pennington, Samuel Ringgold Ward, Henry Bibb, and Frederick Douglass, were fugitive slaves whose formative years and antislavery educations were spent on southern plantations, and not in organizations dedicated to moral suasion. By the 1850s, the roles of black women in the movement expanded, and such activists as Harriet Tubman, Sojourner Truth, Mary Ann Shadd, Francis Ellen Watkins Harper, and Sarah Parker Remond became professional abolitionists (as orators, writers, and Underground Railroad operatives) in their own right.

What emerged was what numerous historians have referred to as "two abolitionisms," one white and one black, the latter characterized by racial independence and strategic pragmatism, and the former, though still committed to antislavery principles, increasingly divided over doctrine such as political action or evangelical reform. Black abolitionists would themselves engage in a great deal of in-fighting, but generally over basic ends, as much as over doctrinal means. Many were also repelled by the racism they encountered from some of their white associates within the movement. The inability of many white abolitionists to comprehend the world in other than moral absolutes, as well as their unwillingness to confront issues of racial prejudice and poverty in the North, drove many black abolitionists toward independent action. A certain logic of responsibility, as well as bitterness toward the behavior of their white colleagues, lay at the root of such separatism. "It is emphatically our battle," declared the highly educated physician-reformer James McCune Smith in 1848, "no one else can fight for us."[5] The two abolitionists educated each other, and were deeply interdependent during the antebellum era. Indeed, many black abolitionists proudly claimed their organizational and ideological roots among the followers of the Massachusetts radical William Lloyd Garrison. But by a combination of moral commitment, a growing political consciousness, and sheer necessity, black abolitionists entered the crucial decade before the Civil War with a deepening sense of how long and complex their "battle" would be.

For antebellum black leaders, the coming of the Civil War would mean the fulfillment of a long-imagined prophecy, but only after a period of crushed hopes. The 1850s were simultaneously a decade of heightened activism and deepening despair among northern blacks. After lifetimes of struggle against slavery and racism, and in the wake of setbacks on the national scene like the Fugitive Slave Act (1850), the Kansas-Nebraska Act (1854), the Dred Scott decision (1857), and southern attempts to reopen the foreign slave trade, northern black leaders suffered both a crisis of faith in America and internal ideological division. By the mid- to late 1850s, African-American intellectuals had reached a cross- roads. Ironically, on the eve of revolutionary changes in their own lives and in American race relations, most black leaders saw a future for their people as dismal as it had ever been. Had disunion and war not come when it did in 1861, it is difficult to know how much longer the bulk of antebellum black leaders could have sustained confidence about their future in America. They had to find their own place on the road to disunion, sustaining them- selves through revitalized resistance, spiritual wellsprings they shared with the slaves, and from events that both spurned and inspired them. In summing up the political crisis over slavery expansion as the crux of Civil War causation, Eric Foner stated, "What was at stake in 1860, as in the entire sectional conflict, was the character of the nation's future."[6] For no people was this more true than African-Americans. At stake for them were not only worldviews based on slave labor or free labor, but whether they even had a place in that future where one or the other worldview might win out.

During the 1850s, warring temperaments, conflicted and strained priorities, impatience, and a growing sense of powerless- ness made black abolitionists as a whole a divided people in a dividing country. They struggled over several fundamental issues: the potential uses of violence as a tactic against slavery and slave catchers; whether black liberation could be achieved within exist- ing American political structures; and emigration from America as an ultimate solution to the burden of futurelessness. Yet their leadership was almost always without traditional political sanc- tion since they served a constituency that could not vote. They labored heroically with the weapons of language—through ora- tory and their own press. Especially through best-selling slave narratives and through their presence on countless platforms, black abolitionists were the best living challenges to the American paradox of slavery and freedom. Some of them did change their world through their voices, but they also discovered the limits imposed by racism, symbolism, and moral suasion. Frederick Douglass described the ironic dilemmas African-Americans faced in the nation's impending crisis. In 1853 he complained that the black intellectual was "isolated in the land of his birth–debarred by his color from congenial associations with whites . . . equally cast out by the ignorances of the blacks." Douglass spoke for most when he concluded that a pragmatic and increasingly radical path was the only alternative for black leadership. "Right antislavery action," wrote Douglass in 1856, "is that which deals the . . . deadliest blow upon slavery that can be given at that particular time. Such action is always consistent, however different may be the forms through which it expresses itself."[7]

Many black leaders insisted that the future of all Americans would be determined by the crisis over slavery and race. The minister and orator Samuel Ringgold Ward aptly asserted that the great question of the 1850s was not "whether the black man's slavery shall be perpetuated, but whether the freedom of any Americans can be permanent." Ward identified a grinding truth that would lay at the root of the Republican party's free labor ideology, the successes of which would begin to lead the country toward disunion, and provide a new kind of political hope for northern blacks. He also anticipated by seven years Abraham Lincoln's haunting claim on the eve of emancipation, in December 1862, that "in *giving* freedom to the slave, we *assure* freedom to the free."[8] The future was, indeed, at stake in the crises of slavery and the Union, and black abolitionists provided a huge body of arguments (to the nation and among themselves) to fuel the debate. Just how the two causes–abolition and preserving or reinventing the Union–would ever coalesce in the interest of black freedom was the central challenge of the 1850s for blacks. It was the subject of both great expectation and great discouragement, appeals to revolution against and reform within the American political system, as well as appeals to abandon America altogether.

THIS DIALECTIC between hope and despair, past and future, took on a new urgency with the passage of the Fugitive Slave Act in

1850. As a response to longstanding southern demands for more stringent federal enforcement of the return of escaped slaves to their owners, this law provided for speedier adjudication of fugitive slave cases, and stripped an ill-fated captive of all legal safeguards, such as jury trial or even a judicial hearing. Accepted by some northern political leaders as part of the sectional truce forged in the Compromise of 1850, the Fugitive Slave Act struck fear into northern black communities and enraged antislavery activists of all kinds. Between 1850 and 1860, an estimated 20,000 blacks fled to Canada to escape capture and re-enslavement. The threat was real, as during the first six years of enforcement, when more than two hundred alleged fugitives were arrested, with only approximately twelve successfully defending their claim to freedom. Perhaps most important in the long run, the Fugitive Slave Act stimulated an organized, and often violent resistance to slave catchers and to the entire legal and institutional structure that upheld such a law. This law, and resistance to it, forced the wrongs of slavery and repression into northern consciousness in a more palpable way than ever before. No longer would fugitive slaves be the "invisible men" of the nineteenth century. The fears and aspirations of the runaway who risked all things mortal to achieve freedom, increasingly immortalized in the slave narratives and in Harriet Beecher Stowe's *Uncle Tom's Cabin* (1852), now conditioned a black and white antislavery community for a struggle that would require new weapons.[9]

Numerous fugitive slave rescues had occurred during the 1830s and 1840s, especially through the work of Vigilance Committees. Such urban organizations as those led by David Ruggles in New York and Robert Purvis and William Still in Philadelphia harbored runaways, fought their legal battles, and engaged in a wide variety of extra-legal, often violent action to protect and spirit fugitives to freedom. American textbooks and folklore know these networks of resistance as the "Underground Railroad."[10] After 1850 many operatives, as well as people freed by this system, would call their work by that famous name as well.

Either way, the anger and panic that hit northern black communities after 1850 gave a new spirit to antislavery resistance. Henry Bibb, himself a fugitive with family still enslaved in Kentucky, spoke more than hyperbole when he reacted to the new law. "If there is no alternative but to go back to slavery, or die contending for liberty," said Bibb, "then death is far preferable." Resolutions condemning the law and appealing for resistance to slave catchers poured from meetings across the North. Providence, Rhode Island, blacks pledged to "sacrifice our lives and our all upon the altar of protection to our wives, our children and our fellow sufferers in common with us." In Philadelphia, blacks passed ten resolutions, concluding with an appeal that demonstrates the decline of moral suasion in the face of new realities. They preferred "only those moral means of truth," said the Philadelphia gathering. But the Fugitive Slave bill was an "unheard of" level of injustice; so they swore to "resist to the death any attempt to enforce it upon our persons." Thus the rhetoric of righteous violence, the art of war propaganda, and the claims for retributive justice that would explode among blacks after the outbreak of the Civil War received a full-throated rehearsal during the resistance to the Fugitive Slave Act of the early 1850s. William P. Powell, an aggressive activist who had protested Jim Crow before the Massachusetts legislature and labored for women's rights and black self-reliance from a pacifist perspective, found the Fugitive Slave Act more than he could bear. By such legislation, Powell concluded, the federal government had "declared war" upon blacks, free and slave, a sentiment shared widely in abolitionist communities. Concerned about the law, and worried about the education of his seven children, Powell moved to Liverpool, England, for ten years, returning to America only when the secession crisis in 1860 prompted new hopes.[11]

In America, rhetoric and reality met in numerous actual rescues of fugitive slaves. Among the most celebrated were the successful rescues of "Shadrach" (Frederick Wilkins) in Boston, in February 1851, Jerry McHenry in Syracuse, New York, in September 1851, and the Christiana, Pennsylvania, "riot," also in September 1851, in which a Maryland slaveowner, Edward

Gorsuch, sought to retrieve four of his escaped bondsmen. In a pitched battle fought between a large crowd of blacks armed with clubs and guns, Gorsuch was killed and his son gravely wounded. The four fugitives, hidden by abolitionists, disappeared into freedom in Canada.[12]

Less celebrated, though equally important, was the unsuccessful effort to free Anthony Burns in Boston in May 1854. Burns was a thirty-year-old fugitive slave who had recently escaped from Virginia. Seized and jailed by the local federal Fugitive Slave Law Commissioner, Burns's case became the subject of an intensive legal, and finally violent, effort to free him. After all legal means were quickly exhausted, including a counter-suit entered against Burns's Virginia owner by black community leader Lewis Hayden, an interracial mob killed one guard in an unsuccessful attempt to break the fugitive out of jail. Boston became an armed camp for a week and a half as President Franklin Pierce ordered federal troops with artillery into the city, making a test case of enforcement of the Fugitive Slave Act. Burns was escorted to the docks by a corps of U.S. Marines, and shipped back to slavery in Virginia, where he would spend four months in a slave pen before being sold. Throughout the ordeal in Boston, hundreds of blacks from that city and surrounding towns kept a vigil around the building that housed Burns. "Through that long week of agony," wrote one observer, "the vicinity of the slave pen [the Boston jail] was thronged by colored men and women, watching from dawn till eve, and some of them the long night through, patiently awaiting . . . the fate of their poor brother in bonds; seeking in every way in their power to show their sympathy for him, and hoping and praying, to the last moment, for his deliverance from the hand of the kidnapper."[13] Such a description demonstrates the circumstances for northern blacks in the mid-1850s: they had experienced a new level of militance and resistance, but in the face of state power, they were left in silent frustration.

More than a "spirit" of resistance was at work in the black response to the crises of the 1850s. Both in rhetoric and reality, the uses of violence and legal defiance had fostered immense experience with what David Ruggles, in one of the founding documents of the New York Vigilance Committee, had called "*practical* abolition." The multitude of letters written to William Still (the Philadelphia leader of the Underground Railroad) during the 1850s by fugitive slaves after they had reached relative safety in the North or in Canada attest to the meaning of freedom to so many ordinary folk. "I hear that the yellow fever is very bad down south," wrote Mary D. Armstead from New Bedford, Massachusetts, in 1855, "now if the underground railroad could have free course the emergrant would cross the river of gordan rapidly[.] I hope it may continue to run and I hope the wheels of the car may be greesed with more substantial greese so they may run over swiftly. . . ." That system never ran by a "free course"; it always operated by a combination of intricate planning, courage, and fear. But Mary Armstead's homespun "greese" metaphor nicely complements the hope embedded in the refrain of the famous Negro spiritual: "Many thousands rise and go, many thousands crossing over. . . ." By 1863, the wheels of the car would be running in ways that thousands of Mary Armsteads had spent lifetimes contemplating. With unending gratitude, another fugitive, John H. Hill, wrote to Still in 1853 to inform him of his arrival and safety in Toronto, attaching a postscript to one letter: "If you know anyone who would give me an education write and let me know for I am in want of it very much."[14] Practical abolition, indeed.

Moreover, in their resistance to the fugitive issue (revived and fueled by John Brown's raid on Harper's Ferry in 1859), black intellectuals forged a body of protest thought that, though not altogether new, in its urgency and radicalism has reverberated down through African-American history ever since. They appealed with scorching irony to the first principles of the Declaration of Independence, especially to the right of revolution. They invoked Patrick Henry's choice between life and death in the face of tyranny, called for days of fasting and prayer in one breath and the killing of kidnappers in the next, and they made the fullest possible use of the natural rights tradition to justify defiance of unjust laws. Above all, they believed they were replenishing a great tradition, not inventing one; they found deep in the bitter well of American irony their own deepest claims to citizenship, in the denial of their freedom a renewed fervor to assert it. Such resistance congealed into arguments so often made that it prompted Benjamin Quarles to conclude that more than anyone else, it was antebellum black abolitionists who refused to allow the United States to ever "derevolutionize the Revolution."[15]

Many black abolitionists took heart from the emerging political antislavery movement, participated in the Liberty and Freesoil parties in the 1840s, and entered an ambivalent but significant relationship with the Republican party in the 1850s. They also found a storehouse of political hope in the antislavery interpretation of the United States Constitution. By the mid-1850s, political abolitionists had advanced the theory by which, at the very least, slavery was judged to be a "local" and not a "national" institution, thereby giving the federal government the authority to abolish human bondage wherever it had exclusive jurisdiction (the District of Columbia, the western territories). Following the lead of white abolitionist Gerrit Smith, many black abolitionists went further, pointing to constitutional guarantees of *habeas corpus* and a "republican form of government" for every state, as well as the Fifth Amendment's declaration that no person could "be deprived of life, liberty, or property without due process of law" as proof that the federal government was constitutionally obligated to abolish slavery everywhere. All knew, no doubt, that constitutional theory would itself never be enough to rid America of slavery. But in trying to imagine a future where blacks would become an equal part of the polity, the antislavery reading of the Constitution and the Republican party's genuine hostility to slavery's expansion were rays of hope in a darkening night of despair in the 1850s. If the Constitution enshrined slavery and made American citizens "mere bodyguards and human fleshmongers," argued Frederick Douglass in 1851, "then we freely admit that reason, humanity, religion and morality alike demand that we do . . . fling from us with all possible haste . . . that accursed Constitution, and that we labor . . . for revolution, at whatever cost and at whatever peril." The political crisis over slavery forced a choice: either America's creeds were a "warrant for the abolition of slavery in every state in the union," as Douglass put it, or the only alternative was violent revolution. Some black leaders had for years suggested that the latter path might be the only recourse (David Walker in 1829 and Henry Highland Garnet in 1843).[16] But this contrast of extreme alternatives became clearer and not merely rhetorical in the 1850s, and it compelled an awareness among black leaders that desperation can be the seedbed of both revolution and a hard-earned political realism.

Perhaps nothing symbolized the plight of blacks in the 1850s so completely, nor caused as much desperation, as the words of Chief Justice Roger B. Taney in the Dred Scott decision of 1857. Black people were "beings of an inferior order," said Taney, "so far inferior, that they had no rights which the white man was bound to respect."[17] Coming from the high court, the denial of black citizenship—which was really the denial of a future in America—had a disturbing air of finality. One black abolitionist said the Dred Scott decision had made slavery "the supreme law of the land and all descendants of the African race denationalized." Mary Ann Shadd Cary, by then leading an emigration movement to Canada, advised her fellow blacks: "Your national ship is rotten and sinking, why not leave it?" Deeply angry, Robert Purvis addressed the annual meeting of the American Anti-slavery Society in New York City shortly after the Scott decision in May 1857. Purvis had "no patience" with any "newfangled doctrine of the anti-slavery character of the American Constitution." He declared himself fed up with "a government that tramples me and all that are dear to me in the dust." Purvis took heart only in "a prospect of this atrocious government being overthrown, and a better one built up in its place." Such rhetoric of revolution among blacks became their best means of understanding the road to disunion that the Dred Scott decision helped so much to build. Writing just after the Scott decision and evoking the economic anxieties that would soon explode in the Panic of 1857, the free-born poet Frances Ellen Watkins Harper wished Americans would have a deeper moral reaction to slavery. Thousands of lives ruined by unrequited physical toil "should send a thrill of horror through the nerves of civilization and impel the heart of humanity to lofty deeds," claimed Watkins Harper. "So it might," she said, "if men had not found out a fearful alchemy by which this blood can be transformed into gold. Instead of listening to the cry of agony, they listen to the ring of dollars and stoop down to pick up the coin."[18] Karl Marx could hardly have said it more poignantly. In this case, the poet understood the political economy; the country was about to experience both a moral and an economic panic in the last years before disunion.

Despair infested black communities in the wake of Dred Scott, but many black abolitionists found in such discouragement the motivation for greater exertions and even more militant rhetoric. J. Sella Martin, the pastor of Joy Street Baptist Church in Boston, drew large audiences with a prepared address on Nat Turner's insurrection, and William J. Watkins, formerly an assistant editor on Frederick Douglass's newspaper, toured the abolitionist circuit with a speech entitled "Irrepressible Conflict." John Rock, the young Boston lawyer, speaking at an anniversary observance of the Boston Massacre in March 1858, announced that he spoke "not simply to honor those brave men who shed their blood for freedom, or to protest the Dred Scott decision," but to "enter into new vows of duty." "Sooner or later," warned Rock, "the clashing of arms will be heard in this country, and the black man's services will be needed." It is easy today to see a clear line of continuity between Rock's rhetoric and the recruitment of black soldiers for the Union army, as well as the war's fortunate ruin of the Dred Scott decision, less than five years later. But in those agonizing years, such clarity was as difficult to achieve in black communities as it was in the larger American political culture. By the end of 1858, Frederick Douglass could only counsel his people to "walk by faith, not by sight."[19]

For some antebellum blacks, the despair of the 1850s found release in the alternative of emigration. In the search for a place where they might find a true sense of belonging, some leaders turned to Canada, the Caribbean, or to West Africa. Several significant movements of black emigrationism emerged in the 1850s. The first, beginning in 1852, was led by Martin R. Delany, a physician and antislavery author and editor from Pittsburgh. In 1854, Delany wielded great influence over the National Emigration Convention that met in Cleveland, Ohio, denouncing all cooperation with white abolitionists and advocating mass emigration to the Caribbean or South America. By 1859, Delany shifted his interest to Africa. He made friendly overtures to Liberia, sought money from white colonizationists (an old movement by then which could date its origins from 1816), and led the celebrated Niger Valley Exploring Party into West Africa. Delany was intensely race-conscious, and after his conversion to emigrationism in 1852, he saw no prospect for blacks, free or slave, overcoming what he persistently called their "degradation" within American society. As a thinker, Delany helped some blacks imagine, if not create, a black "nation" beyond the pressures and realities of their American lives. As for so many others, the Civil War would be a major turning point in Delany's career; by 1865, he would be the first black commissioned field officer in the Union army.[20]

A second emigration movement was led by Mary Ann Shadd Cary, the eldest of eighteen children of Abraham Shadd, a prominent black shoemaker and abolitionist in Wilmington, Delaware. As a child, Mary Ann Shadd moved to Pennsylvania where she was educated in a Quaker school. She eventually took up residence in Canada in 1850, and with Samuel Ringgold Ward founded the newspaper the *Provincial Freeman*. Shadd was a tireless advocate of women's rights and education, and through her long lecture tours of the North, as well as her newspaper, she became perhaps the most persistent voice of Canadian emigration, a cause spurred by events and geography in the 1850s, as well as by arguments.[21]

A third movement appeared with the African Civilization Society in 1858, led by the Presbyterian minister Henry Highland Garnet. As early as 1850 Garnet, a former fugitive slave from Maryland and an eloquent participant in the black convention movement, developed ties to the English free-produce movement. He modeled his own organization on the plan to develop West Africa's economic potential, especially through cotton production. The African Civilization Society was biracial, closely linked to white philanthropy, and very controversial among free blacks. Beginning in 1859, a fourth phase of emigrationism focused on Haiti. With Christian missionary zeal, the Haitian Emigration Bureau was led by the black Episcopalian James T. Holly of New Haven, Connecticut, and the Scottish-born journalist from Boston, James Redpath. In 1860–61 the Bureau had several agents working in cities across the North, published its own newspaper, the *Pine and Palm*, and stirred considerable interest among free blacks.[22]

Emigration schemes caused great rancor among black leadership by the eve of the Civil War. The majority of black abolitionists, often led by James McCune Smith and Frederick Douglass, had either denounced or ignored Delany's plans from their inception. Garnet's organization was especially controversial; opposition meetings were held all over the North in 1859–60, some collapsing into bitter exchanges and even fist-fights. The bitterness of the debate over emigration was a measure of the fundamental commitments on both sides and the sheer frustration blacks faced in the 1850s. In whatever form this debate took—claims to "birthright" as American citizens, the "redemption" of Africa, the reinforcement or overcoming of white racism, or simply the individual emigrant's desire to make a new start in life—it was always a struggle to imagine a future, a place where black folk could find livelihood and secure social identities. Typical of black opposition to emigration was an 1853 Illinois state convention that denounced "all attempts . . . to expatriate us from the land of our birth," yet went on to write more than thirty resolutions condemning slavery, calling for self-reliant uplift, and demanding full political and civil rights.[23] However divisive, black responses to the crises of the 1850s were driven both by strife and expectation.

The role the slaves themselves played in causing the Civil War can never be precisely determined. But collectively, by both their mere presence and their concerted actions, they exerted enormous pressure on the sectional conflict of the 1850s. Through a combination of peasant patience, daily resistance, and occasional overt rebellions, slaves became, however consciously, participants in the *political* crisis surrounding their fate. From Nat Turner's insurrection in 1831 through the frenzied aftermath of John Brown's raid in 1859, white Southerners could never really contemplate the slavery question—its existence or expansion—without considering the potential of violent unrest in their midst. The political stakes for slaveholders grew in proportion to their deepening economic commitment to slave labor, but the stakes also increased in relation to their declining sense of physical security. Proslavery ideology became increasingly intransigent, as well as more radical in its suppression of civil liberties and its quest for self-protection, as white Southerners felt threatened by a combination of alleged northern "abolition emissaries" and by their own insubordinate slaves.[24]

As many white Southerners found public and private ways to admit, the fear of insurrection and general insecurity in the slave regime were not merely abolitionist literary inventions. As early as 1832, in Virginia's harrowing debate over emancipation conducted in the wake of Nat Turner's rebellion, James McDowell asked the unpopular question: "Was it the fear of Nat Turner, and his deluded, drunken handful of followers, which produced such effects?" "No sir," answered McDowell, "it was the suspicion eternally attached to the slave himself—the suspicion that a Nat Turner might be in every family, that the same bloody deed might be acted over at any time and in any place. . . ." Similarly, in January 1859, a South Carolina judge, while sentencing a man convicted of aiding a slave's escape, provided a revealing insight into the fundamental insecurity at the base of proslavery ideology. After declaring slaves to be a "description of property" that government was bound to "protect," Judge Francis Withers lectured the defendant: "Slaves are capable of being seduced . . . capable of evil purposes as well as good. They are, to a certain extent, free agents. They have brains, nerves, hands, and thereby can conceive and execute a malignant purpose. When, therefore, you . . . succeed in corrupting a slave, in swerving him from allegiance, what have you done but turn loose an enemy to society in its very bosom."[25] Even before John Brown touched off a wave of southern hysteria in the fall of 1859, it is clear that the image of Nat Turner had never left the white southern psyche. Neither had the nameless "free agents." Something in the slaves themselves, and in the contradictions of the system that controlled their "brains," "nerves," and "hands," left many slaveholders with what historian Steven Channing has called an "undiminished anxiety," a psychological disposition that transformed a desperate need for *race control* into a political movement for secession.[26]

Put simply, the potential of slave unrest in relation to political crisis had a good deal to do with why the war came. In the late 1850s, especially during election seasons, white Southerners became increasingly concerned about the level of political awareness among their slaves. The extraordinary intensity and sectional hostility of the 1856 presidential election, the first such canvass in which the antislavery Republican party made a bid for power with the candidacy of John C. Fremont, caused widespread insurrection rumors and some bloody reprisals against alleged slave rebels in Tennessee and other states.[27] In the sectional crisis over slavery, perception was becoming reality for many Americans. As southern editors increasingly condemned the alleged "secret missionaries" sent by the Republicans to inform the slaves "that Fremont's election would be the signal of their liberation," the slaves were listening. Few slaves may have ever known or met an abolition emissary, but that their masters could not stop talking about or preparing for such specters was exciting, if unsettling, news in the quarters and the fields of slaves' daily lives. Sectional fear had become racial fear for white Southerners. And slaves themselves could hardly avoid noticing that the world of politics—its rallies and rituals—had become the place where white folks debated the fate of black folks. Sarah Fitzpatrick, an ex-slave born in 1847 in Alabama, recalled the late 1850s as a time of fear mixed with knowledge. "I 'member fo' de war," said Fitzpatrick, "us chillun use' ta go out in de evenin' an' watch de white fo'ks drill. Dey thought 'Niggers' didn't un'erstand whut wuz gwin' on, but dey knowed whut it meant, dey wuz jes' scaid to say anythin' 'bout it."[28]

Of even greater significance was the wave of slave insurrection panics and reprisals that swept the South after the Harper's Ferry raid in 1859 and 1860. As Clarence Mohr has carefully demonstrated for the state of Georgia, John Brown laid bare the deepest racial fears and social insecurities of white Southerners. Widespread reports of slave arson and broader insubordination, suppression of free speech and attacks on northern salesmen and travelers, and a general "mob psychosis" took over the political and social lives of Georgians during the election year of 1860. Such hysteria was fueled even more by the Texas insurrection panic of the summer of that year, in which approximately fifty blacks and whites died in vigilante violence.[29]

Historians continue to debate whether actual slave conspiracies caused such eruptions in the southern social fabric in 1860. But politics, as we continue to learn, is a process of warring perceptions rooted very often in real ideas. Then as now, John Brown, as well as the numerous alleged slave "ringleaders" of revolts who were executed during the year before secession, were far more important as symbols than as realities. What is certain is that white Southerners were deeply worried about maintaining a social order under great duress. Southern editors especially warned about the presence of blacks at political meetings in 1860. A Rome, Georgia, editor tellingly cautioned against the "loose and unguarded discussion before negroes, of the political excitement of which they are the cause." In the cotton belt, the *cause* seemed to be everywhere. A Macon, Georgia, white resident described the problem as many must have seen it by September, 1860. "Every political speech" in the presidential campaign, he said, "attracted a number of negroes, who, without entering the Hall, have managed to linger around and hear what the orators say until the bell rings, when they leave. They do not congregate in sufficient numbers to make an unlawful assembly, but scatter themselves around—some at the hall door and some

in the streets. . . ."[30] Slaveholders continued to assure themselves that theirs was a system based on familial relationships,
white paternalism and black loyalty, at the same time they
described a world teeming with thinking, breathing rebels from
within and without. Civil wars are always, perhaps, rooted in
the deepest and most tragic of contradictions. In towns and on
plantations, the South's racial order, as well as its political economy, was fundamentally threatened in 1860, whether the Republican party intended it in quite such a combination or not.

The manner in which two generations of fugitives pushed
their way into freedom and into the political center of the
national "house divided" may demonstrate even more how slaves
themselves anticipated the war, or at least envisioned the political strife at its core. That story was told over and again in the
slave narratives, which were testimonies not only to the romantic travail of escape, a genre the nineteenth century cherished.
But former slave autobiographies were also the foundation of an
African-American literary tradition; they were demonstrations
of the will to be known, and the will to be free, through the
power of language. The best of the slave narratives were "jer-
emiads," warnings about the impending doom of American
society because of the evil of slavery, at the same time they were
anguished appeals to the American creeds of liberty and justice.
The slave narratives were testaments about the meaning of freedom and of the consequences of its denial. They garnered a wide
readership in the 1850s, and in their antislavery shock effect,
their content became more severe as the sectional crisis deepened. The narratives were in many ways political sermons, chas-
tising the South for its crime of slavery, while also calling the
nation back to its promises and insisting that Americans as
a whole listen to the pleadings of ordinary slaves. Those
who would understand the problem of slavery, wrote Solomon
Northrup, must empathetically "toil" with the slave "in the
field—sleep with him in the cabin—feed with him on husks . . .
know the *heart* of the poor slave—learn his secret thoughts . . .
sit with him in the silent watches of the night—converse with
him in trustful confidence, of 'life, liberty, and the pursuit of

happiness.' . . . ."³¹ Black abolitionism, especially through the stories told in the slave narratives, had tried to enter American hearts and minds in just such a way for two decades before Fort Sumter. Moreover, Solomon Northrup and that Rome, Georgia, editor, who felt the *cause* of political excitement all around him, would probably have understood, if not appreciated, each other's use of irony. The first principles of the Declaration of Independence were precisely where all sides would eventually look in attempting to understand or avoid the causes of war.

The role slave narratives played in Civil War causation will remain part of the elusive question of the place of abolitionism itself in bringing on the conflict. But, as critic William L. Andrews has argued, slave narrative writers were "guerrilla" soldiers "of the pen," analyzing their own alienation from America, while simultaneously demanding a home within it. Their argument with America, their persistent exposure of the evil of slavery, their search for order amidst the potential chaos of broken lives, and their preservation of a sense of irony in the face of oppression tell us much about what the coming of the Civil War and emancipation would mean to blacks. In his 1855 autobiography, *My Bondage and My Freedom,* Frederick Douglass left the following timeless explanation of his hatred of slavery and desire for freedom: "The thought of only being a creature of the *present* and the *past,* troubled me, and I longed to have a *future*—a future with hope in it. To be shut up entirely to the past and present is abhorrent to the human mind; it is to the soul—whose life and happiness is unceasing progress—what the prison is to the body."³² In his yearning to have a future, Douglas captured the collective mood of his people on the eve of the Civil War. His prison metaphor might be applied both to the social condition of African-Americans and to the political condition of the United States. A thoroughly tragic but new future—one with hope in it—was about to emerge.

The conflict that would bring that new future was part of a culture of expectation in black communities, slave and free, during the prewar era. As so much recent scholarship has argued, American slaves fashioned a culture that, at its religious and folk foundations, was a means to manipulate and survive a world of irrepressible strife. Nineteenth-century American slaves conducted their lives without any modern distinction between sacred and secular; they worked, loved, hated, and dreamed in a universe of song, folktales, and religious metaphor, not transmitted merely in otherworldly terms. Their culture was, as historian Lawrence Levine has put it, "forged on the hard rock of racial, social, and economic exploitation and injustice. . . ." But how hard was the rock? How movable or unmovable in different contexts? Did the slaves pound on that rock with their labor by day, at most chipping away at the infinity of its weight, while walking around it by night living in an inner world of folk belief that allowed them to sustain their dignity and sense of a future? How many found "a home in that rock," and how many were crushed by it? The study of slave culture as resistance has been an attempt to evaluate the shape and weight of that rock. Slave songs, as well as slave narratives, are replete with the idea of a quest for a sense of "home," a world where power relationships might be reversed, where the slaves' God might enter history and overturn its injustice. "Going home" to the slaves was not only a religious metaphor for death and heaven fatalistically expressed; it was a way of imagining how the temporal world might be different. In its broadest terms the coming of the Civil War needs to be seen against this backdrop: a "theater," if you will, as William H. Seward described the country in his famous "Irrepressible Conflict" speech, but one where the slaves were not merely a chorus singing mood music, but people who had thought seriously about a coming catastrophe.[33]

Drawing upon the prophetic books of the Old Testament, Christian slaves were able to invent their own alternative history, to weave Moses and a sense of chosenness, Daniel and the lion's den, Joshua at the battle of Jericho, and a host of other stories into countless visions of deliverance. The time and location of such deliverance were, of course, never really the point. Sorrow and joy marched together in the same cadences of transcendence; the coming might be here, or it might be in a hereafter. Harriet

Beecher Stowe once heard Sojourner Truth sing, "There is a Holy City," and remarked that her performance possessed an other-worldly "fervor of Ethiopia, wild, savage, hunted of all nations." But Stowe was also amazed at how real Sojourner's "burning after God" appeared, how compelling was her "stretching her scarred hands towards the glory to be revealed." The belief structure of antebellum African-American religion must be taken seriously; it was one way blacks improvised and found a place in the land of the Dred Scott decision. As historian Albert Raboteau aptly wrote, "the story of Israel's exodus from Egypt helped make it possible for the slaves to *project a future* radically different from their present" (italics mine).[34] Slaves had rejected Justice Taney's opinion long before he wrote it. They had sung, chanted, stomped, and written of a future that no Supreme Court, collapsing second American party system, or even the armies of 1861 could prevent from fulfillment. The temporal freedom that the coming of the war would seem to make possible only meant that their faith had served them well. When the war came, white Americans in North and South would harken to a millennial faith and a religious view of history, not unlike that of the slaves, in order to understand the scope of their conflict.

When blacks, slave and free, reflected ahead to the possibility of their emancipation, they did so with a combination of millennial expectation and considerations of everyday life. Slaves often feared their would-be liberators, such as John Brown, because no one knew better than they of the bloody results of insurrections, however planned. A combination of a peasant sense of fear, cunning, and self-protection guided the vast majority of slaves through their daily lives. They were about the business of preserving their own bodies and souls, and learned, in historian Nathan Huggins's telling phrase, that "fear could be managed." But they had real expectations of what freedom would mean when it did arrive. As the emancipation process during the war would reveal, the ex-slaves seized upon the chance to control their own labor, their own persons, and the integrity of their own families. Temporal control and spiritual sustenance: both elements of black life had always been difficult to obtain, but absolutely crucial to survival. Spiritual and socio-political life were not separate matters to most antebellum blacks. "The idea of a revolution in the conditions of the whites and blacks," wrote slave narrator Charles Ball, "is the cornerstone" of black religion. And, as the sectional crisis reached the breaking point in the late 1850s, one of William Still's Underground Railroad correspondents wrote to him from Baltimore asking "what time was it when israel went to Jerico i am very anxious to hear for thare is a mighty host will pass over and you and i my brother will sing hally luja i shall notify you when the great catastrophe shal take place. . . ."[35] As the war came, blacks from all backgrounds seemed to know what time it was.

As several historians have portrayed it, the secession crisis of 1860–61 was a time of great fear. The deepest anxieties of northerners and southerners were at stake, as both sections came to view each other in conspiratorial terms. By this time, the notions of a "Slave Power" conspiracy in northern minds and a "Black Republican" conspiracy in southern minds each had long histories. The political process that had produced such conspiratorial consciousness, in its rational and irrational dimensions, was something that blacks, slave and free, had observed, interpreted, and helped to shape. Frederick Douglass remembered the secession winter as an example of the "depths" to which a "noble people can be brought under the sentiment of fear."[36] White fears, born of irreconcilable visions of the future, mingled now with black fears of whether there was a future, in the same tragic story.

After the attack on Fort Sumter, black leaders in the North responded in a variety of ways. Some urged immediate support for war, others favored caution or outright resistance in the face of the Lincoln administration's refusal to accept black enlistments. A few maintained that the hostilities would never be more than a quarrel between white men that would not free any black people. But amid uncertainty, all were deeply interested, and most knew that somebody was going to Jericho. By late summer of 1861, James McCune Smith captured decades of expectation as well as the meaning of the moment. "We are concerned in this fight and our fate hangs upon its issues," said Smith. "The South must be subjugated, or we shall be enslaved." Whatever the current policies, Smith asserted, "circumstances have been so arranged by the decrees of Providence, that in struggling for their own nationality they [white northerners] are forced to defend our rights. . . ." The conflict, the level of political disorder, the break with the past and the chance to imagine a new, re-invented American republic that so many black abolitionists had come to desire, whatever the consequences, was now at least at hand. "At last our proud Republic is overtaken," wrote Frederick Douglass immediately after Fort Sumter. Douglass spoke to the past, present, and future. "Now is the time," he announced, "to change the cry of vengeance long sent up from the . . . toiling bondsmen, into a grateful prayer for the peace and safety of the Government." Black abolitionists had rarely spoken of the United States government in such warm terms. But in spite of untold "desolations" he feared the war would bring, Douglass now saw the hope of "armed abolition" conducted in a sanctioned war against the South. Above all, he saw the central meaning of the war for all Americans in a crisis that, willed or not, "bound up the fate of the Republic and the fate of the slave in the same bundle."[37]

Comprehending the full meaning of that mutual fate, as well as understanding why it took war on such a horrible scale to make African-Americans free, have also been the central legacies of the conflict ever since.

4

The Crisis of American Democracy

The Political System and the Coming of the Civil War

WILLIAM E. GIENAPP

*M*ore than 130 YEARS after Confederate batteries opened fire on Fort Sumter, Americans are still haunted by the meaning of the Civil War. The conflict had such a profound impact on the nation, its society, institutions, and values, that few would deny its central importance in American history. Yet paradoxically the Civil War has stubbornly resisted incorporation into the mainstream of America's historical experience. Whether historians have viewed the war as a singular and ultimately incomprehensible exception to the normal operation of the country's political system, have pointed to vast unseen and uncontrollable forces as the cause of the war, or have blamed the nation's political leaders for blundering into a war that could have and should have been avoided, underlying all these interpretations is an unspoken faith in democracy as a superior form of government; only rarely has the war been considered as an understandable product of America's democratic political system.

The problem of the origins of the Civil War is too complex to be treated in all of its facets here. Instead, in this essay I intend to focus on two problems. First, what was the relationship between the structure of American politics and the coming of the war? How did the Constitution, the evolution of politics institutions, the nation's political culture, political ideology, and the spoken and unspoken rules that governed American politics facilitate the outbreak of war? And second, why did the party system realign in the 1850s? Why did the Jacksonian party system suddenly disintegrate in this decade, and why was it replaced by a new sectional alignment? Why was the Republican party the beneficiary of the collapse of the old party system, and why did the party come to power in 1860? Together, these problems–the structure of American politics and the antebellum party realignment–provide a way to assess the relationship between the American political system and the origins of the war. However much social and economic developments fueled the sectional conflict, the coming of the Civil War must be explained ultimately in political terms, for the outbreak of war in April 1861 represented the complete breakdown of the American political system. As such, the Civil War constituted the greatest single failure of American democracy.

IN EXAMINING the underlying causes of the sectional conflict, one must begin with the existence of slavery. Without slavery it is impossible to imagine a war between the North and the South (or indeed, the existence of anything we would call "the South" except as a geographic region). Nor is it possible to imagine slavery existing in 1861 if it were not based on race. If the slaves in the South had been white, the abolitionist movement would have encountered far less resistance, and slavery, if it had survived the American Revolution, would certainly have disappeared sometime before 1860.

To agree that racial slavery was an indispensable cause of the Civil War doesn't take us very far, however, in understanding the origins of that conflict. Slavery, after all, was considerably older than the Republic, and for over half a century following adoption of the Constitution, the institution had only sporadically been an issue in national politics, and it had never dominated state politics in either section.

Fundamental to the growing crisis between the North and the South was the rise of the slavery issue in American society. This development was rooted in a number of changes in American society in the first half of the nineteenth century: population trends, the economic development of the two sections, the transportation revolution, the uneven impact of modernization, the romantic movement, the spread of evangelical Protestantism, the reform impulse, and the geographic expansion of the country. Given the nature of the revivals of the Second Great Awakening, the changes in American Protestantism during these years, and the impact of romanticism, the emergence of some kind of militant antislavery movement in the North was inevitable. There was nothing accidental about the appearance of abolitionism in the 1830s. The movement did not depend on some chance event or the presence of any particular individual.[1]

The rise of abolitionism, however, did not make it inevitable that slavery become a political issue. Abolitionists initially rejected political action against slavery in favor of moral suasion, and party leaders were anxious to keep slavery out of partisan politics. Indeed, the leaders of the second party system consciously tried to suppress the slavery issue and isolate it from partisan divisions. A decade of agitation by the abolitionists and proslavery partisans in the South failed to make slavery a vital, pressing concern in national politics.

Instead, it was the politicians themselves, as part of the struggle for control of the two major parties, who ultimately injected the slavery issue into national politics. The key development was the introduction in Congress in 1846 of the Wilmot Proviso, which prohibited slavery from any territory acquired from Mexico, by a group of Van Burenite Democrats who were angry with President James K. Polk and his southern advisers. Once the slavery issue, in the shape of the question of its expansion into the western territories, entered the political arena, it proved impossible to get it out. The issue took on a life of its own, and when politicians tried to drop the issue after 1850, they discovered that many voters were unwilling to acquiesce.

A second critical development, intimately related to the first, was the crystallization of rival sectional ideologies oriented toward protecting white equality and opportunity. Increasingly, each section came to see the other section and its institutions as a threat to its vital social, political, and economic interests. Increasingly, each came to think that one section or the other had to be dominant. Informed by these ideologies, a majority of the residents of each section feared the other, and well before the fighting started the sectional conflict represented a struggle for control of the nation's future.

IT FELL TO the political system to adjudicate differences between the sections and preserve a feeling of mutual cooperation and unity. And for a long time the political system had successfully defused sectional tensions. Because it brought northern and southern leaders together, Congress was the primary arena for hammering out solutions to sectional problems. In various sectional confrontations—the struggle over the admission of Missouri as a slave state in 1819–21, the controversy over nullification and the tariff in 1833, the problem of the status of slavery in the territory acquired from Mexico in 1850, and the struggle over the proslavery Lecompton constitution in 1858— Congress had always managed to find some acceptable way out of the crisis.

Yet the American political system was particularly vulnerable to sectional strains and tensions. One reason was the institutional structure of American politics. The Civil War occurred within a particular political institutional framework that, while it did not make the war inevitable, was essential to the coming of the war.

Integral to this institutional framework was the United States Constitution. While some aspects of the Constitution retarded the development of sectionalism, it contained a number of provisions that strengthened the forces of sectional division in the nation. No constitution can anticipate all future developments and conclusively deal with all controversies that subsequently arise. The purpose in analyzing the Constitution's role in the sectional conflict is not to fault its drafters or condemn it as a flawed document, but rather to indicate the importance of certain of its clauses for the origins of the war.[2]

One significant feature of the Constitution was its provision for amendment. Lurking beneath the surface in the slavery controversy was white Southerners' fear that the Constitution would be amended to interfere with the institution. In advocating secession after Abraham Lincoln's election, Governor Andrew B. Moore of Alabama predicted that the Republicans would quickly create a number of new free states in the West, which "in hot haste will be admitted to the Union, until they have a majority to alter the Constitution. Then slavery will be abolished by law in the States."[3]

No one could foresee in 1861 the number of states that would be formed out of the western territories, and few Americans believed that the country's geographic expansion was nearing an end, but if the fifteen slave states remained loyal to slavery, no constitutional amendment abolishing slavery could be ratified even today (at present 38 states would have to approve of such an amendment, and if Texas had at some point been divided into as many as five states, as the terms of annexation allowed, ratification of an antislavery amendment would be even more unlikely). Moreover, one might ponder what effect the proposed thirteenth amendment forever guaranteeing slavery in the southern states, which passed Congress in 1861, would have had on the sectional conflict if it had been approved in 1820 or 1833.

The Constitution's fundamental ambiguity on a number of matters involving slavery that eventually became sources of sectional controversy also stimulated the growing conflict between the North and the South. These points included the status of slavery in the territories, the power of Congress over the institution in the District of Columbia, whether the power of Congress to regulate interstate commerce extended to the slave trade, whether it was a state or federal responsibility to return runaway slaves, and whether Congress could impose conditions on a new state or refuse to admit a new slave state to the Union.

But the most crucial ambiguity of the Constitution was whether a state had the right to leave the Union. Whereas the Articles of Confederation had proclaimed the Union to be perpetual, the Constitution contained no such statement. Indeed, nowhere did it discuss whether a state could secede or not. In the absence of any explicit provision, neither the nationalists nor the secessionists could present a conclusive argument on the subject. In upholding the perpetuity of the Union, Abraham Lincoln conceded that the language of the Constitution was not decisive.

"Perpetuity is implied, if not expressed, in the fundamental law of all national governments," he declared in his first inaugural address. "It is safe to assert that no government proper, ever had a provision in its organic law for its own termination."[4]

The Constitution's silence on this matter contributed to the intensity of the debate over secession, for it allowed Southerners to plausibly maintain that secession was a legal right of each state under the Constitution, a belief that fueled southern extremism. The point is not that Southerners were wrong when they upheld the right of secession. Indeed, the proponents of secession had a strong constitutional argument, probably a stronger argument than the nationalists advanced. Instead, the point is that if it had been agreed that there was no right of secession under the Constitution and the advocates of southern independence had been forced instead to defend their cause on grounds of the natural right of revolution, they would have had much less success in winning the support, even momentarily, of moderate and conservative Southerners.

The presidency occupies a central place in evaluating the institutional framework of the war's origins. Andrew Jackson fundamentally transformed the office by taking a more activist role in shaping legislation, appealing directly to the people for support, and portraying the president as the people's representative in the federal government. The presidency became the focus of partisanship, and although subsequent presidents generally were not as active or forceful as Jackson, parties placed great importance on controlling the office. Under Jackson's influence, the presidency became the symbolic center of the federal government, and perhaps it is therefore not surprising that the states of the Deep South seceded in response to the outcome of a presidential election.

Had the delegates at Philadelphia created an executive council, as many critics wished, less weight would have been attached to control of the executive branch. Given the nation's experience under the Articles, however, the creation of a single executive is understandable. More critical was the method they devised for electing a president. Although Jackson claimed that the president represented the people, he was not directly elected by the voters. Anxious to insulate the presidency from popular pressures, the delegates at Philadelphia created the cumbersome electoral college to select a president. This was a major mistake that played directly into the hands of sectional extremists.

In the long run, the creation of the electoral college, and especially adoption in the nineteenth century of the winner-take-all principle, played a crucial role in the coming of the Civil War. In maneuvering for partisan advantage, parties jettisoned election of presidential electors by congressional district in favor of awarding all of a state's electoral votes to the candidate with the most popular votes (these votes, of course, were not cast directly for the presidential candidate, but instead for a slate of party electors pledged to a particular candidate). In the presidential elections from 1844 to 1860, only once, in 1852, did the winning candidate poll a majority of the popular vote. Yet beyond adopting the Twelfth Amendment, which separated the election of president and vice president in the electoral college, Congress made no changes in the procedure for selecting the president.

The consequence of bloc voting by states was not only to magnify the importance of the largest and most heavily populated states, which controlled the most electoral votes, but also to make a sectional party feasible. With its support confined to the North, the Republican party could never have won a popularly based presidential election. Indeed, in 1860 Abraham Lincoln won less than 40 percent of the votes cast, but because his support was overwhelmingly concentrated in the North, which had a majority of the electoral votes, he was victorious in the electoral college. Under the winner-take-all principle, Lincoln received 98 percent of the North's electoral votes although he won less than 54 percent of the popular vote in the free states.[5] A sectional northern party could carry a national election only under a system such as the electoral college which translates a popular plurality into an electoral majority.

Because of the electoral college, the establishment of state boundaries, which was done with little forethought, had enormous significance for the coming of the Civil War. The direct popular election of president would have negated the historical accident of state boundaries. Voting in such states as Ohio, Indiana, and Illinois in the North, or Alabama, Mississippi, and North Carolina in the South, followed sectional lines, and thus drawing state boundaries differently can produce dramatically different results (this analysis inevitably ignores the potential impact of a state's heritage and political culture on partisanship). Had smaller states been created, such as Thomas Jefferson had suggested in the 1780s, the outcome of the 1860 election might have been different (recombining the 1860 votes approximately along the lines of Jefferson's proposed states indicates that Lincoln might still have won enough electoral votes to be elected, but the margin is so close that it is impossible to be certain).[6]

What made the electoral college such an anachronism was not the winner-take-all principle but rather the development that it reflected: the rise of political parties. The drafters of the Constitution had not envisioned party contests for the presidency, and hence they had not taken this extra-constitutional institution into account in creating the electoral college. The development of political parties linked to large number of voters through intensely held partisan identities dramatically transformed the nature of presidential elections. Rather than selecting the most qualified man from the leading figures of the nation, the electoral college became a mere formality to ratify the decision of party nominating conventions and the electorate. The Founders cannot be faulted for not foreseeing the development of parties, but the fact remains that in creating the electoral college they inadvertently made possible the formation of a powerful sectional party such as the Republican party. The election of a Republican president in 1860 was the only likely event on the political horizon that had the potential to precipitate secession and war.

The Twelfth Amendment provides that in the event no candidate has a majority of the electoral votes, the House of Representatives, with each state casting one vote, is to select a president from the three candidates with the highest number of electoral votes. The House that would make this decision was a lame duck body, having been elected two years earlier and its term due to expire in a few months. This provision was of vital importance in shaping party strategies in the 1860 presidential election. The only hope to deny Lincoln a victory was to throw the election into the House; the outcome in such an eventuality was unclear, but it seemed certain that Lincoln could not win. Having the House select the president represented the only chance of victory for either John Bell on the Constitutional Union ticket or John C. Breckinridge, the southern Democratic candidate. The expectation of a deadlocked presidential election was a central consideration in the disruption of the Democratic party at Charleston in 1860, and also for the formation of the Constitutional Union party. A number of schemes were discussed to manipulate the electoral vote with this end in view. Some southern radicals hoped to prevent any selection in the House and have the Senate elect the Vice President, who would then be the acting president. They calculated that the Senate, where the South had more strength, would likely select Joseph Lane, Breckinridge's running mate, as Vice President.

As this possibility suggests, the creation of the vice presidency, which John Adams, its first incumbent, dismissed as "the most insignificant office that ever the invention of man contrived or his imagination conceived," was unfortunate.[7] Over the years, the vice presidency has been an indisputable source of political entertainment. But in the event of the president's death, the vice presidency ceases to be a laughing matter, and its occupant is of crucial importance. In the two decades before the Civil War, two vice presidents succeeded to the presidency upon the death of the president. Millard Fillmore was a competent if undistinguished president; John Tyler was an utter disaster. More important, neither could ever have been elected president on his own merits. The creation of the vice presidency subjected the nation to a dangerous gamble. If the vice presidents had been men of talent and distinction, as the Founders intended, then the consequences of a president's death would not have been so momentous. But the office quickly became a haven for second-rate politicians. A system to elect a new president upon the death of the incumbent would have been far superior.

Another important factor in the eventual outbreak of war was the decision of the constitutional convention to set the presidential term at four years with the possibility for re-election. This feature allowed presidents to remain in office pursuing harmful policies after they had been repudiated by the electorate. The most obvious examples were Franklin Pierce and James Buchanan. In the ensuing congressional elections, Democrats met a resounding defeat after passage of the Kansas-Nebraska Act in 1854 and the attempt to admit Kansas under the proslavery Lecompton constitution in 1858, yet Pierce and Buchanan continued in office. Under a ministerial system such as exists in many parliamentary democracies they would have been removed after these elections. A similar situation prevailed in John Tyler's administration. Tyler's incessant warfare with the Whigs in Congress enabled Democrats to regain control of Congress in 1842, yet short of impeachment there was no way to remove "His Accidency," who had no significant popular support.

Also important was the Democratic party's adoption of the paralyzing two-thirds rule for its national conventions. Enacted in 1844 to prevent Martin Van Buren's nomination, the requirement that a candidate receive two-thirds of the votes in order to be nominated, which continued in force at subsequent conventions, made it impossible for the Democratic party to pick a strong candidate. Prominent party leaders inevitably made enough enemies to be denied the nomination. Except for the choice of James K. Polk, a dark horse, the party failed to nominate forceful men for the presidency in this period. In addition, the two-thirds rule gave the South a veto over the party's presidential candidate, yet the South alone could not elect a president. This situation proved particularly damaging in 1860, when southern delegates blocked Stephen A. Douglas's nomination. Douglas was certainly the strongest candidate the party could run as well as the most popular Democrat in the country, yet southern intransigence prevented his nomination by a united party.

What we might term the American political tradition also shaped the sectional conflict and ultimately contributed to the failure of the political system. In the nineteenth century republicanism gave way to democracy as the central American political creed. After 1820, the democratic reform movement expanded the suffrage by abolishing property requirements in favor of white manhood suffrage, made many more offices elective, and reduced or abolished property requirements for office-holding. At the same time, by extolling the wisdom of the common people and contending that public policy should reflect the popular will, this movement fundamentally changed the relationship between voters and political leaders. Rather than being independent, leaders were expected to follow the desires of the majority, as expressed in election results, and ambitious politicians soon learned that to win office they needed to portray themselves as the champion of the people's interests against their aristocratic enemies.

These changes created a much more volatile political system. Widespread suffrage, heated party campaigns, and closely competitive elections caused turnout to soar, so that in the last two decades before the Civil War, over 70 percent of the eligible voters regularly cast ballots in presidential elections. Moreover, turnout was also high in state and congressional contests, far eclipsing comparable figures in the twentieth century; in some states, something like 90 percent of the eligible voters participated in antebellum elections. With a larger, less sophisticated electorate, wily politicians manipulated popular passions and stimulated popular fears, particularly by emphasizing alleged threats to equality and opportunity. This tactic was especially prevalent in the South, where extremists repeatedly whipped up sentiment to defend slavery by catering to the fears of non-slaveholders that emancipation would destroy white equality. These easily aroused popular fears, which exploited the status slavery provided to poorer whites, placed tremendous pressures on moderate southern politicians.

The uniqueness of the nation's political calendar in the antebellum period further contributed to political instability. Unlike today, nineteenth-century elections occurred at widely varying times. Congressional elections, for example, took place over an eighteen-month period. In a number of states, local and county elections often occurred in the spring, and state elections were held at a different time than national elections.[8] As a result, a much larger part of the year was filled with political campaigning. Incessant electioneering kept popular emotions high and allowed little time for tempers to cool or feelings to subside. Edward Everett, the famous Massachusetts educator, admitted that "frequent elections keep us in hot water."[9]

Although democracy increasingly shaped the nation's political culture in these years, republicanism, which was the heritage of the American Revolution, had a long-term impact as well. The main legacy of republicanism for the antebellum period was not its fear of commerce, which had largely disappeared by mid-century, but rather its deeply ingrained fear of power, and more particularly its conspiratorial mentality. Inheriting a belief in conspiracies from the Revolutionary generation, nineteenth-century Americans continued to fear conspiracies among those in power to destroy liberty. Antebellum political rhetoric was steeped with allusions to conspiracies. By the 1850s, this underlying belief was expressed by the two sectional symbols of the Slave Power and the Black Republicans—each portrayed as an illegitimate organization and hence a threat to the Republic—but they were hardly unique. Rather, this basic fear could be discerned in the Democratic party's attack on the money power, in Whigs' emphasis on the threat of the executive veto, and in the Anti-Masonic movement's assault on Masonry. The Civil War generation merely reshaped this longstanding tradition to its own ends, redirecting fear from the demons of the Jacksonian era to the new threats of the sectional antislavery Republican party (the Black Republicans) and the aristocratic slaveholding class (the Slave Power).

The final aspect of the antebellum political system that requires comment is the process by which Americans voted in this period. In the absence of state-printed ballots, political parties printed their own list of candidates, usually on distinctively colored paper and often with a party symbol, which party workers distributed to voters at the polls. After making any changes they desired, voters deposited this slip in the ballot box (the paper's color disclosed which party each voter supported). Secret, state-printed ballots would not be the norm until the Progressive era.

The unforeseen consequence of this procedure was to greatly increase the threat of independent candidates and the number of important third parties. The major handicap confronting third parties and independent candidates today is access to the ballot. Sharing a common interest to limit competition and isolate dissident groups, the two major parties in the early twentieth century devised rules to thwart independent candidates and block the creation of third parties. Contemporary independent candidates have to spend large sums of money and divert considerable energy to the time-consuming process of qualifying for a place on the ballot. In the antebellum period, all that a candidate needed to run for office was a printing press and a group of loyal volunteers to distribute ballots. The result was a host of independent candidates and third parties that contested countless elections from the local level all the way up to the presidency. The prevalence of third parties undermined political stability and put pressure on the major parties to cater to the wishes of zealous groups and single-minded crusaders. Unlike today, parties did not feel secure from grass-roots insurgency, a situation that eventually played into the hands of extremists who agitated sectional issues.

The ease of conducting political campaigns in the antebellum period was also important for the development of the sectional conflict. The parties controlled nominations and used that power to keep radicals out of power. But insurgents did not have to capture control of an existing party in order to contest an election. Instead, they could simply launch a new party. Today such a step is legally cumbersome and necessitates vast sums of money. But little money was needed to run a campaign, even at the national level, before the Civil War. The Republican National Committee raised about $50,000 in 1856 for its first national campaign, and the Democrats (who had to conduct a campaign in the South as well) spent about twice that amount.

Unpaid volunteers did most of the work, and the major means of disseminating information was through party newspapers, which required little capital investment, especially for weeklies published in small towns. A group of dedicated supporters, armed with a printing press and the willingness to work, was sufficient to mount a campaign. As a result, third parties were a persistent threat to the established parties.

The most important third party of the period, and indeed the most successful third party in American history, was the Republican party. Its emergence in 1856 as a major alternative to the Democrats dramatically intensified the sectional conflict, and the party's victory in 1860 – the last time a new party has carried a presidential election in American history – began the final rush to civil war.

As the response to Abraham Lincoln's election in 1860 indicates, the party realignment of the 1850s played a major role in the coming of the war. As long as the nation harbored two major national parties, it was difficult to imagine a political deadlock of the magnitude necessary to produce civil war. A party system based on two national parties offered the greatest security to the South. And indeed, the Jacksonian party system deliberately suppressed the slavery issue in order to prevent sectionalism from threatening the Union. Martin Van Buren, who had been badly shaken by the bitter sectional debate over Missouri's admission in 1820, conceived of the Democratic party at its birth as an intersectional organization that would keep the slavery issue down and direct public attention to questions of economic development and federal power.[10] The rise of the slavery issue in the 1840s had shaken the party system and momentarily detached a number of disgruntled voters in the free states, but the party system – and the Union – gained a narrow escape through the Compromise of 1850. With the fall-off in the antislavery Free Soil vote in the North, and the rejection of secession in the Deep South, the party system appeared to have survived intact, and commentators anticipated that popular interest would shift from sectional issues to other matters.

Then abruptly and without warning, the party system re-aligned. The realignment of the 1850s produced a serious escalation of the sectional crisis. By the time this realignment had run its course, the Whig party had disappeared, the Democratic party was badly weakened, and a new organization, the sectional Republican party, had become the strongest party in the nation. The rise of the antislavery Republican party to national power precipitated the final sequence of events that led to war.

The existence of a competitive party system is essential for a political democracy, since it is impossible to sustain democracy for any period of time based on a one-party system. Consequently, in a democracy, it is necessary that opposition parties be accepted as legitimate. A majority of Southerners, however, refused to accord the Republican party this standing, and thus from their perspective the party's presidential victory in 1860 represented more than simply one party assuming national power in the place of another. In the face of this denial of the Republican party's legitimacy, elections took on an extreme life-or-death kind of quality. For these Southerners, a Democratic defeat was not perceived as a momentary setback, easily reversed at the next presidential election. Instead, it was deemed a fateful defeat, the disastrous consequences of which could not be avoided. Thus it is no exaggeration to say that the creation of the Republican party, and its emergence as a powerful political organization, was one of the most crucial links, if not *the* most crucial link, in the chain of Civil War causation.[11]

There was nothing inevitable, however, about the rise of the Republican party. Another set of events in the 1850s might have led to a different outcome, and thus the historian must analyze these developments from the perspective of the time, with due allowance for chance and contingency, rather than reasoning backward from the war's beginning in 1861. The Republican party's growing strength did not foreclose the possibility of avoiding war, but it significantly narrowed the range of options and limited the ability of political moderates to defuse the slavery issue in national politics.

The antebellum party realignment was neither the first nor the last such upheaval in American history, but no other realignment has had such decisive consequences. In some important ways, the Civil War realignment was unlike the shuffling of voters' preferences in the 1890s and the 1930s, for it involved two distinct phenomena that occurred simultaneously. On the one hand, the Whig party collapsed and disappeared as a competitive organization. At the same time, the Republican party was born and eventually succeeded the Whigs as the Democratic party's primary opponent. The usual view is that the death of the Whigs and the rise of the Republican party stemmed from the same cause—the issue of the extension of slavery—and thus the Republican party rapidly and almost inexorably assumed the Whigs' place in the two-party system. According to the traditional interpretation, the slavery issue, particularly the passage in 1854 of the Kansas-Nebraska Act, which opened the remainder of the Louisiana Purchase to slavery, accounted for both the demise of the Whigs and the success of the new Republican party, and hence heightened sectionalism produced the realignment of the 1850s.

This interpretation, however, is far too simple, and even a cursory examination of voting patterns in the free states indicates that it is erroneous. One needs to ask why, if northern voters were angry over passage of the Kansas-Nebraska Act, they abandoned the Whig party when every northern Whig senator and representative had opposed the bill. Why did the Democratic party, which was responsible for this law, survive, while the more strongly antislavery Whig party disappeared? And if the slavery issue accounted for shifts in voters' preferences in this decade, why was the Republican party, which sought to capitalize on antislavery and anti-Nebraska sentiment in the free states by opposing the expansion of slavery, so weak in its first years of existence? Indeed, why did experienced observers as late as the beginning of 1856 predict that the party would soon go the way of all antislavery parties and disappear?

In analyzing this political upheaval, historians have concentrated on the wrong actors and the wrong party: The key to the onset of realignment were the actions of voters and not party leaders, and it was the anti-Catholic, anti-immigrant Know Nothing party and not the Republican party that played the decisive role. The Know Nothing party's strength easily eclipsed that of the Republican party initially, and the causes of the Know Nothings' initial success and eventual failure determined the course of realignment.

The collapse of the Whig party constituted the first phase of the realignment of the 1850s. The party had been badly battered by the slavery issue during the previous decade. Deep divisions separated northern and southern Whigs on the issue of slavery and its expansion, divisions that were acutely apparent in the struggle in Congress over the Compromise of 1850, and which resurfaced again in the 1852 national convention. When the party jettisoned sectional issues in favor of once again running a military hero for president, the result was a decisive defeat, as Winfield Scott managed to carry only the four most loyal Whig states in the country.

Scott's drubbing was especially disheartening, because Whigs had never recovered psychologically from Henry Clay's defeat in 1844. Gallant Harry's loss to James K. Polk, a considerably less distinguished opponent, convinced many Whig leaders that the party could carry a national election only with a popular military hero as the candidate. Now with that road seemingly closed, Whig spirits plummeted.

The Whig party was also singularly unlucky in its choice of presidents. William Henry Harrison, the party's first president, died soon after taking office, and Zachary Taylor, who was elected in 1848, was stubborn, politically inexperienced, had only weak ties to the party, and like Harrison died in office. Their successors were unfortunate choices. Only nominally a Whig to begin with, John Tyler soon broke with the party's leaders in Washington, and under Millard Fillmore party factionalism worsened. In addition, the party had lost many of its traditional issues, and in the prosperity spawned by the California gold rush, economic questions no longer provoked sharp partisan divisions.

With Whig spirits low, the furor over the Kansas-Nebraska Act in 1854 offered the party a golden opportunity to regain national power. In 1854 Congress again took up the question of organizing the remainder of the Louisiana Purchase west of Missouri and Iowa. By the terms of the Missouri Compromise, slavery had been forever prohibited from this region, but under pressure from a group of radical southern senators, who bristled at this reproach to southern equality and who believed that the southern portion of this area could be made into a slave state, Democratic leaders agreed to repeal the 1820 compromise. The Pierce administration endorsed Senator Stephen A. Douglas's Kansas-Nebraska bill, which established two territories in the region and stipulated that the residents of these territories, at some unspecified time, would be allowed to decide whether they wanted slavery or not. National party leaders decided to make this idea, known as popular sovereignty, an official principle of the Democratic party.

Antislavery northern Democrats joined northern Whigs and Free Soilers in protesting the proposed repeal of the Missouri Compromise, but despite widespread northern opposition, the Kansas-Nebraska bill passed Congress in May. Some antislavery congressmen advocated the formation of a new party dedicated to stopping the expansion of slavery and restoring the Missouri Compromise, and in several states an attempt was made in 1854 to launch the Republican party. Most northern Whigs, however, held aloof from this movement because they were convinced that the suddenly revived slavery issue would enable their party to regain its former strength. Party strategists confidently believed that Pierce and Douglas had saved the Whig party.

What checked any Whig comeback and led to the party's rapid demise was the emergence in the early 1850s of ethnocultural issues, particularly temperance and nativism, in northern politics. The liquor issue ripped the traditional Whig coalition to shreds in a number of northern states when zealous drys mounted a crusade to enact statewide prohibition laws. With many voters already torn loose from their traditional partisan loyalties, the nativist movement, which had briefly manifested some political strength during the previous decade, suddenly surged to the forefront in the wake of the massive influx of immigrants, many of whom were Catholic, that began in 1846 and continued at an accelerating pace in the early 1850s. The secret Order of the Star Spangled Banner, an anti-Catholic, anti-immigrant society headquartered in New York City, embarked on a program of national expansion in 1853. The following year, with lodges in a number of states and membership expanding at a rapid rate, the society's leaders decided to challenge the major parties and run independent candidates for state offices and Congress. In an effort to ridicule supporters of this movement, Horace Greeley, the editor of the *New York Tribune*, dubbed them Know Nothings because members were instructed if asked about the society to say, "I know nothing." Despite the scorn of veteran politicos such as Greeley, the new party, which attacked the political power of Catholics and immigrants, made an impressive showing in the 1854 fall elections. Taking the name the American party, it continued to expand and run state and local candidates in preparation for a concerted campaign to win the presidency in 1856.

The rise of the Know Nothings, who capitalized on anger over the repeal of the Missouri Compromise, impatience with the existing parties, bigotry against Catholics and immigrants, and the social and economic dislocation of the period, sealed the fate of the Whig party, as thousands of loyal Whigs suddenly abandoned the party for the nativist cause. Countless Democrats defected as well, but because the Whig party had always contained a powerful nativist wing, it suffered much more extensive losses. Whiggery disappeared in a number of states and in many others was reduced to a mere shell of its former organization; throughout the North and the Deep South, where northern Whigs' hostility to slavery was fatal to the Whig cause, the party ceased to be politically competitive. Only in a few border states was there much support for the idea of trying to revive the party, but without significant northern backing, this movement was hopeless. Eventually most southern Whigs, seeking an alternative to the Democrats, joined the

Know Nothings and then supported a series of opposition movements after 1856.

Yet the Know Nothing movement, which had destroyed the second party system, proved to be ephemeral. The party had done extraordinarily well in its first campaigns in 1854, winning several states and establishing itself as the dominant opposition party to the Democrats. The party's success continued in 1855, especially in the North. Yet by the end of 1856 the party was on its deathbed. Finishing last in the presidential election, the party had lost most of its northern constituency to the Republicans and had been relegated to the status of a third party, holding the balance of power in several free states but unable to carry any. Likewise in the Deep South, the Know Nothings, while challenging Democratic power, could not control any state. The party's strength was confined to the border states, and even here it soon gave way to a more generalized anti-Democratic Opposition movement.

The Know Nothings' fall was as meteoric as their rise. A number of factors contributed to the party's decline. For one thing, the party had portrayed itself as a new organization that would drive party hacks from power, yet it was quickly taken over by professional politicians. Moreover, once in office party members proved woefully incompetent. The party failed to deliver on its promises to reform the political system, and it could not point to enactment of any significant legislation to weaken the power of Catholics or immigrants. In addition, the party was hurt by charges of bigotry and the violence of party gangs during elections; its secrecy also generated accusations that it was incompatible with a democratic political system. But the most important reason for the party's collapse was its inability to handle the slavery issue. Republicans in the North and proslavery radicals in the South kept up a constant drumbeat on the slavery issue, making it impossible for the Know Nothings to dodge sectional issues, especially when they tried to conduct a national campaign in 1856. Northern and southern Know Nothings could not unite on a platform because of wide disagreement on the slavery extension issue. When southern Know

Nothings prevailed and adopted a platform endorsing the Kansas-Nebraska Act, northern delegates bolted the convention. The subsequent nomination for president of Millard Fillmore, a tired political face and a sectional moderate who attempted to sidestep the slavery issue, intensified northern disaffection in 1856, and rank-and-file members went over to the Republicans in droves. The consequence was a significant proportion of previous Know Nothings—in some states a majority—cast Republican ballots in November.

Weakened by these defections, Fillmore finished a distant third in the 1856 election with 22 percent of the vote, trailing both James Buchanan, the Democratic nominee (45 percent), and John C. Frémont, the Republican candidate (33 percent). Fillmore ran a respectable race in the South but managed to carry only Maryland, a victim of the intensifying sectional conflict and the growing fears of the southern electorate. Alarmed that the strong Republican performance in the northern state elections in September and October foreshadowed Frémont's election in November, large numbers of southern moderates deserted Fillmore to vote for Buchanan. Had they remained faithful to Fillmore, the election might have been thrown into the House. Instead, Fillmore's poor showing sealed the fate of the American party. While he polled 44 percent of the southern vote, he secured only 13 percent in the North, where the Know Nothings' strength had always been concentrated. With the American party wrecked in the free states, it was futile to attempt to maintain it as a national organization. It ceased to run candidates in most states, and by 1860 had disappeared, another casualty of the Civil War realignment.

The decline of the Know Nothings was paralleled by the symbiotic rise of the Republican party. The party experienced an inauspicious birth. Efforts in 1854 to organize the party failed in most northern states, and it managed to carry only two minor states, Wisconsin and Michigan. Although the Republican movement made some headway in the 1855 northern state elections, the party's outlook remained bleak. Indeed, with less than a year until the next presidential election, the party lacked functioning organizations in half of the free states, and it was notably weak in several heavily populated states, which were essential for a sectional party to win national power. "Nobody believes that the Republican movement can prove the basis of a permanent party," commented one Democratic paper late in 1855.[12]

The 1856 presidential election, however, produced one of the most remarkable turn-arounds in American political annals. Frémont led all candidates in the North, carrying all but five free states, and finished second in the national totals. Seemingly headed to an early death at the beginning of the year, the Republican party had nearly elected a president in its first national campaign. This astounding performance established the Republicans as the major alternative to the Democrats in the country's two-party system. In three short years, Republicans had positioned themselves as the successor to the Whigs in the two-party system.

The surge of Republican strength in 1856 derived from two sources. First, the party capitalized on the divisions and discontent within the Know Nothing party. Party platforms and spokesmen openly bid for nativist support by adopting nativist proposals and employing nativist rhetoric and code words, particularly against Catholics. Countless nativist voters who wanted a party that was both antislavery and anti-Catholic found a comfortable home in the Republican ranks. More important, the party was helped by the continuing turmoil in Kansas, where free state and proslavery partisans established rival governments and soon began fighting. The disorder in Kansas, the caning of Senator Charles Sumner of Massachusetts by Representative Preston S. Brooks of South Carolina, southern filibustering enterprises, and the sectional deadlock in Congress all breathed new life into sectional feeling. As a sectional, antislavery party dedicated to breaking the political power of the South, and especially the Slave Power, the Republican party naturally benefited most from these issues. The result was a stampede of northern anti-Democratic voters into the Republican party in the spring and summer of 1856.

The 1856 results represented an ominous turn in the sectional conflict. In the aftermath of Frémont's showing, the nation for the first time confronted the real possibility that an antislavery sectional party might gain national power. Unlike the Liberty and Free Soil parties, the Republican party was not simply a third party, holding the balance of power in a few states and electing a handful of congressmen. Instead, by the end of 1856 it controlled most northern governorships and legislatures, had elected a large number of congressmen, and had almost captured the White House in its first national campaign. In order to undercut the suddenly robust Republican party, the new president, James Buchanan, and Democrats in Congress had to dampen sectional issues, end the Kansas controversy by bringing that territory into the Union as a free state, play down expansionist sentiment and suppress filibustering movements in the South, and appeal to northern conservatives who had supported Fillmore in 1856. For the future of the Union, it was essential to check the Republican party's growth and beat back its challenge in 1860.

For obvious reasons, voters are unwilling to support indefinitely a party that has no chance of winning national office, and Republican leaders believed that they had one or at most two more chances to demonstrate that they could elect a president, something no sectional party had ever done, before the party's supporters abandoned it. Scrutiny of the 1856 election results indicated that if Frémont had carried Pennsylvania and one other state he had lost, or if he had carried the other four (New Jersey, Indiana, Illinois, and California) without Pennsylvania, he would have been elected. Therefore, the Republicans' goal during the next four years was to hold on to the states that they had carried in 1856 while capturing those free states that they had lost. The Republicans' 1860 presidential campaign began as soon as the 1856 outcome was known.

The events of the next four years played directly into the Republicans' hands. Few parties have ever been handed more advantages or been aided to a greater extent by their enemies than were the Republicans between 1857 and 1860. Indeed, so many things went the Republicans' way that the party seemed to be, in the words of one historian, "a favored child of destiny."[13]

In March 1857 the Supreme Court issued the Dred Scott decision, which ruled that Congress had no power to prohibit slavery in the territories (thereby negating the Republican party's main platform plank). An economic panic commenced in late summer, and while it was not severe nationally, thanks to the general prosperity of the South, the industrialized North was hard-hit. As the administration unsuccessfully tried to stimulate the economy over southern opposition, many northern conservative businessmen joined the Republican party, which now added several economic planks, including a protective tariff, to its platform. A religious revival that began in 1857 and extended into 1858 inevitably galvanized temperance sentiment, anti-Catholic feeling, and moral opposition to slavery, all of which found a natural outlet in the Republican party.

Even worse, Buchanan endorsed the fraudulent proslavery Lecompton constitution and, ignoring the sharp objections of Stephen A. Douglas and northern Democrats, endeavored to admit Kansas as the sixteenth slave state in the Union. The result was a titanic struggle in Congress in 1858 that led to the rejection of the Lecompton constitution by both Congress and the voters of Kansas and left the president humiliated, his administration politically crippled, and the Democratic party torn asunder. Following his re-election to the Senate, Douglas was the favorite to secure his party's 1860 presidential nomination, and his candidacy increasingly symbolized the deep division between northern and southern Democrats. Southern Democrats vowed that they would never accept Douglas, who had opposed the Lecompton constitution, as the party's nominee, and southern ultras in Congress and in several states now demanded a federal slave code to protect slavery in the territories (and thereby make meaningful slaveholders' right, upheld in the Dred Scott decision, to take their property with them into the territories). Douglas and northern Democrats retorted that slavery was a state institution, and vowed they would never accept such a code. With the Democratic party's national unity in shreds, Republican prospects in 1860 seemed brighter than ever.

The only major event during Buchanan's term that had the potential to weaken the Republican party was John Brown's raid on Harpers Ferry, Virginia, in 1859. Had any prominent party leader been implicated in Brown's fantastic attempt to foment a slave insurrection in the South, the Republican party might have been fatally damaged. Despite persistent southern accusations, however, no important party leader was involved in the planning of Brown's invasion, and following his capture Republican leaders hastened to repudiate the raid, which the 1860 Republican platform denounced as "the gravest of crimes." Republicans were thus able to minimize the potential damage of Brown's raid.

Aided by these events, the disruption of the Democratic national convention at Charleston, and the nomination of Abraham Lincoln, a moderate, for president, the Republican party won an easy victory in 1860. Lincoln carried every free state except New Jersey, which he divided with Douglas, and had a clear majority in the electoral college despite winning only 39.9 percent of the popular vote.

The Republican party's first national triumph sounded the death knell of the Union. Between December 21, 1860, and February 1, 1861, before Lincoln had even been inaugurated, the seven states of the Deep South seceded from the Union. Efforts to find a suitable compromise in Congress failed, as all proposals except a proposed thirteenth amendment forever guaranteeing slavery in the southern states were rejected. Congress adjourned with a sense of futility and hopelessness. Six weeks later, the Civil War began when Lincoln dispatched a relief expedition to Fort Sumter in Charleston harbor, South Carolina. Confederate leaders chose to open fire on the federal garrison in the fort rather than let the Union fleet land supplies. The attack on Fort Sumter galvanized public opinion in both sections, and men and women fervently rallied to the cause of the Union or the Confederacy. Matters had moved beyond compromise. In April 1861, Northerners and Southerners alike rejected the democratic process and turned to war to resolve their differences. The disruption of the Union and the outbreak of war represented the ultimate failure of American democracy.

WHY HAD the political system failed? The party system had successfully contained sectional animosities for a long time, only to falter abysmally in this final crisis, which it had not come close to solving. This failure had momentous consequences, for the American party system was the major mechanism to deal with and defuse the sectional conflict. For one thing, it placed certain limits on dissent. Party members were not free to take any position concerning sectional confrontations. Instead, they had pay some heed to the national ramifications of their ideological stance and behavior, since whatever the party did in one state affected the party's welfare in other states.

Prior to the rise of the Republican party, the two major parties were national organizations, with a constituency drawn from both sections. The need to agree on a national platform promoted the idea of compromise and sectional harmony. As a result, parties often emphasized the personalities of presidential candidates over issues and channeled popular emotions behind candidates and party symbols rather than rigid ideologies. Because parties must unite a diverse national constituency, the American party system, as a number of political scientists have commented, works best when fundamental issues are not at stake. Over the long sweep of time, race has been the most divisive problem in American society, and the party system has never effectively handled this issue in its various forms.

One of the important qualities of the antebellum political system was that it had no effective means to control political outsiders. The party system could impose discipline on those who attempted to rise through the party ranks, since it was designed to restrain individuality and reward party loyalty and service. But beginning in the 1830s, abolitionists and southern radicals seized upon the slavery issue to advance their causes. The abolitionists were oblivious to party control, for they had abandoned the two major parties as hopelessly proslavery. Even those who turned to political action and founded the Liberty party in 1840 and the Free Soil party in 1848 operated as loose cannons in the political system. They had no interest in controlling either of the major parties. Instead, they used their position of holding the balance of political power in several states to advance their agenda through the traditional political system of logrolling, and they used their seats in Congress for the purposes of agitation rather than legislative accomplishments.

The proslavery Calhounites were not as independent of the party system, since John C. Calhoun continued to nurture unrealistic presidential ambitions. Much like the political abolitionists, however, his supporters served as a balance-of-power third party in southern politics, maneuvering for factional advantage in various states. They had little success in promoting Calhoun's national aspirations, but they adroitly kept sectional issues alive in southern politics. Any sign that a southern politician was wavering on the protection of slavery brought a prompt attack from southern hotspurs. In order to survive politically, southern politicians responded in kind. The result was to give southern politics an overheated intensity.

Safely ensconced in public office because of his solid support in South Carolina, Calhoun recklessly pursued the same policy in national politics. He seized on the abolitionist mailing campaign of 1835 to demand suppression of antislavery agitation in the North. He pounced on the antislavery petitions to Congress to demand enactment of the so-called gag rule, automatically tabling these petitions without consideration. He constantly looked for any opening to raise the cry that southern institutions were threatened and that the South had to unite in the interest of self-preservation. As secretary of state, he deliberately linked the slavery issue to the annexation of Texas, and in response to the Wilmot Proviso he constructed the ingenious constitutional argument that slavery was legal in all the territories of the United States. Following his ouster from the Jackson administration, his erratic course was one of tortured twists and turns as he maneuvered in national politics, and up until his death in 1850 he repeatedly agitated sectional issues for personal and political advantage, oblivious to the long-term consequences of such action.

Calhoun's death removed the last restraints on southern radicals, both in his home state of South Carolina and throughout the South. These men did not share Calhoun's devotion to the

Union, and they were not interested in national power. Instead, following passage of the Compromise of 1850 many took as their goal southern independence and worked assiduously for that end throughout the 1850s. Others who were less committed to secession were nevertheless determined to press the North to the wall on the slavery issue, arguing that the South had to secure ironclad guarantees for its institutions.

This relentless agitation was part of the maneuvering for advantage in state politics. The drive to repeal the Missouri Compromise, for example, grew out of the bitter rivalry between David Rice Atchison and Thomas Hart Benton in Missouri politics.[14] Southern radicals staked everything on forcing slavery into Kansas. When they failed, their bitterness deepened and hardened. Their demands culminated in the call for a federal slave code, something that could never be obtained in the poisoned atmosphere of 1860 and which violated the southern position since the beginning of the sectional conflict that slavery was strictly a state institution. This demand ultimately tore the Democratic party apart along sectional lines. The purpose of the agitation of this question was not, as southern extremists claimed, to thwart Douglas's assertion (known as the Freeport Doctrine) that regardless of the Dred Scott decision, the residents of a territory could keep slavery out by simply refusing to protect it. Rather, it was to get rid of the hated Douglas as the Democratic party's presidential candidate. Following the break-up of the Charleston convention over the southern demand for a congressional slave code, one angry southern delegate insisted, "The struggle over the platform was a mere sham; the real contest was about the candidate. Douglas out of the way, the platform was of no consequence to the central managers who combined for his destruction!"[15] Aided by the inept Pierce and Buchanan administrations, southern fire-eaters operated freely in the 1850s and eventually smashed the Democratic party from within and without.

Compounding the difficulty of containing southern radicals was the absence of a two-party system in South Carolina. A number of factors combined to prevent development of a party system in the state, including the state's majority black population, white fears aroused by the Denmark Vesey conspiracy, the economic and social unity of the state's slaveholding aristocracy, its aristocratic state constitution, the governor's lack of power, the absence of statewide electoral contests, and the fact that the legislature selected the governor and the state's presidential electors. But the most important reason was the state's crushing defeat in the nullification crisis, which forever discredited Jackson in the state and established Calhoun, who up to then had been a moderate in the state's politics, as the political dictator of South Carolina. The only position one could take in South Carolina politics and hope for office was to be more rabid on the slavery issue than Calhoun.[16]

The consequences for the sectional conflict of South Carolina's failure to develop a legitimate two-party system were immense. It placed the state outside the bounds of the national party system and allowed the state to chart its own political course in these decades. Moreover, it rendered the state's politicians immune to party discipline and the demands of party interest. It also encouraged radicalism in the state's politics, both institutionally (since there was no national party organization to restrain it) and intellectually (since the surest way to power in the state was to champion the special interests of slavery, South Carolina, and the South by denouncing Northerners as unfaithful to southern institutions). Fire-eating demagoguery took the place of genuine electoral competition. Thus throughout the sectional conflict South Carolina's leaders were oblivious to the concerns and needs of political leaders elsewhere and pursued a narrow state interest with a single-minded intensity. It was not just coincidence that the one state without a two-party system was also the most radical state in the Union.

The disappearance of a competitive two-party system in the Deep South after 1856 also served to radicalize politics in that region. With no powerful party to fight at home, politicians in these states directed their attacks instead on the hated northern Republican party, which prompted an increasing focus on national rather than state issues. Party factionalism became rampant, rhetoric intensified, and fire-eating grew apace. As a result, public opinion in the Deep South was much more extreme by 1860 than it had been four years earlier, a development that had fateful consequences for the Union.[17]

The American party system was further destabilized by the existence of third parties. In the years before the Civil War, for reasons already discussed, third parties were a persistent feature in American politics. Because antebellum politics was state- and not national-oriented, strength in a single state could translate into important political gains. The need to prevent third parties from forming, or to satisfy the supporters of existing parties, prevented the two dominant parties from permanently suppressing divisive issues. Moreover, third parties were a constant danger to the major parties' electoral support. Temperance was an example of an issue forced into the political arena by political outsiders against the wishes of party managers. So were slavery and nativism. Once these issues entered the political arena, they were difficult to dislodge, since they had a zealous group of supporters who placed morality above political calculations. The close balance between the two parties, and the ease of forming third parties, allowed committed supporters to intrude these issues into the partisan system.

Moreover, unlike today, third parties in the antebellum period did not invariably aim for national power. Instead, many concentrated on state and local races, because political power was concentrated in state and not federal government.[18] This emphasis also facilitated building parties from the ground up rather than from the top down. The new Republican party, for example, spent two years establishing state organizations before conducting its first national campaign; the same was true of the Know Nothings. Unlike modern third parties, these parties were not dependent on a single political leader, whose defeat or retirement ended the movement; a similar outlook also prevailed among Calhoun's supporters, many of whom were more committed to his goals of a politically united South and forcing northern concessions on slavery than they were to promoting his personal career. Instead, these were ideological causes, spawned and sustained by the crusading enthusiasm of their supporters.

As a result, third parties and independent candidacies were a major means to mobilize discontent in the antebellum electorate. As party ties weakened in the late 1840s and early 1850s, the number of multi-candidate contests increased, shifting among voters intensified, and political instability increased. The Liberty and Free Soil parties in the North, and the Calhounites and southern nationalists in the South, shook the party system in the 1840s. Temperance parties in a number of northern states, and pro-compromise Union coalitions in the southern states in 1850–51, further disrupted traditional voting alignments. Eventually a third party, the Know Nothings, destroyed the Jacksonian party system, and another third party, the Republicans, was the ultimate beneficiary of this development.

The Republican party differed from other third parties in that it had to control Congress and the presidency to achieve its goals. Republicans could first organize at the state level, but they had to ultimately create a strong party on the national level in order to stop the expansion of slavery and limit the political power of the South. Republican organizers, however, enjoyed two advantages over new parties today. First, congressional incumbents lacked the decisive advantages that they now enjoy in terms of name recognition, campaign funds, and media exposure. Moreover, most districts adhered to some sort of rotation rule, so congressional terms of service were shorter and turnover higher. Because they did not have to challenge mostly well-financed, deeply entrenched incumbents, Republicans were able to quickly elect a number of congressmen who served as the nucleus for the developing national party organization.

The other advantage was that antebellum presidential campaigns were national in name more than scope. Presidential campaigns were really run by state committees, working in only loose cooperation with other state organizations. The National Committee functioned as a national fund-raising body and provided some direction to the campaign, but except for campaign funds and speakers, most states were left largely to take care of themselves. Thus it was far easier for state-based parties to conduct a national campaign in this period.

Given the threat posed by political outsiders and third-party movements, party leaders had to handle the slavery issue cautiously. They needed to strengthen sectional moderates and weaken extremists in both sections. It was also essential that they preserve a party system based on two national political parties, which offered the minority South its surest protection. In pursuing these goals, political leaders failed miserably.

Constrained by attitudes and fears of the electorate, politicians did not have a completely free hand in dealing with the sectional conflict, and it is not my purpose to resurrect the argument that selfish politicians blundered the nation into a needless war. But it is an inescapable fact that except for rare but extremely crucial moments party leaders, not voters, drove the political system, and their decisions and actions had a vital impact on the sectional conflict. It was they who politicized issues and framed the choices before the electorate, and it was the leaders, not the voters, who made the crucial policy decisions. It made a difference for the country whether Henry Clay or James K. Polk was elected president in 1844, or that James Buchanan pursued the policies that he did. Politicians were not simply victims of forces that they could not control, and throughout most of the sectional conflict their hands were not effectively tied by popular passions.[19]

The passing of the second generation of the Republic weakened the forces of sectional adjustment in the country. The generation of Clay, Webster, and Calhoun had fashioned the great legislative · compromises that defused various sectional crises, but after 1850 they were replaced by a new generation of political leaders less fearful of sectional agitation and less willing to compromise. As the strident debates of the late 1840s and the 1850s revealed, Congress was no longer a center of sectional moderation and good will.

It increasingly fell to the presidency to heal the sectional breach and unite the country. Instead, the presidents from Tyler to Buchanan committed a series of serious mistakes and made a number of miscalculations. In dealing with the sectional crisis, the antebellum presidents were probably no worse as a group than most presidents in American history. But the problems these presidents confronted were especially severe, and the consequences of their mistakes and failures were much more profound.

In some ways, presidential power was more limited before the Civil War than in the modern era. Presidents generally did not exercise great influence over Congress, and there certainly were limits to their ability to shape legislation or force Congress to follow their lead. In the struggle over the Compromise of 1850, Zachary Taylor had enough strength to block passage of Henry Clay's plan, but he lacked the power to get his own proposal approved. Similarly, in the contest over the Kansas-Nebraska bill in 1854, Pierce helped secure enough northern votes to pass the bill, but nearly half of the northern Democrats defied the administration and voted against the bill. Finally, administration pressure, including the resort to outright bribery, was inadequate to push the Lecompton constitution through the House in 1858.

In other areas, however, the president had considerable power to inflict damage. One example was in the territories, where he appointed the major officials (subject to Senate confirmation) and controlled the U.S. troops stationed there. Taylor's saber rattling over the New Mexico-Texas boundary dispute nearly led to armed conflict with Texas and complicated Congress's search for a resolution to this dispute. A similar situation prevailed in Kansas, where Pierce's one-sided policies significantly exacerbated the problems in that troubled territory. Pierce appointed incompetent federal officials, refused to remove southern partisans from office, including the hot-tempered territorial chief justice Samuel Lecompte, and used the army in a one-sided manner to undercut the free-state movement. His appointment of Andrew Reeder, a minor Pennsylvania Democrat, to the key post of territorial governor was a grievous error in judgment; even worse was his selection of the ineffectual and easily terrified Wilson Shannon as his successor. Neither had the strength or wisdom to deal with trouble-makers on both sides. Much more successful was John W. Geary, who pursued more even-handed policies, but he resigned after it was clear that he had lost the confidence of the administration because of criticism by proslavery advocates. Buchanan made an excellent choice in Robert Walker for territorial governor, but under pressure from southern Democrats he eventually abandoned Walker and repudiated his pledge that the people of Kansas would be allowed to vote on the Lecompton constitution; in so doing, he ruptured his party in two. Better appointments and stronger presidential support for policies to end the turmoil in the territory would have done much to remove the Kansas issue from national politics.

The other area where presidential power could be particularly harmful was foreign policy. When peaceful efforts to acquire California and New Mexico failed, Polk provoked a war with Mexico to achieve his territorial aims, and the acquisition of territory soon became entangled with the question of the expansion of slavery. Likewise, Pierce and Buchanan recklessly pursued the acquisition of Cuba from Spain, oblivious to how their actions exacerbated sectional tensions. Pierce also followed an erratic course concerning filibustering expeditions to Latin America, at first seemingly winking at them and then intervening to block them.

When William Henry Harrison was elected president in 1840, no one believed a civil war was remotely likely. The country was in the midst of a major depression, sectional issues were not salient, and economic policies were the most pressing questions confronting the country. But Harrison's unexpected death elevated Vice President John Tyler to the presidency. Nominated without any regard for his qualifications, Tyler was ill-equipped intellectually and personally to be president. Following his break with the Whigs in Congress, Tyler took up the annexation of Texas as the way to win a second term as an independent candidate. A proslavery ideologue, he pushed this issue without proper concern for the potential threat it posed to the Union and the party system. The manipulated emergence of the Texas issue in national politics badly divided both parties and increased sectional mistrust.

Tyler's Texas ploy transformed the sectional conflict. Thereafter the expansion of slavery was the central issue dividing the sections; the links between foreign and domestic policies tightened; and party leaders exploited sectional issues and exacerbated sectional fears in their struggle for party dominance. James K. Polk's expansionist policies and personal duplicity further divided the Democratic party, discredited the doctrine of Manifest Destiny, convinced a significant body of northern public opinion that territorial expansion was part of a proslavery plot, and embittered northern public opinion. If Polk pursued pro-southern policies and paid insufficient heed to northern concerns, Zachary Taylor erred in the other direction, ignoring southern fears and stubbornly clinging to his solution to the territorial question in the face of strong southern opposition. Only Taylor's death prevented the crisis from erupting in 1850. Millard Fillmore helped get Clay's compromise measures approved, but his patronage policies and personal vendetta against antislavery Whigs deepened the divisions in the Whig party. Still, the party system seemed resilient and appeared to have weathered this latest sectional storm.

More serious were the shortcomings of Pierce and Buchanan. Of the two, Pierce deserves the greater censure. Inheriting a reasonably stable situation, the hesitant New Hampshire Democrat pursued a set of policies that exacerbated sectional animosities and strengthened extremists in both sections. His nomination was a disaster, proof of the folly of adopting the two-thirds rule in the first place (only such a rule would have enabled such a little-known candidate to be nominated in a rush on the 49th ballot by the exhausted delegates). Pierce's patronage policies deepened party factionalism; his endorsement of the Kansas-Nebraska bill alienated countless northern Democrats; his one-sided policies in Kansas kept the territory in constant turmoil and inflamed public opinion in the North; and his reckless pursuit of the acquisition of Cuba alarmed Northerners and further discredited American expansionism.

Recognizing the consequences of elevating the hapless Pierce from relative obscurity to the presidency, the Democrats in 1856 nominated James Buchanan, an old party wheelhorse, for president (only Douglas's withdrawal, however, enabled Buchanan to gain the requisite two-thirds majority, otherwise yet another nonentity would have been selected). When he took office, Buchanan faced a much more difficult task than Pierce had four years earlier. Unlike Pierce, Buchanan confronted a powerful sectional party, deep sectional animosities, and much more intense popular fears in both sections. One should not minimize the problems Buchanan inherited. Yet despite his cautious nature, he persistently adopted policies that made the situation worse. It is difficult to explain his political blindness beyond his close emotional and personal ties to southern Democrats, his indifference to the slavery issue (like many who did not care about this question, he found it hard to understand the feelings of those who did), and his personal dislike of Douglas. Whatever the reasons for his behavior, Buchanan's policies strengthened the Republican party. His repudiation of his pledge that there would be a popular vote on the Lecompton constitution, his attempt to force that constitution through Congress without seeking some accommodation with the anti-Lecompton Democrats, his agitation of the Cuba question, his attempt to acquire additional Mexican territory by establishing a "protectorate" over its northern provinces, and his personal feud with Douglas, which he persisted in to the party's detriment, were all serious errors of judgment. The consequence of his one-sided policies and fratricidal war against Douglas was the rupture of the Democratic party at Charleston, an outcome in which his closest associates played a key role. The division of the Democratic party was one more nail in the Union's coffin.

The process of nominating presidential candidates was badly flawed. Tyler and Fillmore were vice presidents nominated without concern for their abilities. Taylor was a war hero without political experience; Pierce was selected because no one knew his views; and Polk secured the nomination only because the two-thirds rule blocked Martin Van Buren, the choice of a clear majority of Democrats. Only Buchanan enjoyed widespread support in the party prior to his nomination, and his presidency was undone by his timid character and lack of political astuteness. Despite his long public career, even Buchanan was nominated only because he had been out of the country as minister to England in 1854 and thus was not personally connected with the repeal of the Missouri Compromise. Of all the candidates nominated for president in this period, Clay was the most qualified to be president, and his defeat in 1844, which stemmed from the Liberty party's vote that cost him the state of New York, was a serious blow to the Union.[20]

The Republican party was no more responsible in its presidential nominations. John C. Frémont, the party's first presidential candidate, was both inexperienced and (as his wartime career amply demonstrated) incompetent. He had only a slim public record at the time of his nomination and was temperamentally and intellectually unqualified for the office. In 1860, the party bypassed its most prominent leaders and selected Abraham Lincoln. Lincoln, of course, turned out to be a great president, but often lost sight of in the luster of his wartime statesmanship are his limited qualifications in 1860. The Republican nominee was no mere prairie lawyer, as critics scoffed, but while he may have once been a railsplitter, by any objective standard he was not presidential timber. He had served one undistinguished term in the House of Representatives, had been out of public office for more than a decade, and had never held an administrative office. He was nominated because the delegates were convinced that he was the strongest candidate the party could run. In selecting him to head the party's national ticket, the delegates gave little thought to Lincoln's qualifications for office and paid no heed to whether he had the ability to handle the crisis that would likely ensue if the Republicans carried the election.

The problems confronting these presidents were not simple and easily solved, but the nation had a right to expect better. It needed presidents who put the national interest above party concerns, sectional harmony above political advantage, meaningful solutions above personal animosities. More concerned about gaining power than exercising it, American political parties have rarely selected men of intellectual distinction and vision to lead the nation; perhaps it is not surprising that the pre-Civil War presidents were inadequate for the task before them.

The nation has been fortunate that in times of extraordinary national crises, such as the Civil War and the Great Depression and World War II, the presidency has fallen on unusually talented individuals, but given the party system's tendency to select less than distinguished candidates, one must wonder whether this luck will not eventually run out. Moreover, the question remains whether more capable presidential leadership earlier could have resolved permanently the sectional conflict.

Overarching these problems was the refusal of southern political leaders to confront historical reality. Defying the clear course of western thought and history in the century, white Southerners refused to accept the end of slavery, however gradual and however distant in the future. Sometime between 1820, with the adoption of the Missouri Compromise, and 1832, with the rejection of emancipation by the Virginia legislature, the South had reached and passed the point of no return. White Southerners could not envision their society without slavery, and they were unwilling to consider, as the Missouri debates showed, any program to end the institution, even gradually. Far from challenging these attitudes, most southern politicians pandered to them, accusing their opponents of being unreliable on the defense of slavery, alarming their constituents by putting the worst possible face on national political developments, and wildly distorting Republican aims by insisting that the party was an abolitionist organization committed to racial equality. This approach drew directly on the heritage of republicanism, with its fear of internal threats to liberty.[21]

The best defense of slavery was to keep it out of national politics and prevent it from becoming a political issue. Since Southerners were a minority, agitation of the slavery question could work only to the South's disadvantage. The wisest course for southern politicans was to avoid discussing the slavery issue in Congress, to ignore the pitifully weak abolitionist movement, and refuse to engage in verbal brawls with antislavery congressmen. But Southerners were generally more impetuous and had a keener sense of honor, and while a number of southern congressmen initially adhered to this policy, they found themselves under mounting pressure at home from proslavery fanatics. Ambitious southern politicians soon learned that casting doubts on an opponent's reliability on the slavery issue was a sure road to political power.[22] As a result, when slavery became an issue fewer and fewer southern congressmen were willing to be silent. Perhaps it was asking too much of human character to remain calm in the face of taunts, insults, and condemnation.

The refusal of Southerners to accept the inevitable end of slavery, however distant, fatally handicapped the ability of the party system to resolve the sectional conflict. Assent to the end of slavery expansion would have represented the first step in dealing with the problem of slavery in a republic dedicated to liberty. But southern inflexibility rendered all sectional compromises simply temporary adjustments rather than lasting solutions. As the futility of the Compromise of 1850 demonstrated, no comprehensive settlement of the sectional conflict was possible in this environment. Instead, the sectional compromises represented a delaying action, postponing the crisis to some later day. Under the best of circumstances, such an approach might have succeeded by gaining time for a group of more realistic leaders to arise in the South, yet as late as 1861 there was no sign of this happening, and southern white attitudes after the war suggest that it was not likely to occur anytime soon. Had there been any realistic way to couple removal of the black population with emancipation, southern whites could have confronted the end of the institution, but as long as blacks were going to remain in the South, southern whites, including nonslaveholders, overwhelmingly supported slavery (it should be added that if emancipated slaves were removed to the free states, there would have been little antislavery sentiment in the North either). At the same time, Northerners' harsh and uncharitable criticism of Southerners weakened southern moderation, stunted the development of more realistic attitudes in the South, and hardened southern resistance to these historic trends.

Belief in the constitutional right of secession, which a growing number of Southerners endorsed after 1846, encouraged southern politicians to resort to political blackmail. Increasingly, they engaged in a dangerous game of brinkmanship, steadily escalating their demands on the North heedless of the consequences. In doing so, they relied on the right of secession to protect the South if this strategy failed. Acceptance of the theoretical right of secession allowed southern politicians to gamble on an all-or-nothing strategy. They had little incentive to compromise or take a broad national view of matters, or even seek northern cooperation, for they could always leave the Union if their tactics led to political disaster. Had the postwar situation prevailed where secession was not an option, southern political leaders would of necessity have behaved much differently.

That the Republican party was not allowed to contest elections in the South also had important consequences. Popular hostility prevented Republicans from campaigning or running candidates outside the border slave states, a situation that increased misperceptions on both sides. Denied access to the southern electorate, Republicans lacked a sound comprehension of southern public opinion, while at the same time they lacked means to counteract the distorted popular image of the party in the South. Most Southerners had never laid eyes on a Republican, and thus their perception of the Republican party and its aims derived entirely from assertions of its opponents. When condemned by Southerners for being a sectional party, Republicans responded that if allowed to campaign in the South, they would quickly develop a southern wing. Southerners defended this interference with the free democratic electoral process as necessary for their self-preservation.

Finally, the party system was hampered by the intensification of popular politics. Politicians and editors rallied popular support by indulging in sectional stereotypes and sectional boasting. They also misinterpreted the aims of their opponents. But while politicians capitalized on and inflamed popular fears in both sections, these fears were not artificially created nor can they be dismissed as mass paranoia. There *was* a Slave Power which *did* wield unusual power in American life, and the Republican party *did* threaten southern interests and the long-term future of slavery.[23] If exaggerated, the popular perceptions of the Slave Power and the Black Republicans nevertheless went to the heart of the sectional conflict.

These popular fears intensified as the decade advanced through an interactive process with events, thereby severely reducing the options available to party leaders and limiting the room for compromise. The Republican victory in 1860 ushered in the final crisis that led to war.

THE SECESSION CRISIS was the point at which all of these factors converged and played out their final ramifications. Southern nationalists seized the moment presented by Lincoln's victory and stampeded the states of the Deep South out of the Union. They capitalized on deeply felt popular resentment to momentarily assume power in southern politics, and while their reign was short-lived, it was sufficient to sunder the Union. In working for southern independence, secessionists had the advantage that they had to carry a state only once to accomplish their objective, whereas their opponents had to retain power without interruption. If it had been necessary for southern nationalists to prevail in a series of elections over an extended period of time, secession probably never would have amounted to more than a dream.

Even with southern emotions at a peak following Lincoln's election, the margin by which secession was achieved was quite narrow. The elections for delegates to the secession conventions were very close in Alabama, Louisiana, and Georgia—indeed, Unionist candidates probably carried the elections in both Louisiana and Georia—and nothing resembling a regular election occurred in Texas. The secessionists' triumph in these elections rested on intimidation of Unionist voters, a light turnout, an unduly abbreviated campaign, and a switch in position by a number of Unionist delegates after their election. Fraud was a factor as well in Texas. In addition, in times of excitement, the party of action has the advantage, and the secessionists were aided greatly by the fact that unlike their opponents they knew exactly what they wanted.

Whether secession represented the wishes of a majority of the whites in the Deep South or was the act of a minority cannot be determined from the existing evidence. Only one state, South Carolina, was irrevocably committed to secession, although disunion sentiment was also strong in Mississippi and probably would have triumphed there in a normal election. Whatever the true division of opinion, the process of selecting delegates to the secession conventions violated the fundamental norms of American democracy. Secessionist military companies constantly drilled prior to the election, whipping up revolutionary enthusiasm; southern radicals threatened Unionist voters and questioned their honesty of purpose; and undecided voters came under heavy pressure to back secession. What the outcome would have been if southern voters had had more time to reflect on their action, and if the voting had been conducted free of intimidation, is unknowable, but there is a good chance that secession would have been rejected in several states of the Deep South, most notably Louisiana and Georgia, and perhaps in Alabama as well. Moreover, except in Texas, where the entire procedure was irregular, none of the original seven states that seceded provided for popular ratification of this decision.[24]

Here again the historical accident of state boundaries played a major role. Had smaller states been created according to Jefferson's earlier plan, secession would have been confined to the black-belt regions of the lower South, and instead of seven out of fifteen slave states seceding, at most seven out of twenty would have left in the first wave. This situation would have certainly strengthened the forces of compromise and reduced secessionists' confidence, although whether the end result would have been any different is questionable. Once it departed, South Carolina did not intend to return to the Union, no matter what the other southern states did, and since the majority of southern states would accept no federal coercion of a seceded state, and since Northerners steadfastly denied the right of secession and insisted on a complete restoration of the Union, it seems unlikely that even under this counterfactual scenario war could have been avoided, although the Union's ability to conduct the war once it began would probably have been enhanced.[25]

Whether the act of a zealous minority or a confused majority, the secession of the Deep South set the stage for the final collapse of the normal political process. James Buchanan remained in office despite the repudiation of his policies in the just-concluded election, but devoid of personal influence or political prestige, he lacked the will to lead. Thoroughly discredited, abandoned by his political friends, and held up to daily scorn and ridicule in the press, he hoped merely to hang on and avoid starting a war until March 4, when he could dump the problem in Lincoln's lap. With his administration in turmoil and his cabinet deeply divided, he proved incapable of responding with any vigor to the escalating crisis.

Meanwhile, all efforts at compromise in Congress between December 1860 and March 1861 failed. By now the two groups that had to make any meaningful compromise—the secessionists of the Deep South and the Republicans of the North—had no interest in accommodation. Secessionists had cast their lot with southern independence and were simply marking time until their states seceded, whereas Republicans refused to compromise with those they considered traitors engaged in lawless behavior. To surrender to southern threats, they were certain, would be the end of majority rule, the essence of democracy itself.

We can see in hindsight that there was no chance for compromise in this session of Congress. Even today, with over a century of hindsight, it is difficult to see what compromise solution would have allayed southern fears and restored the Union. Differences were increasingly seen in abstract terms—questions of right, honor, and equality. Matters had passed beyond the possibility of compromise.

Crucial to the breakdown of the party system in this final crisis were fundamental miscalculations on both sides. When the war began, neither side envisioned a conflict that would last four years, cost the nation more than $20 billion in national treasure, and produce the loss of over 620,000 lives. Each was convinced that the other side would not fight, or that if there was a war, it would be short—essentially one battle. Furthermore, Confederate leaders discerned definite advantages from a war, which they believed would force the hand of the upper South and precipitate these states' secession. Adding the upper South would greatly strengthen the Confederacy in terms of size, population, resources, wealth, and military capacity. And perhaps most important, underlying to each side's willingness to fight was the belief that it would win. After years of bitter sectional rivalry, it was almost with a sigh of relief that the residents of both sections greeted this final resolution.

In April of 1861 both sides went to war to save democracy as they understood it. For southern secessionists, at stake was the right of self-government and the fundamental right of southern whites to control their own destiny. For the North, the war was a struggle to uphold the democratic principles of law and order and majority rule, as expressed in a fair and free election, as well as preserve the Union, which they believed was inseparably linked to democracy. In endorsing the decision for war, few Northerners appreciated the fundamental irony that they were ready to kill their fellow Americans in order to prove that democracy was a workable form of government.

5

The Divided South,
Democracy's Limitations,
and the Causes of the Peculiarly
North American Civil War

WILLIAM W. FREEHLING

*D*EMOCRACY HAS BECOME the most coveted American export. The cold war has been won; the democratic way vindicated. Throughout yesterday's totalitarian half of the globe, long-repressed voices demand freedom of speech, free elections, and majority rule. As the twenty-first century approaches, Americans have seemingly lived up to their seventeenth-century forebears' ambition: to become a City Upon a Hill for all the world to emulate.

Such ideological imperialism, however, has sometimes ill-served this nation. In striving to spread their supposedly ideal political system, Americans on occasion have generated foreign policy disasters, especially in Vietnam. So now more than ever, historians must remind their fellow citizens that democracy, like all things human, is no universal panacea. American democracy indeed could not peacefully resolve our own gravest social problem, slavery. It is a telling historical irony that of all the New World slavocracies, only slaveholders in the United States lived in an advanced republic, and only the United States required a civil war between whites to abolish slavery for blacks.

Despite that singularity of the American Civil War, violence sometimes accompanied emancipation in less republican New World regimes. Abolition in Haiti evolved out of an equally singular civil war, in that case between slaves and slaveholders. Agitation over emancipation also led to some bloodshed in Cuba. So too, slaveholders' rage at not receiving recompense for their slaves helped inspire a revolution in Brazil after emancipation. But nowhere else in the Americas did slaveholders rise in revolution before emancipation, accepting the risks of a military showdown with nonslaveholders.

The southern slaveholders' unique acceptance of trial by warfare demanded unique self-confidence. Secession required both nerve and the perception of power. The Brazilian and Cuban slavocracies could have no such nerve in the 1870s and 1880s, after watching U.S. slaveholders go down in flames in the 1860s. Nor did their nondominant position in their respective political power structures embolden Cuban or Brazilian slaveholders with the illusion that they could win a civil war.

Latin American slaveholders also lacked illusions about their worldwide economic power. No Caribbean or South American planter imagined that his European customers would intervene on his side in a New World civil war. Fantasies that European customers would bolster King Cotton's army, however, rarely dominated the secessionists' thinking. Rather, U.S. slaveholders' unique political power inside a peculiarly advanced republic above all else instilled in them the illusion—and for a long while the reality—that they could control slavery's fate.[1]

Or to be more accurate, the minority of slaveholders inside the U.S. majoritarian republic swung between feelings of infuriating powerlessness and perceptions of imperial powerfulness, as they exerted their unusual leverage over slavery's destiny. On the one hand, some ideological and institutional aspects of U.S. republicanism empowered nonslaveholding majorities to assault the slaveholding minority. Because of the possibility of majority control, U.S. slaveholders were potentially as much at the mercy of outside forces as were Latin American slaveholders, who could only postpone their less democratic governments' emancipation decrees. On the other hand, some aspects of the U.S. republican system, as embedded in the Constitution, empowered the slaveholder minority to resist emancipation in a manner impossible elsewhere in the Americas. The southern minority's power over the northern majority inspired a new northern word, the most charged in the antebellum political vocabulary: *Slavepower.*

The term connoted the driving force of the U.S. sectional controversy: the slaveholders' arguably undemocratic power over northern white citizens no less than over southern black slaves. All of the resulting thrusts for power—the northern majority's disavowal of the Slavepower's dominion over whites, the southern minority's secession from the Union after the northern majority rejected Slavepower rule, fugitive slaves' escape from their masters, the Border South's defiance of Deep South disunionism, the North's reversal of slaveholders' secession from the Union—all this unraveling of a republic and coercive reconsolidation stemmed from the foundations of American democratic practice and belief. But America had become an ugly City Upon a Hill, demonstrating that the world's most advanced republic could end slavery only by one of the bloodiest fratricides in human history.

I

THE DIVERGENT U.S. and Latin American roads toward emancipation began with dissimilar colonial settlements. During the seventeenth century, England, the most republican of the European colonizing nations, sent to the North American mainland by far the largest percentage of nonslaveholding settlers to be found in any New World area containing large numbers of slaves.[2] Because of that comparatively huge white republican population, the thirteen colonies had special leverage to resist English metropolitan impositions on colonial republicanism; and out of that resistance came the American Revolution and the first New World liberation from Old World control. With the establishment of the federal Union, the Revolutionaries encased one of the most extensive slaveholder regimes in the Americas inside the most republican nation in the New World.

Within the republican Union, advanced Anglo-American antislavery ideas could especially flourish—if abolitionists could mobilize the majority of nonslaveholders. Yet within the Union, the minority of slaveholders had a special New World power to protect themselves—if they could mobilize the masses. Nowhere else in the New World did slavery's fate hang on popular mobilization.

A second peculiarity in colonial settlement of the future United States ultimately threatened slaveholder mobilization of southern public opinion. Just as a higher proportion of non-slaveholding whites peopled the original thirteen colonies than could be found in other New World locales with large numbers of slaves, so only North American colonists planted slavery primarily in nontropical areas. Anglo-American economists have always echoed the Latin American colonials' conventional wisdom that tropical climates spawned the largest plantation profits. Seventeenth- and eighteenth-century English settlers, however, considered the climate of the most tropical part of North America, the Lower South, too cool for sugar and coffee, Latin America's profitable plantation products. North American colonists turned to other tropical crops for the Georgian and South Carolinian swamplands and Sea Islands on the Atlantic coast. In these Lower South tropics, huge slave gangs grew rice, indigo, and Sea Island cotton.

Nowhere west of the Lower South's coastal swamps, however, could these crops be lucratively extended. The most far-flung North American eighteenth-century slaveholder enterprises instead thrived northward, still farther from the sugar-and coffee-producing tropics. North of South Carolina—in Middle South latitudes—North Carolina and especially Virginia planters raised primarily tobacco. North of the Middle South—in Border South latitudes—Delaware and especially Maryland planters raised less tobacco and more grains. Farther yet from the tropics—in the most southern part of the eventually free-labor North—Pennsylvania, New Jersey, and New York grain farmers used some slaves; and in New England, a few Puritans utilized house slaves. In late-eighteenth-century North America, the coolest locale of New World slaveholders, almost four slaves out of five lived north of the more tropical Lower South.

As the eighteenth century gave way to the nineteenth, an invention and a law pressed U.S. slavery toward tropical habitats. Eli Whitney's invention of the cotton gin in 1793 impelled the movement of slaveholders toward Lower South frontiers. Fourteen years later, in 1807, the federal government's closure of the

African slave trade contracted the Cotton Kingdom's source of slaves. Unlike mid-nineteenth-century tropical developers in Cuba and Brazil, the two other large New World slavocracies, cotton planters could not legally buy slaves from Africa. But only U.S. slaveholders could purchase slaves from their own northerly, relatively nontropical areas, which had concurrently fallen into chronic economic recession.

A slave drain ensued, especially from the more northern South to the more southern South. Between 1790 and 1860, some 750,000 Middle and Border South slaves traveled downriver to the Cotton Kingdom. The Lower South, which had had 21 percent of U.S. slaves in 1790, had 59 percent in 1860. Maryland and Virginia, with 60 percent in 1790, had 18 percent in 1860. Some 37 percent of Lower South white families owned slaves in 1860, compared with only 12 percent in the Border South, down from 20 percent in 1790.[3]

At the same time that the more southerly U.S. slaveholders expanded toward Latin American-style tropical locations, the more northerly U.S. slavocracy contracted toward Latin American-style antislavery ideas. The Latin American slavocracies lacked the power to defy worldwide antislavery currents in the manner of Lower South slaveholders. Latin slaveholders instead gave ground grudgingly, stalling for more time to reap profits, mostly through the passage of so-called free-womb laws. These edicts freed only slaves born after a given law's enactment and only after they reached a distant target age, usually eighteen or twenty-one. These laws set a clock ticking toward the end of slavery.

The clock ran slowly, satisfyingly so from Latin American slaveholders' perspective. A slave born even a day before a law was passed would never be freed, which meant that slavery could profitably persist for at least fifty years. As for lucky slaves born at the right time, they were lucklessly doomed to involuntary servitude throughout their youth; and by the time they were twelve years old, black children toiled hard in the fields. A series of Latin American regimes with relatively few slaves, including Chile, Peru, and Venezuela, first tried delaying emancipation through free-womb laws. Then in the two Latin American countries with large slave populations, Cuba's Moret Law (1870) and Brazil's Rio Branco Law (1871) brought the free-womb tradition to climax.

Nowhere did free-womb emancipation work as slowly as entrepreneurs had hoped. Abolitionists and slaves pressed for a faster end to the system. Slaves born only a short time before passage of a free-womb law deployed especially angry resistance. In response, slaveholders often bargained individually with their slaves, scheduling freedom for each before the law freed any. Slaves, in return, promised to labor willingly during the interim.

These bargains drew on older Latin American manumission traditions. Latins had long liberated favorite slaves under certain conditions: when a master and a cherished black woman had a sexual relationship; when beloved mulatto offspring had resulted from such a union; or when a slave had given especially valued economic service. The combination of free-womb laws, expanded manumissions, intensified abolitionist attacks, and more widespread slave resistance finally toppled the regimes in Cuba in 1886 and Brazil in 1888—or before these slavocracies' respective free-womb laws had freed any slave.

These Latin American patterns, shunned in U.S. tropical areas where slavery was concentrating, had originated in U.S. temperate areas where the institution was dwindling. Free-womb emancipation bore a different title in the United States—post-nati emancipation—but only the name was different. In 1780, Pennsylvania enacted the hemisphere's first post-nati law. In 1799, New York followed suit, as did New Jersey in 1804. In 1817, New York followed up its preliminary post-nati law in the later Cuba/Brazil manner, declaring an end to the institution ten years hence.

South of these belatedly emancipated Middle Atlantic states, slaveholding states never passed a post-nati law. The Border South, however, emulated another aspect of Latin American gradualism: individual manumissions. Different nations took censuses of their populations in different years, which makes comparisons imprecise. Still, a similar pattern of manumission is clear enough. In 1830, 19.5 percent of black residents of the Border South were free, compared with 23 percent in Brazil (in 1817–18) and 46 percent in Cuba (in 1846). Two Border South states manumitted their slaves at rates faster than the Latin American norm. By 1830 in Maryland, 34 percent of the resident blacks were free, as were 83 percent of Delaware's blacks.[4]

But just as post-nati laws penetrated no farther south than the Middle Atlantic states, so manumissions flourished no farther south than the Border South. While 21 percent of Border South blacks were free in 1860, the percentage sank to 7 percent in the Middle South and 1.5 percent in the Lower South. The Border South manumission story was a subplot of the larger tale: that U.S. slavery was incrementing waning in northern nontropical habitats but rapidly strengthening in southwestern tropical locales.

With slavery swiftly concentrating southward and slowly fading northward, different social attitudes and political priorities developed. Lower South slaveholders came to call slavery a probably perpetual blessing, while Border South masters persistently called the institution a hopefully temporary evil. So too Lower South political warriors cared more about perpetuating slavery than the Union, while Border South leaders would compromise on slavery in order to save the Union. Still, even in Delaware, where over 15,000 slaves in 1790 had shrunk to under 2000 in 1860, slaveholders resisted final emancipation. In Maryland, where manumissions plus slave sales to the Lower South had halved the percentage of white slaveholding families, the increasingly outnumbered slavocracy counterattacked desperately in the mid-1850s, futilely seeking to re-enslave the freed blacks. Concurrently, in Missouri, the state's even faster declining fraction of slaveholders counterattacked still more desperately, unsuccessfully seeking to establish slavery in neighboring Kansas.

In the mid-nineteenth century, then, slaveholders overwhelmingly controlled the Lower South, which had been belatedly but massively developed. The slavocracy somewhat less solidly controlled the Middle and Border South, where percentages of slave owners were slowly dropping. But even in the

Border South, vestiges (and sometimes defiant concentrations) of the old relatively nontropical slavocracy occasionally fought to salvage a fading system. The mature Slave South had a tropical base of states, containing large slave populations, and several layers of buffer zones to the north, with less tropical conditions and less proslavery commitments and fewer slaves in each successive tier above.

Yet despite this degree of geographic disunity, no other New World slavocracy could muster as united a front against worldwide antislavery currents. The difference between slaveholders' unity, albeit incomplete, in the United States and their utter disarray in Brazil is especially revealing, for similar experiences yielded dissimilar outcomes. In both countries, a once-flourishing northerly slaveholding region fell into decline and sold many of its slaves to a newly flourishing southerly region. In the United States, the Upper South Tobacco Kingdom sold hundreds of thousands of slaves to the Lower South Cotton Kingdom. In Brazil, the Northeastern Sugar Kingdom, which in 1822 had held almost 70 percent of the country's slaves, transferred equally huge numbers of blacks to the South Central Coffee Kingdom, which by the early 1880s owned 65 percent of Brazil's slaves.[5]

There the similarity ended. In Brazil, the old sugar provinces, despite a population still 15 percent enslaved, led the movement for free-womb abolition, with the Ceará region in the vanguard. When the national Chamber of Delegates voted on the Rio Branco free-womb bill in 1871, the Northeastern sugar provinces favored gradual emancipation, 39–6, thus canceling out the South Central coffee provinces' 30–12 vote against.[6] The Border South, in contrast, usually voted with the Lower South on slavery propositions in Congress and never enacted a postnati law.

A more intense racism fueled the U.S. slaveholders' greater capacity to mobilize a united front. Because Latin American racial attitudes toward blacks were less hidebound than in the United States, greater tolerance for free-womb emancipation, for mulattoes, and for individual manumissions—and less willingness to fight a civil war over the issue—pervaded Latin American slavocracies. Because U.S. racism was so extreme, a more unified slaveholding class and more support from white nonslaveholders—and thus a greater capacity to fight a civil war—infused the Slave South.

Behind the more severe U.S. racism lay in part a different heterosexual situation, itself another result of the largest white migration to an important New World slavocracy. English colonists to the future United States migrated far more often in family groups and/or with equal numbers of unmarried males and females in the entourage than did colonists headed farther south, who more often sought their fortunes as unattached males, with only slaves available for sexual liaisons. More frequent and less taboo interracial sexual intimacies resulted south of British North America, which led to more mulattoes and less insistence that the world be rigidly separated into black and white.

Politically no less than biologically, U.S. slaveholders preferred nothing between black and white. The very basis of black slavery, in so republican a regime for whites, had to be a rigid color line. The Old South had to cleave advanced republicanism for whites totally from abject slavery for blacks. That black and white separation mystified Brazilian quasi-republicans, to say nothing of Latin American nonrepublicans. Only U.S. slaveholders, in short, considered *free black* an oxymoron.

Some historians doubt that racism was more culturally deep-seated in the United States than south of the border. That position founders before the greater U.S. taboo surrounding miscegenation and the far greater desire to deport blacks from antebellum America than from any other New World slavocracy. But the comparative power of cultural racism *before* slaveholders politically mobilized is unimportant to the comparative history of emancipation, for uniquely in the United States, slaveholders had to mobilize nonslaveholders, and racism was their most potent weapon. After southern slaveholders had used the distinction between equality for all whites and inequality for all blacks to rally the nonslaveholders, southern racism inarguably had become an especially powerful idea.

The racial foundation of Southwide unity, however, was a two-edged sword. For racism to unite nonslaveholders and slaveholders, the black race had to be significantly present. With the slave drain to the Lower South and the movement of European whites to such northerly slave states as Maryland and Missouri, Border South blacks became steadily less visible. As for that highly visible group of blacks in northern Maryland and Delaware, the free blacks, their energetic labor and law-abiding deportment demonstrated that racial control hardly required slavery.

That conclusion had proved fatal to slavery in northern states, where percentages of blacks had declined. In the colonial period, New York had had slave proportions in the 1860 Border South's range, about 15 percent of the total population. As New York's slave percentage had dwindled toward 5 percent, sentiment for post-nati emancipation had grown. Mid-nineteenth-century Border South states were in no immediate danger of becoming a New York, much less a Brazilian Ceará. But given the Border South's waning percentage of blacks, its Latin American-style manumissions, its propensity for thinking of slavery as a temporary evil, and its commitment to Union-saving compromises on the institution, could the Lower South rely on its northern hinterlands' future loyalty?

On the answer hung the Slave South's capacity to be that unique New World slave regime: the one that could defy an emancipating century rather than settle for a few more decades of slaveholder profits. Latin American slavocracies lacked not only the South's intensely racist reasons to stonewall antislavery but also its political basis for confidence that emancipation could be routed. The Latin American slavocracies were either too vulnerable to black insurrection (as in Haiti), too much under the power of European empires (as in the French and British West Indies and in Spanish-owned Cuba), or too small a minority (as in Venezuela and Peru) to command their fate inside a government that could abolish slavery. True, the Latin American regime closest in type to the southern slaveholders, the Brazilian slavocracy, also possessed a powerful minority in a partly parliament-ruled (and partly monarchical) nation. But

Brazilian slaveholders, compared with their more intransigent U.S. counterparts, were too divided against each other over slavery's future, too lacking in a rigid racism that might control the nonslaveholders, and too fond of a *regime des notables* to risk enfranchising and mobilizing the "nonnotables." Unable to mount a united front, in or out of parliament, the Brazilian slavocracy could only postpone emancipation with Rio Branco laws.

The Old South, in contrast, had various powers to command a majoritarian democracy despite its minority status—*if* all fifteen slave states hung together and the Border South did not go the way of New York, or worse, Ceará.

Numbers indicate how much was at stake in that *if*. The seven Lower South states of 1860 (South Carolina, Georgia, Florida, Alabama, Mississippi, Louisiana, and Texas, with 47 percent of their population enslaved) could not fight off the eighteen northern states (containing 61 percent of the American population) without the enthusiastic support of the four Middle South states (Virginia, North Carolina, Tennessee, and Arkansas, with 32 percent of their population enslaved) and the four Border South states (Maryland, Delaware, Kentucky, and Missouri, with 13 percent of their population enslaved). Those buffer areas above the Lower South could come under siege—the siege of democratic public opinion. Would the Border South remain foursquare behind slavery and the Lower South, even if the slavocracy's northern hinterlands came to possess scantier and scantier percentages of blacks?

That question transcended the Border South. The slaveholders' worst internal problem involved not a single localized place but a regionwide lopsided distribution of blacks. While the Border South was the most widespread locale with a relatively low percentage of slaves, some areas farther south also contained few blacks; and everywhere a paucity of slaves allowed more nonslaveholder hostility toward slaveholders. Wherever blacks were concentrated, whites drew together, however much the poor resented the rich, for lowly whites despised lowlier blacks even more than they resented lordly masters. But whenever blacks were scarce, race hatred intensified class hatred, for nonslaveholders preferred to have neither autocrats nor blacks around. A relatively slaveless situation, while most prevalent in the Border South, also predominated in western Virginia, in eastern Tennessee, and in piney woods and semimountainous areas of the Lower South. Here the Border South predicament came closer to home to worried Lower and Middle South slavocrats. Could upper-class ideology command lower-class loyalties in areas where no racial tensions united the whites?

II

STRUGGLES FOR ideological command often take a dialectical form of charge and response. In the United States, intensified versions of white republicanism and antiblack racism generated a dialectic about slavery different than that in Latin America. At the heart of the difference lay two fears foreign to Latin America. First, slavery and the slavery issue might destroy an advanced white men's republic. Second, emancipation might also devastate a white republic unless freed blacks were removed.

The North American dialogue about emancipation began with the foundation of U.S. republicanism, the Declaration of Independence. When the Founding Fathers asserted that *all* men are created equal, they immediately confronted a moral dilemma: their long unquestioned institution of slavery had become an anomaly in the republic they sought. Thomas Jefferson of Virginia, author of the Declaration and a large slaveholder, believed that all men would and should rise up against so antirepublican a horror as slavery. He thus feared that slave insurrection would disrupt white republics unless white republicans freed blacks. He also worried that southern republican leaders would become irresponsible tyrants if youths learned to exercise power by lashing dissolute blacks. Thus did the U.S. slavery controversy early take its special tack: Whites would always worry not only about whether blacks ought to be freed but about how white republicanism could be preserved.

Yet if Jefferson called slavery antithetical to republicanism, he considered racism compatible with the Declaration of Independence. Whites and blacks, thought Jefferson, were innately different. Whites allegedly possessed a keener abstract intelligence; blacks a keener sexual ardency. Ex-slaves, he further worried, would be eager for revenge and ex-masters determined to repress the avengers. If slaves were freed and remained in the United States, "deep-rooted prejudices entertained by the whites" and "ten thousand recollections, by the blacks, of the injuries they have sustained" would "produce convulsions, which will probably never end but in the extermination of one or the other race."[7]

Thus to preserve white republics, freed blacks had to be deported. The dangerous alternative was to keep blacks enslaved. Jefferson's conviction that emancipation must be conditional on removing blacks, the first thrust in the U.S. dialectic on abolition, was rare in Latin America.[8] An insistence on race removal would have ill-suited Latin American nations, where individual bargains between masters and slaves slowly led to a third class of semifree blacks and a fourth class of free blacks. The supposed necessity that U.S. slaveholders must choose between enslaving or removing blacks also misfit the situation in Delaware and Maryland, where black freedmen formed an orderly working class. But because U.S. slaveholders saw the world through the lens of a rigid non-Latin-American-style racism, the successful manumissions in Maryland and Delaware went unacknowledged, even unseen, as if the phenomenon of orderly free blacks *could* not happen and therefore *had* not happened. Instead, that more common Upper South phenomenon, the removal of slaves by sales to the Lower South, became the model for further action in the selling region. Proposals for stepping up the removal of blacks from the Upper South included expulsion to Africa, deportation to the Caribbean, and legislatively induced accelerated sales to the Lower South through the passage of post-nati laws.

By sometimes campaigning for Latin American-style post-nati proposals, with the non-Latin American purpose of forcing the removal of blacks, Upper South emancipators demonstrated again the U.S. slave regime's oddity in hemispheric perspective. In Latin America, free-womb laws were *nationally* enacted. Thus slaveholders in one part of the nation could not subvert emancipation by selling the bondsman before his emancipating birthday to another part of the nation. But in the United States, where only states passed post-nati laws, a slaveholder could sell his soon-to-be-freed slaves into permanent thralldom by transporting them to a state that lacked the law. Thus could one state remove its blacks, with slave purchasers in another state paying to "whiten" the selling state's population.

Some northern masters first discovered this singular black removal process. After their states passed post-nati laws, nineteenth-century New York and New Jersey slaveholders often sold their slaves down South before an emancipating birthday. Few northern legislators cheered such a cynical evasion of abolition. Most northern masters also deplored the loophole, but New York slaveholders still used it perhaps two-thirds of the time, thus permanently enslaving thousands of blacks whose future freedom had been decreed.[9]

This process, unintended by northern legislatures, became the deliberate intention of southern not-so-antislavery legislators when they appropriated the post-nati proposal. Southern propositions for the ploy began in the Virginia antislavery debate of 1831–32, an episode that ironically has been mistaken for the end of southern consideration of abolition. In the wake of Nat Turner's slave revolt, the most successful (although still abortive) slave uprising in the United States, Thomas Jefferson Randolph, Jefferson's favorite grandson, proposed to the Virginia legislature that slaves born after 1840 be freed on their eighteenth (women) and twenty-first (men) birthdays. Thus far Randolph's proposal was standard Latin American-style free-womb emancipation. But Randolph's bill added the condition, alien to Latin America, that the state must remove the freedmen to Africa. Randolph's speech for the historic proposal also featured the cynical prediction, more alien still south of the U.S. border, that many Virginia masters would sell slaves to the Lower South before emancipating birthdays. Thus, Randolph cheered, masters would profitably remove slaves from Virginia at no cost to state coffers.

Randolph's proposal led to a famous state crisis, for Virginia's largely nonslaveholding areas rallied behind Jefferson's grandson in defiance of slaveholding areas. Never before in the history of the Slave South, and never again until western Virginia seceded from Virginia during the Civil War, was the potentially dangerous antagonism between slaveless and slaveholding geographic zones more obvious, for here western Virginian nonslaveholders sought to impose emancipation on eastern Virginia planters. Earlier, eastern squires had built a bulwark against the nonslaveholder threat. They had insisted that slaveholders have more seats in the Virginia House of Delegates (lower house) than eastern Virginia's white numbers justified. The underrepresented western Virginians responded, as did later Northerners, that the Slavepower thus enslaved *them*. These nonslaveholders preferred that all blacks depart the commonwealth. Then true white democracy would replace Slavepower dominion in Virginia. So western Virginians cheered Thomas Jefferson Randolph's black removal proposal.

After two weeks of debate, the Virginia House of Delegates rejected a variation of Randolph's proposal by a vote of 73–58. The margin against antislavery would have shriveled to one vote if the slaveholders had not held those extra legislative seats. The shaky anti-Randolph majority warned that even after masters had sold off some blacks, state-financed removal of other slaves would bankrupt the government. Nor should the government bully masters into selling bondsmen by placing post-nati deadlines over capitalists' heads. But Randolph's none-too-proslavery opponents, also desiring an altogether white Virginia, predicted that masters' capitalistic decisions would dispatch Virginia slaves southward without the threat of post-nati laws. Thomas R. Dew, then Virginia's most famous advocate of slavery, was pleased that all Middle South slaves would eventually be sold to the Lower South, for Virginia was "too far north" for slavery.[10]

Dew's proposed remedy, removing slaves by altogether-voluntary private sales, could keep slavery and blacks too far north for a long time. Thomas Jefferson had proposed a swifter way to deport blacks: a federal constitutional amendment that would authorize compulsory emancipation and colonization to be financed by federal land sales, a richer source of funds than state taxation. Throughout the nation, antislavery moderates perpetuated this scheme for liberating slaves while also whitening the republic. The persistent admirers of Jefferson's black removal plan included the Border South's favorite statesman, Henry Clay; the Republicans' favorite politician, Abraham Lincoln; and the North's favorite novelist, Harriet Beecher Stowe. A national volunteer organization, the American Colonization Society, used private donations to establish a rather unstable African colony, Liberia, to receive American blacks. In those unusual days of a federal budgetary surplus, the national government had excess funds to help with the financing. But South Carolina threatened secession if Congress even discussed the possibility. So the debate stopped before much was said.

III

IN POST-JEFFERSON AMERICA, as in post-Nat Turner Virginia, that first thrust of the U.S. dialectic on slavery, the abolition-conditional-on-removal argument, was yielding little black removal, save the slave drain southward, which was not antislavery at all. Thus did the conditional antislavery polemic, unusual in Latin America, generate its opposite, also uncommon in Latin America: northern extremists' exasperated attack on black removal and on all conditions that must be observed before slavery could be immediately abolished.[11] William Lloyd Garrison's *Liberator* articulated this assault on procrastination, beginning in 1831. Black deportation, Garrison wrote angrily, was as outrageous as black slavery, for blacks were created equal. Furthermore, democracy must abolish slavery or slavery would abolish democracy, for masters with sinful absolute power and a republic with salutary limited power were deadly foes.

The black-removal idea lay forever discredited among northern antislavery extremists after Garrison's savage assault. But here as everywhere, posterity should never confuse the northern extremists with the northern mainstream. The argument that antislavery must be conditional on removing black freedmen retained thousands of northern supporters for every Garrisonian and hundreds of thousands of Upper South supporters with scarcely a southern Garrisonian to be found. The debate between Garrison's unconditional immediatism and Jefferson's conditional gradualism would persist until deep into the Civil War. Then blacks' wartime utility helped the Garrisonians rout the long-more-powerful Jeffersonian black-removal tradition.

Jefferson's and Garrison's positions, while clashing on black removal, agreed that black slavery poisoned white democracy. That concurrence did not augur well for the slaveholding minority. White racist nonslaveholders, the majority of citizens in the South and in the nation, had to be deterred from believing that black slavery endangered white democracy and/or that blacks could safely be removed. Thus conditional and unconditional antislavery together generated, in the next phase of the United States' unique dialogue on slavery, the predictable proslavery response: Without slavery, both blacks and democracy would expire.

Although proslavery Latin Americans also sometimes dwelled on blacks' alleged inferiority, the racial argument for *black* slavery was more necessary in a white men's republic, and race-based arguments were more central in U.S. proslavery polemics. South of the United States, proslavery articulations emphasized more strongly the color-blind message that abolition portended *social* upheaval. Proslavery polemicists in the United States characteristically added that emancipation portended specifically *racial* upheaval. The Lower South slavocracy compared blacks to orangutans and gorillas. Such barbarians, went the ugly argument, would revert to African cannibalism if freed.

But though this argument for *black* slavery was almost always front and center, a few proslavery theorists wrought the final uniquely U.S. rationale: Not "mere Negro" slavery but slavery per se was especially right in a republic, regardless of its special rightness for blacks. This color-blind aspect of the U.S. proslavery argument reaffirmed the Latin American emphasis on social upheaval and added an emphasis on political upheaval. Abolition would unhinge not just the society but also the republic, according to the peculiarly U.S. version of color-blind proslavery.

This nonracial proslavery argument reversed Jefferson's racist antislavery thesis. Early experience in despotism over blacks, Jefferson had argued, would corrupt republican leaders of whites. Defenders of color-blind paternalism countered that the plantation system trained the best men to command lesser blacks and thus to command lesser whites. Inferiors of any age or sex, class or color, needed patriarchal direction, lest children revolt from parents, wives leave husbands, lower classes assault upper classes, and especially lest patriarchal republics degenerate into depraved mobocracies.

These, then, were the prime ideological contestants on the issue of slavery in the mid-nineteenth-century United States: antislavery moderates, who would abolish slavery only if free blacks were deported; antislavery extremists, who denounced the black-removal condition; advocates for race-based slavery, who denounced freedom for blacks; and advocates for slavery per se, who would extend paternal authority beyond blacks to whites of lesser status, partly to salvage patriarchal republicanism. This ideological pattern, when laid over the geographical pattern of slaveholding locations in the United States, indicates how majoritarian democracy could menace the Lower South minority. The color-blind argument that slaveholders must rule nonslaveholders outraged the southern (and northern) nonslaveholding majority, as western Virginians had shown in 1832. The far more politic (and thus far more frequent) color-based argument that slaveholders must control blacks played into the rigid racism that everywhere differentiated the U.S. slavery controversy from other New World varieties.

But racist ideology remained a fragile basis for universal proslavery opinion. American whites in areas with few or no slaves preferred to live among no blacks at all. The race-based argument that blacks must be enslaved would thus become academic to Middle and Border South moderates if they thought their region's blacks could be removed somewhere else, including to the Lower South. Proslavery persuasion, in short, could not permanently consolidate the South's quasi-consolidated northern extremities. How, then, could Lower South zealots banish antislavery opinion from those vulnerable hinterlands?

IV

THE MORE REPUBLICAN U.S. slavocracy ironically outdid their less republican Latin American counterparts in eradicating antislavery opinion. Inside Spanish-owned Cuba, the Old World metropolitan authority, not the New World provincial slaveholders, usually dictated which opinion was to be silenced. Inside quasi-republican Brazil, where slaveholders constantly argued antislavery with one another, the ruling class could hardly silence its own debate. Discussion thus raged uncontested in Rio de Janeiro, the heart of the Coffee Kingdom. In U.S. areas with heavy slave populations, in contrast, local lynch mobs violently repressed supposedly incendiary discussion. American republicanism, in the black-belt South, meant that all ideas could compete in the open—except antislavery.

Local closure of antislavery discussion, however, could not transcend its local basis of legitimacy. Democratic agitation most menaced the Border South with fewer slaves, not the Lower South with more; and according to southern dogma, each neighborhood could police only itself. No slaveholders' mob could lynch a man inside a nonslaveholders' community, and no Lower South mob could violate Border South white dissenters.

Nor could Border South whites altogether deter their most threatening black dissenters—fugitive slaves. Group insurrectionists in the United States, though momentarily more terrifying than individual runaways, were less numerous. They were also less threatening, for whites knew that slave conspirators had few guns and some potential turncoats. In contrast, individual slaves, when they escaped without telling another black, could not initially be betrayed and could liberate themselves before the master could react. A solitary slave could most easily reach the North from the Border South, as Maryland's Frederick Douglass, the most famous fugitive slave, demonstrated. Although less than 1 percent of Border South slaves annually escaped to the North, their loss cost their masters over $100,000; and if more Frederick Douglasses freed themselves, more Border South slaveholders might cash in their investments at Lower South slave auctions before still more blacks could flee. Then Border South white moderates, whom Lower South extremists could neither convince nor lynch, might agitate harder for further removal of blacks.

Thus fugitives achieved more than their own freedom in the seemingly apolitical act of running away from masters (and from millions of enslaved brethren). The runaways advanced the political process that led to war and emancipation. Particularly Border South fugitives illuminated the slavocracy's geographic area of weakness—an illumination that provoked border masters into initiating Union-shattering political controversies. The slaveholders' political answer to border fugitives lay in the national forum, for only national laws could consolidate the line between South and North, as well as the barrier between slavery and free democratic discourse.

The electoral numbers might seem to have forbidden slaveholders from wielding national governmental power to deter border fugitives or otherwise consolidate their outposts. During pre-Civil War controversies, around 70 percent of U.S. whites lived outside the Slave South, and around 70 percent of southern white families did not own slaves. In those overwhelming numbers lay the slaveholders' potential peril. But the democratic system, as ever both threatening and empowering for a besieged minority, long enabled the master class to protect its borderlands and dominate Yankee majorities.

The federal Constitution provided the minority's most obvious defensive weapon. Abolitionists often conceded that the Constitution protected slavery, not least because it authorized Congress to pass fugitive slave laws. The Constitution also contained many restrictions on majority antislavery action, includ-- ing the ultimate one: a forbidding amendment process. Three-fourths of the states have to agree on a constitutional amendment before it becomes operative. If all fifteen slaveholding states had voted against any future emancipation amendment, the free-labor states would have had to swell from 18 to 45 and the Union from 31 to 60 states before abolitionists could have triumphed by this route. Moreover, if Texas had split itself into five slave states, as Congress authorized it to do any time after its admission to the Union in 1845, the resulting 19 slave states could not have been outvoted on a constitutional amendment until a 76-state union had been achieved. Armed with these numbers, the Slavepower minority apparently could stand forever behind unamendable constitutional bulwarks.

Proslavery forces accordingly appealed constantly to constitutional prohibition of majoritarian impositions. John C. Calhoun's doctrine of the concurrent majority took this dogma of "majorities-shall-not" to its logical extreme. Calhoun asserted that every minority must unanimously concur before a numerical majority could pass constitutional law. In 1832, Calhoun's state, South Carolina, transformed this logic into action. In the so-called Nullification Controversy, South Carolina declared the national numerical majority's protective tariff null and void in that state. Only the Compromise Tariff of 1833 stopped President Andrew Jackson from militarily imposing the countervailing postulate: When majorities decide, minorities must obey.

By the 1840s, Calhoun had come to see proslavery utility in Jackson's majoritarian postulate, for the nullification dogma of majorities-shall-not provided an arguably useless constitutional protection. Unless a congressional majority, for example, provided coercive mechanisms to enforce fugitive slave laws, Yankee rescuers of slaves could raid the Border South and flout the Constitution's fugitive slave clause. Then slaveholders in the four Border South states might sell their slaves to the Lower South. Were the 15 slave states to shrink to 11, an antislavery constitutional amendment could be enacted against slave states' wishes in a not-so-far-off 44-state Union, instead of in an incredibly distant 60-state or impossibly distant 76-state Union.

This potential Border South problem illustrated the slaveholders' provokingly small margin for error. Totally to control ¹¹⁄₁₅ of slaveholders' territory and largely to control the other ⁴⁄₁₅ of their world would have been a miracle in any other New World slaveholding regime. But U.S. slaveholders, unlike Latin American counterparts, were seeking to stonewall the Age of Emancipation, and the singular effort would fail if the slaveholders' large degree of control over their most vulnerable four states weakened. In part for that reason, southern extremists, including Calhoun, came to eschew the doctrine of federal hands off slavery and to urge that federal hands be heavily laid on, especially in the borderlands, to protect the slaveholders' interests there. National majorities must annex Texas on the Lower South's flank, admit Kansas on the Border South's edge, and ensure the return of fugitive slaves who escaped over any border.

Two more empowerments of the southern minority long enabled slaveholders to maneuver congressional majorities into fortifying southern outposts. First, the Constitution let the slaveholding states count three out of five slaves, in addition to all whites, when the number of southern congressmen and presidential electors was calculated. Thus in 1860 the Slave South, containing 30 percent of the nation's white citizens, had 36 percent of the nation's congressmen and presidential electors. That extra power (which had first prompted the coining of the word *Slavepower*) turned southern defeat into victory on key occasions, including the election of Virginia's Thomas Jefferson over Massachusetts's John Adams to the presidency in 1800, the Missouri Controversy, the Gag Rule Controversy, and the Kansas-Nebraska Controversy.

Second, national political parties gave a 30 percent popular minority with a 36 percent congressional minority the leverage to secure another 14 percent or more of congressional votes. Especially the dubiously titled Democratic party became a bulwark of the slavocracy. The party could be entitled "democratic" only in the way the American Revolution could be called socially revolutionary: if white men alone counted as Americans. Just as the Founding Fathers' principal emancipation policy, antislavery conditional on black removal, commenced a nonrevolutionary crawl toward black freedom, so the Democratic party's leading ideology, egalitarian democracy for white men only, consolidated undemocratic dominion over Native Americans, blacks, and women. Andrew Jackson's agenda included enslaving blacks, dominating females, removing Native Americans from land coveted by whites, and treating as equals only white male adults. Jackson's egalitarianism, for white males only, won him huge majorities in the Lower South but progressively smaller majorities at every step northward and fewest majorities in New England. That voting distribution gave the Democratic party a majority control in the nation and Southerners a majority control in the party. Thus when slavery controversies emerged in national politics, Southern Democrats could use the leverage of the nation's usually dominant party to demand that Northern Democrats help consolidate the slavocracy's frontiers.

A powerful minority of southern reactionaries, gathered around Calhoun in South Carolina and eastern Virginia, usually remained aloof from the Democratic party. They espoused the most extreme proslavery argument, that patriarchs should rule not only blacks but all poorer persons. They scorned American electioneering with its, so they thought, party demagogues appealing to the passions of white plebeians. These eighteenth-century-style aristocratic republicans feared even the southern-dominated Democratic party. They doubted that southern spoilsmen would insist that northern spoilsmen support extreme proslavery legislation. They prophesied instead that demagogical Northern Democrats would persuade demagogical Southern Democrats to dilute proslavery legislation. Then all Democrats would secure national electoral triumphs and patronage feasts.

Calhoun suspected the Whig party even more. He knew that while Democrats won in the South more often than in the North, Whigs won in the North more often than in the South. Thus though Southerners held the balance of power inside the Democracy, Northerners held the balance of power inside Whiggery. Worse, the Border South's most popular politician, Henry Clay, favored Jefferson-style antislavery, conditional on deporting black freedmen. According to Clay's utopian scenario, Border South moderates would edge away from Lower South extremists, fuse with northern antislavery moderates in the Whig party, and secure national funding for removal of blacks.

If national politics were to reverse Clay's preferred course, Southern Democrats had to insist that Northern Democrats support the fullest proslavery protection. Southern Whigs also had to repel the Northern Whigs' slightest conditional antislavery overture. To goad southern waverers toward maintaining the necessary intransigence, proslavery warriors possessed yet another empowering gift from a democratic political system. When a besieged democratic society fears attack from outside and softness within, crusaders demand that trimmers prove their loyalty. The nineteenth-century cry that Southerners must not be soft on slavery, like the twentieth-century cry that Americans must not be soft on Communism, aimed at shaming private doubters into public displays of solidarity. Then a unanimous South might force the national parties to back proslavery laws.

Southern politics periodically became a three-ring loyalty circus. Southern Democrats accused Southern Whigs of treasonous alliances with antislavery Yankees. The accusers had a point. Northern Whigs, unlike Northern Democrats, composed the majority in their party, and they would never compromise on slavery-related matters. Southern Whigs, in retaliation, accused Southern Democrats of disloyally compromising on proslavery laws. These accusers also had a point. To secure Northern Democrats' proslavery votes, Southern Democrats often had to compromise a little. Calhounite aristocratic republicans meanwhile damned Southerners in both egalitarian republican parties for disloyally compromising the South.

Ironically, northern extremists were southern extremists' best allies in these loyalty contests. Garrison's righteous denunciations, aimed at all who opposed unconditional emancipation, damned all Southerners, whether they hoped to remove or to retain slaves. Southern moderates, enraged at being called sinners, passionately joined proslavery extremists in resenting the slur on their honor. On the subject of Yankee holier-than-thouism, Henry Clay sounded like John C. Calhoun.

Southern loyalty contests worked such "democratic" magic most effectively in Washington, D.C. Back home, Lower South extremists and Border South compromisers lived hundreds of miles apart. But in Washington, they crowded into the same boardinghouses. Here Yankees called Southerners sinners to their faces, and any Southerner who cherished his self-esteem and honor, went the tribal cry, must show the colors. In such an atmosphere, when Lower South militants demanded the Border South's support for slavery's expansion, the less militant Southerners usually felt compelled to go along. When border slaveholders demanded federal protection, the Lower South always went along. When a united South demanded proslavery legislation, Northern Democrats usually acquiesced, lest their party, their nation, and their national political aspirations be damaged. But Northern Democrats' appeasement of minority demands instead put the National Democratic party, the Union, majoritarian republicanism, and the appeasers' northern re-election prospects at ever-greater risk.

V

THE GAG RULE CONTROVERSY, the first national slavery crisis after Garrison's emergence, introduced the deadly process. In 1835, antislavery zealots petitioned Congress to abolish slavery in Washington, D.C. The petitions inadvertently demonstrated that abolitionists constituted a fringe group outside the northern mainstream. Only a tiny fraction of Northerners signed the appeals, and a large number of signers were women, barred from the electorate.

Nevertheless, the petitioners reshaped national mainstream slavery politics. Their Garrisonian tone, insulting to Southerners, would have been counterproductive in Latin American countries, where slaveholders and abolitionists often negotiated gradual manumissions and free-womb laws. But in a U.S. world where Lower South extremists rejected any form of gradualism, the Garrisonian holier-than-thou polemics evoked a violent southern response. That provocative response shook northern complacency about the slavery issue more than any abolitionist could.

The slaveholders' provocative demand was that petitions for congressional action against slavery must be barred from congressional deliberations. Antislavery must not be discussed in secret committees, much less publicly. To justify this repression of democratic debate, Southerners emphasized that congressional discussions might swell northern antislavery sentiment, increase the Upper South's distaste for the institution, incite slave insurrection and flight, and rob Southerners of that self-esteem and pride necessary to defend themselves. By attempting to gag congressional debate, Southerners tried to impose on the nation their regional version of republicanism: all ideas, *except* antislavery, were open to discussion.

Northerners responded that republicanism would lie in ruins unless *all* ideas could be debated. Representative republicanism especially would become a mockery, said Northerners, unless citizens could request that their representatives discuss whether slavery, an arguably antirepublican institution, should exist in the republic's capital city. The southern gag rule tactic, an irrelevant strategy in largely undemocratic Latin America, thus immediately produced the key non-Latin American question: Were slavery for blacks and democratic procedures for whites compatible? From that question, an otherwise rather isolated abolitionist movement would spread in the North, and the U.S. slavery controversy would assume its irrepressible–and non-Latin American–form.

In the Gag Rule Controversy as ever afterward, Southern Whigs, Southern Democrats, and Calhounites competed to secure the most thoroughgoing protection of slavery, whatever the North's understanding of democratic niceties. That southern competition escalated the pressure on Southerners' northern party allies. In 1836, Northern Democrats, exhorted by the southern majority in their party, agreed to enact a gag rule after they had watered it down. Northern Whigs, in the majority in their party, denounced any gag rule, watered down or not. Southern Whigs, unable to secure proslavery legislation, scoffed that the Democracy's watered-down gag rule was ineffective. Calhounites, opposing all national parties, condemned all southern compromisers as disloyal. Southern Democrats, now besieged from all southern sides as soft on the issue, subsequently demanded tighter gag rules. Northern

Democrats succumbed, but with ever-increasing resentments, in ever-smaller numbers, and at ever-greater risk of losing northern support.

The most airtight of the Democratic party's gag rules, passed in 1840, forbade the House of Representatives from receiving, much less considering, antislavery petitions. To the embarrassment of Southern Whigs, the Northern Whigs, led by Massachusetts's ex-president John Quincy Adams, refused to be gagged. Adams relentlessly attacked Northern Democrats as the Slavepower's slaves. The issue, he said, was not black slavery but white republicanism. The minority South must not rule the majority North. The slaveholding minority must not gag republican citizens. A viable republic must allow all ideas to be discussed. Northern Democrats must represent the majority North, sustain white men's democracy, and repeal the minority South's antidemocratic gag rule.

In December 1844, Northern Democrats finally acted to protect their home base. By voting down all gag rules, after eight years of caving in to ever-tighter gags, they signaled that the southern minority could push Northerners only so far. This denouement of the Gag Rule Controversy also signaled that northern and southern antiparty extremists had unintentionally collaborated to weaken their mutual foe: national party moderates. Just as the Garrisonians' antisouthern insults had helped southern extremists rally moderate Southern Democrats, so proslavery diehards' antirepublican procedure had helped northern extremists rally moderate Northern Democrats.

Without inadvertent aid from Southrons and when agitating about just black men's rights, Garrisonian polemicists had converted only a tiny minority of the very conservative, highly racist antebellum Northerners to crusade against slaves' antirepublican plight. But with the aid of provoked Southerners and when agitating about white men's rights too, abolitionists had raised northern consciousness about slavery's inherently antirepublican nature. By demanding a gag on the discussion of that one issue, slaveholders had confirmed one aspect of the abolitionists' case: The preservation of southern-style black slavery meant the annihilation of northern-style white republicanism. These dynamics of northern consciousness-raising ultimately forced those key northern appeasers, Northern Democrats, to join Northern Whigs and northern extremists in opposing all gags, just as the dynamics of southern consciousness-raising forced southern moderates to join southern extremists in seeking ever-tighter gags. Then neither centrist national party could find a middle position between the two sections' different versions of republicanism. And in any democracy, the erosion of the vital center can be the first step toward civil war.

VI

IN 1844, AN OMINOUS second step was taken. Southern Democrats surrendered on the gag rules, partly to press Northern Democrats to support the annexation of the then-independent Republic of Texas. Slaveholders' fight to save slavery in Washington, D.C., could and would successfully continue, whether Congress debated abolitionists' petitions or not. Meanwhile, Southern Democrats thought that they must immediately annex Texas, of whose population only 20 percent was enslaved in the early 1840s. That was a Border South percentage of slaves. But this time, the borderland with a low proportion of slaves abutted the slaveholders' southwestern flank, thick with slaves. A Texas republic with relatively few slaves, Southerners worried, might submit to English antislavery blandishments in exchange for diplomatic protection. Then an emancipated Texas, under English control, would beckon fugitive slaves from the Lower South. In contrast, an annexed Texas, under U.S. control, would consolidate the Lower South frontier. In early 1844, Secretary of State Abel P. Upshur, a Virginia Whig, started negotiations toward an annexation treaty. In April, after Upshur's death, John C. Calhoun completed the negotiations and President John Tyler, another Virginia Whig, asked the Senate to ratify the treaty. In June, when the administration could not secure the necessary two-thirds majority for ratification, Tyler and Calhoun urged Congress to admit the proposed slave state by a simple majority of each house.

A Southern Whig administration had proposed a border safeguard. But as usual, only the National Democratic party could pass prosouthern legislation. Northern Whigs, as usual, denounced the southern proposal. Southern Democrats, however, induced reluctant Northern Democrats to replace the lukewarm annexationist New Yorker, Martin Van Buren, with the strongly annexationist Tennessean, James K. Polk, as the party's presidential candidate in 1844. After Polk won the election, Southern Democrats, now pressured by Southern Whigs to do still more for the South, successfully insisted that reluctant Northern Democrats not only admit Texas to the Union but also allow the annexed state, any time in the future, to divide itself into five slave states. Four years later, a resentful Van Buren bolted the Democratic party, arguing that white men's majoritarian democracy must be protected from minority dictation. Van Buren ran for president on the Free-Soil ticket, hoping to stop slavery from spreading into federal territories.

At midcentury, while Van Buren sought to contain the Slavepower in the South, Southerners sought to stop the flight of slaves to the North. In 1850, border Southerners proposed a new fugitive slave law, especially designed to protect the South's northernmost hinterlands from northern slave raiders. The proposed law contained notorious antirepublican features, as the North (but not the South) defined republicanism. Black fugitives were denied a jury trial, as they were in the South (but not in the North). Any nonslaveholder could be compelled to join a slave-chasing posse in the manner of a southern patrol—an outrageous requirement in the North.

In the face of the southern minority's latest attempt to impose on the nation southern-style republicanism, Northern Whigs again balked. But again Northern Democrats reluctantly acquiesced, and again the minority South, using the National Democratic party as a congressional fulcrum, had gained protection of vulnerable frontiers. When Southerners subsequently attempted to extradite captured fugitives from the North, the new procedures returned the alleged slaves 90 percent of the time. But in the remaining cases, northern mobs blocked the return of the

escapees. The well-publicized stories of rare fugitive slave rescues dramatized Garrison's most telling lesson: Southern-style
power over blacks damaged northern-style republics for whites.
The Kansas-Nebraska Act of 1854 drove the lesson home. Once
again a vulnerable slaveholders' hinterland, this time the Border
South's Missouri, with only 10 percent of its population enslaved,
demanded protection of its frontier. Proslavery Missourians urged
that slaveholders be allowed to enter the uninhabited territory to
their west, Kansas, if Congress opened the area for settlement.
Missouri's senator David R. Atchison claimed that if free laborers
controlled Kansas, Missouri slaves would flee to Kansas sanctu-
aries; the number of Missouri's still-scarce antislavery politicians
would increase; and worried Missouri slaveholders would sell
their slaves southward. The erosion of Missouri slavery would
then spread east to Kentucky, Maryland, and Delaware, toppling
slavery in the South's northern outposts.

Before any citizen could come to the federal area west of
Missouri, Congress would have to authorize migration. Before
slaveholding citizens could come, Congress would have to repeal
the Missouri Compromise of 1820, which had prohibited slavery
in all Louisiana Purchase territories north of the 36° 30' line.
That man-made geographic boundary continued westward from
the latitude of Missouri's southern border, thus barring slaveholders from living west of Missouri, once Congress allowed
settlement there. Stephen A. Douglas, the Northern Democrats'
leader in the post-Van Buren era, warned Southerners that repeal
of the Missouri Compromise would raise "a hell of a storm." But
most Border South Democrats adamantly demanded repeal, the
Lower South rallied to the cause, and another borderite, Southern Whig Senator Archibald Dixon of Kentucky, insisted that
Southern Democrats go all the way for slavery.

Douglas, although a Northern Democrat, could not with-
stand this latest competition within the South to be most
southern. Above all, he wished to open the Kansas-Nebraska
area for white settlers, an objective that would achieve his own
goals: a revitalized Democratic party, its presidential nomination, and a West open to white entrepreneurs' economic devel-

opment, especially railroads (including one in which Douglas owned shares). But not enough southern congressmen would vote for a Kansas-Nebraska bill, inviting settlers to come, unless the bill honored *their* anti-Missouri Compromise proposal that slaveholding and nonslaveholding settlers alike be permitted. Their stance, they pointed out to Douglas, sustained *his* Popular Sovereignty principle. According to Douglas's dogma, local populations, not distant congressmen, should have sovereignty over local institutions. Then Washington congressmen of 1820 should not have dictated Kansans' labor arrangements in 1854; and this misguided bar to settler sovereignty and to slaveholding settlers must be repealed.

So Douglas, pressed to repeal a Missouri Compromise measure that violated his principles, agreed to sponsor a Kansas-Nebraska bill that sustained Popular Sovereignty. No pre-Civil War moment was more revealing. Douglas was as convinced as any Southerner that supposedly superior whites should evict supposedly inferior Native Americans from the West and that the enslavement of supposedly inferior blacks was no Northerner's moral business. Yet Southern Democrats had to pressure Douglas to be Douglas, for their shared program bore the taint of Slavepower domination. And this astute majoritarian politician did not want to be labeled a tool of the minority.

Nevertheless, he had to risk the noxious designation. What became known as *his* Kansas-Nebraska Act, passed by a Douglas-rallied National Democratic party plus a majority of Southern Whigs, repealed the Missouri Compromise ban on slavery in Kansas Territory, located due west of Missouri, and in Nebraska Territory, located due north of Kansas. Any settler with any form of property could come to these two territories, declared the law, and the majority of settlers in each territory would decide which institutions should thereafter prevail. This most important of all mid-nineteenth-century American laws authorized slaveholding migrants to move to Kansas, seek to make it a slave state, and thus protect the Border South's western flank, just as Texas Annexation had fortified the Lower South's western frontier and the Fugitive Slave Law guarded the Border South's northern extremities. Douglas's law also invited the Democrats' northern opponents to claim that the Slavepower minority, in its anxiety to quarantine border slavery from neighboring democratic currents, had again bullied a congressional majority in the manner of an imperious dictator.

In 1854, in the perspective of the Slavepower's influence on Douglas and on the Kansas-Nebraska Act, the uncertainty of the Border South's long-run commitment to slavery hardly seemed disastrous. Although Border South vulnerabilities existed, Southerners worked to overcome them. The resulting national legal antidotes seemed promising. The Kansas borderlands were open to slaveholders. Border South conditional antislavery advocates rarely campaigned and almost never collaborated with Northerners. A few spectacular rescues aside, nine times out of ten northern communities returned captured slave fugitives to the South in compliance with the Fugitive Slave Law. While neither proslavery polemics nor vigilante mobs had totally consolidated the South, national laws had apparently secured tolerably safe Border South outposts, to say nothing of an ultra-safe Texas hinterland. Majoritarian democracy and the National Democratic party guarded an enslaving minority's frontiers.

VII

IN THE NEXT SIX YEARS the northern majority would revoke the minority's domination of the republic, making problems inside the southern outposts more threatening. A similar phenomenon would happen during the Civil War. Halfway through that war, as halfway down the road to disunion, the slaveholders' internal world would seem well enough consolidated and their external attackers well enough contained. But in the antebellum years after 1854, as in the wartime years after 1863, disagreements inside the slavocracy would seem more lethal as northern assaults became more alarming.

In post-1854 politics, the South's most vulnerable instrument was the national party. Long useful in passing the slaveholders' favorite legislation, it had lately buckled under the weight of the minority's attempts to seek ever-more domination over the majority. Northern Democrats' resentment of the minority's demands had led to the 1844 defeat of the gag rule and to Van Buren's 1848 revolt. Despite Van Buren's defection, most Northern Democrats remained in the fold, and the National Democracy remained largely intact.

In the early 1850s, however, the National Whig party collapsed. Until the middle of the century, Lower South Whigs had hoped that Northern Whigs would relent on slavery-related matters. But after Northern Whigs said no to the Fugitive Slave Law, no to the Kansas-Nebraska Act, and, all too often, yes to the rescue of fugitive slaves, the Southern Democrats' charge rang all too true: Southerners who cooperated with Yankee Whigs might be secretly soft on slavery. After the Kansas-Nebraska Act, Whiggery lost all credibility in the Lower South.

Whiggery simultaneously lost some northern credibility. Old Whig rhetoric did not sufficiently convey many Yankees' twin indignations in 1854: hostility toward new immigrants and loathing for the Kansas-Nebraska Act. The anti-immigrant nativist impulse had been eroding northern Whiggery even before the Kansas-Nebraska Act finished off Lower South Whiggery. Since the early 1840s, an unprecedented wave of European migrants had begun arriving in the North–some 300,000 annually. The North's predominantly Protestant natives, usually English in origin and often Whiggish in politics, considered the newcomers too Irish or German, too Catholic, and too enraptured with the southern-dominated Democratic party. A fusion of northern immigrants and southern slaveholders, many native Yankees thought, bid fair to destroy American republicanism, using as the agent of destruction the deplorably named *Democratic* party.

A countervailing fusion swiftly transpired. Northern campaigns against immigrants and the Kansas-Nebraska Act, originally separate matters, partly funneled into one deliberately named *Republican* party in time for the presidential election of 1856. The Republicans' first presidential campaign almost swept enough northern votes to win the White House, despite the lack of southern votes. Some Northerners especially welcomed most

Republicans' secondary mission: to serve free laborers' economic interests. Republicans often saw southern and immigrant economic threats as similar. Impoverished immigrants could displace Yankee wage earners by accepting low wages, just as affluent slaveholders could displace Yankee farmers by making Kansas a slave territory.

But most Republicans considered free republican government more endangered than free labor capitalism. Here again, they saw immigrants and Southerners as related perils. Immigrants, not educated in American schools, supposedly voted as the pope or Democratic city bosses instructed, just as Northern Democrats, swollen in power by immigrant support, supposedly voted as the Slavepower instructed. In confronting these intertwined political dangers, Republicans emphasized containment more than abolition. Nativists in the 1850s did not usually urge abolition of immigration in order to save American jobs. Rather, they sought to contain foreigners from voting for many years in order to save the American republic. So too, Republican campaigners did not usually emphasize abolition of slavery, with or without expulsion of free blacks. Instead they usually stressed that the spread of slavery to the new territories must be contained, lest the slaveholding minority further control the national majority.

The events of the mid-1850s enhanced the longstanding northern suspicions that slaveholders menaced American white majoritarianism. In 1856, South Carolina's congressman Preston Brooks, by beating Massachusetts's senator Charles Sumner unconscious on the Senate floor, recalled southern attempts to gag congressional debate. Simultaneously, southern vigilantes, by marauding in Bleeding Kansas neighborhoods, reminded Yankees of lynch mobs in southern neighborhoods. In 1857–58, Southerners, by attempting to impose Kansas as a slave state on the northern congressional majority, rekindled memories of the imposition of Texas annexation. Then also Southern Democrats had handed aspiring Northern Democrats such as Martin Van Buren an infuriating ultimatum: Give us our slave state or forfeit your national political ambitions.

Republicans' drive to contain the imperious masters' alleged travesties against white men's republicanism shrewdly seized on Garrison's popular denunciations of sinning despots, while just as shrewdly shedding his unpopular demand for immediate abolition. Republicans often called absolute power over blacks a sin against Christianity, against free-labor ideology, and against the Declaration of Independence. But their anti-Slavepower rhetoric made minority domination of white republics the intolerable crime. Republicans would confine slaveholders to the now-existing slave states, like rats in a cage. Then the Slavepower's undemocratic domination would poison neither the free-labor economy nor republican deliberations in the nation and its territories.

Occasionally, Republicans such as Abraham Lincoln talked of probing inside the poisonous cage to secure the ultimate extinction of slavery. But this sporadic Republican rhetoric remained vague on *how* party leaders meant to achieve abolition. On the few occasions when they dropped hints about how the confinement of slavery to the South would escalate into emancipation, the Lincolns speculated about voluntary southern collaboration. They would impose nothing on the sinning region. Rather, they would help Southerners remove blacks, probably first from the Border South and with federal funding for deportation.

This Republican rhetoric showed how much (and how little) William Lloyd Garrison had triumphed. Lincoln's mainstream rhetoric appropriated Garrison's extremist vocabulary about southern sinfulness, his conception that free-labor and slave-labor economies were antithetical, his demand for inclusion of blacks in the Declaration of Independence, his hopes for slavery's extinction, and his detestation of slaveholders' imperiousness. Still, Republicans' condemnation of the Slavepower's tyrannizing over whites, not Garrison's condemnation of slaveholders' tyrannizing over blacks, had been most responsible for spreading moral outrage about slaveholders from the northern extreme to the northern mainstream. The average Northerner rejected Slavepower imposition on *him*. But most Northerners were as fearful as ever that federally imposed abolition would break up the Union, jeopardize national commerce, and lead northern blacks to demand *their* egalitarian rights.

The Republicans' resulting caution outraged Garrison. He loathed Lincoln's political formula: Always emphasize containment of the Slavepower and occasionally add a vague hope of slavery's ultimate extinction. Garrison equally detested Lincoln's emphasis on the slow transformation of public opinion North and South, even if abolition was delayed a hundred years. Moreover, Lincoln's program for achieving the delayed extinction of slavery was exactly the one Garrison had furiously denounced in 1831. Lincoln, like Henry Clay and Harriet Beecher Stowe, was back with Thomas Jefferson, advocating the removal of slavery *and* freed blacks from the republic with federal funds—and seeking southern consent before doing either.[12]

This strategy, if anathema to Garrison, was exactly the highly conditional form of antislavery gradualism that southern extremists most feared. The Border South deplored immediate emancipation without removal of blacks. But the offer of a northern hand to help consenting whites transport blacks gradually out of the South—that could be seductive among black-hating Border South nonslaveholders. In the face of the Republicans' clarity about containing southern sinners like lepers and their hints about helping southern softhearts cure a black plague, the Lower South response escalated. At the southern extreme, particularly in South Carolina, secessionists wanted out of this hateful Union, not territorial expansion within it. But the far more numerous southern moderates preferred to stay in the Union if they could expand their territory, particularly the territory bordering on their vulnerable outposts.

The Southern Democratic majority on the U.S. Supreme Court provided the clearest protection for slaveholders' right to expand into the nation's territories. In its notorious Dred Scott decision (1857), the Court pronounced the Republican party's containment program unconstitutional. Congress could not bar slavery from national territory, ruled the Court, for slaves were property and seizure of property violated the due process clause of the Constitution. Alarmed Republicans replied (and apparently believed) that a second Dred Scott decision would follow. Since citizens of one state had the rights and immunities of citizens of another state, the Court allegedly would next empower slaveholders to take (human) property into northern states!

If Republicans needed post-Dred Scott evidence that Southerners meant to extend slavery into northern latitudes, southern insistence on admitting Kansas as a slave state in 1857–58 seemed to provide it. The Kansas-Nebraska Act had allowed both Southerners and Northerners to come to the area, with the majority of settlers to decide on an eventual state's constitution and its labor arrangements. Three years later, when Kansans applied for admission to the Union as a state, northern settlers predominated. But the minority of southern settlers demanded admission as a slave state anyway, despite the majority of Kansans' frenzied objections. This time, Stephen A. Douglas defied the Southerners, for they were asking him to abjure his Popular Sovereignty principle that the majority of settlers should determine their own institutions. Despite Douglas's protests, the U.S. Senate voted 33–25 to admit Kansas as a slave state, with most Northern Democrats casting their usual prosouthern vote. The House then rejected a proslavery Kansas, 120–112.

Southerners, enraged at their first congressional loss on a major slavery issue since gag rule times, principally blamed the 40 percent of House Northern Democrats, admirers of Douglas, who had voted against them. Two years later, at the first of two 1860 Democratic National Conventions, Lower South Democrats insisted that the party platform contain anti-popular-sovereignty language on slaveholders' rights in the territories. Douglas and his supporters balked, just as Martin Van Buren had balked at southern control of the party during the Texas episode. But this time, when the key Northern Democrat said no to Slavepower rule, Lower South convention delegates walked out. At the subsequent Democratic convention, Northern Democrats barred those who had left from returning as accredited delegates.

With the split of the National Democratic party, the minority South lost its longstanding leverage to secure majority laws protective of its hinterlands. The need never seemed greater. When the House of Representatives rejected a proslavery Kansas, six Upper South ex-Whigs voted with the North. Had they voted with the South, the slaveholders' 120–112 defeat would have been a 118–114 triumph. The episode again illuminated one reason for southern defensive maneuverers' frantic quality: Even a small amount of southern internal disunity could destroy slaveholders' national dominion. To control all but six of 91 Slave South congressmen would have been a degree of dominance unthinkable in any other New World slavocracy. But the minority's control of 93 percent of its regime was not enough to impose Kansas on the majority. Only a little erosion at the fringes could undercut the slaveholders' chance, not found elsewhere in the New World, to bring an antislavery century to a standstill.

At the time the six deserters helped defeat a proslavery Kansas, other departures from proslavery solidarity arose. For many U.S. slaveholders, the most profitable expansion seemed to lie southward toward Latin America. Yet when southern adventurers sought to annex Nicaragua and Cuba, many South Carolina and Upper South slaveholders decried such Caribbean expansion as folly, indeed as piracy. More revealingly still, antebellum Southerners intemperately clashed over the fastest rising Lower South political movement of the 1850s, the crusade to reopen the African slave trade. Proponents of moving Africans to America wished to reverse southern thinking about population movement. Border Southerners should not advocate removal of African Americans from the civilized United States. Africans should instead be removed from the barbarism of the Dark Continent. So too, the Border South should not sell its too few slaves to the Lower South. Lower South slaveholders should instead buy slaves from Africa so that slaves could be kept up North.

Every southern region a permanent slavocracy! Every border Southerner a devotee of perpetual slavery! Reopening the African slave trade seemed to offer the most hopeful remedy yet for uncertain southern commitment. But hope swiftly gave way to a sinking realization: that instead of permanently fortifying a slightly shaky Border South, the proposed panacea drove the more northern and the more southern South further apart.

Border South masters denied that slavery would be bolstered in their region if Lower South masters could buy cheap Africans. Instead, the more northern South would find its slaves devalued and its slave sales ended; and then its rationale for complicity in slavery would evaporate.

More ominous still for Lower South slaveholders who wished to import Africans in the 1850s, the Border South preference for exporting African Americans grew stronger. From the perspective of those who wanted an all-white, all-free-labor South, slave sales had removed blacks from the Upper South too slowly. Thomas Jefferson, and after him Henry Clay, had suggested a faster solution: federally financed colonization to the Caribbean or Africa. Although these emancipation-and-removal schemes still inspired Upper South support, the post-nati Upper South heresy, popularized by Thomas Jefferson Randolph in the Virginia debate of 1832, grew in importance in the 1850s. Cassius Clay in Kentucky and Frank Blair, Jr., in Missouri, the two most politically powerful Border South heretics, campaigned in their respective states for a legislative decree of freedom for future-born slaves when these blacks reached a distant birthday. Like Randolph earlier, Blair and Clay cynically hoped that slaves would be sold southward before emancipating birthdays. Let Lower South masters pay to remove the Upper South's blacks!

Despite that enticement, Kentucky voters trounced Cassius Clay's bid for governor in 1851. St. Louis voters, however, sent Blair to Congress in the mid-1850s. Simultaneously, Maryland voters overwhelmed a slaveholders' counteroffensive designed to re-enslave free blacks. And in North Carolina, Hinton R. Helper's *Impending Crisis in the South: How To Meet It* was published in 1857. Helper urged the southern nonslaveholder majority to serve both its own economic interests and America's racial interests by deporting slaveholders' blacks. With this publication, the 1850s, not the 1830s, had become the Upper South's great age of dispute over removing slaves.

More important, in the 1850s for the first time, northern leaders threatened to make southern black-removal programs national in scope. Northern Republicans printed hundreds of thousands of copies of Helper's emancipation-by-removal scheme. Did Republicans, many Southerners wondered, thereby hope to provoke a southern white lower-class revolt against the slaveholding class? Meanwhile, many Northern Republicans, including Lincoln, endorsed the Thomas Jefferson-Henry Clay colonization proposal. Did the Lincolns thereby seek a national collaboration between conditional antislavery moderates in the North and in the Upper South? Lincoln's hero, the Border South's Henry Clay, had dreamed of exactly that fusion in the now-expired Clay-Lincoln Whig party.

Such a post-Whig party collaboration across sectional lines could have a new partisan foundation. Although in the Lower South most ex-Whigs joined the Democrats, in the Upper South ex-Whigs formed a powerful Opposition party that defeated the Democracy in a number of elections. These Upper South Oppositionists, never happy about being de-Whigged, wished again to form a southern wing of a national party. They approached Northern Republicans. If Lincoln's party would cease its insulting condemnation of slavery, they would accept a fusion with Republicans on some black-removal platform. And that politically powerful advocate of black removal, St. Louis congressman Frank Blair, Jr., became a Republican; he helped secure 17,028 Missouri votes, 10 percent of the state's total, for Lincoln in 1860. In addition, 24 percent of Delaware voters cast their ballots for Lincoln.

Lincoln, who also disliked being de-Whigged, would have liked to build a national Whiggish party on this promising Border South foundation—a preference he later signaled by placing a couple of Border Southerners in his cabinet.[13] But with no southern votes needed to gain the presidency, the biggest northern issue in the 1860 election remained the southern minority's domination of the white man's majoritarian republic. Upset over the recent southern triumph in the Dred Scott case and near-triumph on the Kansas issue, the majoritarian section now meant to rule like a majority. That determination could be seen in the Northern Democrats' rejection of the Lower South's demand for a proslavery platform at the party's conventions and in the northern electorate's sweeping affirmation of Lincoln's leading message: that the *Republican* party must keep the South from destroying *republicanism*. Yet the question remained, after Lincoln's election in November 1860, would the southern minority now truly destroy the republic by withdrawing its consent to be ruled by the victorious majority?

VIII

BEFORE SOUTHERN SECESSIONISTS could escape the northern majority, they had to win over their own majority. If some Southwide Gallup poll had inquired whether Southerners wished to secede immediately after Lincoln's election, the secessionists' vote likely would have been down in the 25 percent range. In the Border South, where secessionists lost even after civil war began, 37 percent of all southern whites resided. Another 31 percent lived in the Middle South, where secessionists lost until civil war began. Even in the Lower South, a slim majority might have voted against secession had a Southwide referendum occurred immediately after Lincoln's election. In late November 1860, only Mississippi and Florida probably would have affirmed the expediency of secession, and only South Carolina assuredly would have done so.

The Southwide majority against disunion in November 1860 fed on conservatives' dread of revolution, on Southerners' patriotism as Americans, and on moderates' doubts that Lincoln could or would threaten slavery. Southern Unionists denounced the president-elect for declaring slavery immoral, for calling its spread to new territory unacceptable, and for terming its ultimate extinction desirable. But Lincoln conceded, Unionists pointed out, that the Constitution barred federal intervention in the South to force slavery's extinction. To re-emphasize this federal powerlessness, Lincoln in his inaugural address supported an unamendable constitutional amendment, already passed by Congress, that would have forever banned federal antislavery coercion in the South. But no constitutional amendment was needed, Unionists added. Lincoln's party did not have a majority in the Senate or in the House or on the Supreme Court. If Lincoln nevertheless managed to act against slavery, the South could *then* secede. Why secede now over an uncertain northern menace, thereby subjecting slavery to certain menace in a civil war?

Secessionists retorted that a stealthy northern majority would initially let Southerners do the menacing. Southern politicians would form a wing of the Black Republican party, dedicated to agitating against slavery, especially in the Border South. South Carolina patricians, the most avid secessionists, considered all agitating parties dangerous. These aristocratic republicans had long taken the proslavery rationale beyond a vision of whites directing blacks. Theirs was a more universal paternalistic conception: The best men should direct lesser humans of all races. To them all national parties portended mobocratic republicanism. Patronage-hungry demagogues would stir up the masses and thus overwhelm disinterested paternalists.

In contrast, Lower South mainstream politicians beyond crusty South Carolina, having long happily participated in national parties, feared not democratic parties in general but a prospective Southern Republican party in particular. They uneasily recalled Frank Blair's delivery of 10 percent of Missourians to Lincoln in the election of 1860, Delaware's 24 percent vote for Lincoln, the more northern South's Opposition party's recent overtures to the Republicans, and Northern Republicans' publication of Helper's call for nonslaveholder war against slaveholders. They knew that Lincoln had patronage jobs at his disposal and that Border South leaders wanted them. They understood that Lincoln, like the Border South's hero, Henry Clay, carried on Thomas Jefferson's vision of emancipation with freedmen's removal financed by the federal government. Lincoln, in short, need not force abolition on the most northern South. He could instead encourage and bribe Border Southerners to agitate for their misty hope of, and his nebulous plan for, removing blacks from a whitened republic.

Nor, warned the secessionists, would Republican efforts for black removal be restricted to rallying a Border South *white* majority. Republicans would encourage slaves to flee the Border South.

With white support melting away and black slaves running away, border slaveholders would dispatch their human property to Lower South slave markets. Then nothing could deter a Border South Republican party. The Slave South, shrunk to 11 states or less and prevented from expanding into new territories, could only watch while northern free-labor states swelled from 18 to 33. In that 44-state Union, concluded secessionists, Republican emancipators would have the three-fourths majority to abolish slavery in 11 states by constitutional amendment.

Southern extremists meant to cancel that democratic drama before the staging began. They would not let northern-style republicanism, with all issues open for discussion, replace southern-style republicanism, in which debate about slavery was impermissible. They would not sit back and watch while a new president used patronage to forge a new centrist position on the forbidden subject. They would not allow Lincoln's method of antislavery, the slow transformation of public opinion, to operate within the South. They had long especially feared democratic agitation in the Border South, that nontropical vestige of seventeenth-century slaveholders' effort to defy tropical geography. Many of the Slavepower's aggressive defenses, including the Fugitive Slave Law and the Kansas-Nebraska Act, had sought to keep Border South whites and Border South blacks separated from contamination by freedom.

Now Lincoln's and the Border South's favorite national solution to slavery—compensated emancipation conditional on federally financed black removal—might establish the most contaminating and indestructible vital center yet. Since gag rule times, southern and northern extremists had unintentionally collaborated to destroy centrist ideological positions and centrist national parties. After twenty years of slavery crises, the Democratic party could no longer find a middle position between that of southern moderates, enraged by Yankee insults, and that of northern moderates, enraged by proslavery ultimatums. But no extremist tactic in the Union might deter a new centrist program, institutionalized in a newly national Republican party. Cries of "traitor" would not deter Border South Republicans, for the region's numerous advocates of black removal thought an all-white Border South exceedingly patriotic. Fear of losing southern elections would not deter conditional antislavery moderates, for Henry Clay Whiggery had done well in the Border South, and Lincoln's party figured to be a rebuilt Whiggish coalition. Furthermore, Border South demagogues could not feast on Lincoln's national patronage. After well-fed politicians started agitating, wouldn't Border South inhabitants agree to remove blacks at federal expense, or Border South masters sell out at Lower South purchasers' expense, especially if more and more of the region's slaves ran away?

For the first time, many Lower South slaveholders felt powerless to answer such questions. Their feeling of impotence rivaled that of Latin American colonists when European metropolitan centers abolished slavery and that of Brazilian coffee planters when sugar planters assaulted the institution. But if Lincoln's election seemed to revoke a democracy's unique invitation for slaveholders to control their fate, the U.S. republican system offered a final invitation for minority self-protection, unavailable in less democratic Latin America. The people of a single colony, the American Revolutionaries had declared, had a right to withdraw their consent to be governed. It was as if the Brazilian coffee provinces had a *right* to secede, which the sugar provinces might feel an obligation to defend.

A *right* of secession, held by a single one of the South's fifteen states! That right did empower a secessionist minority to force the southern majority's hand on the expediency of secession. But to force-feed secession to the antisecessionist majority, secessionists had to abort the southern Unionists' favorite idea: a region-wide southern convention, where a Southwide majority would veto immediate secession. Secessionists instead wanted the most secessionist state to call a convention to consider disunion. If the most secessionist state seceded, other southern state conventions would have to decide not whether secession was *expedient* but whether a seceded state could be denied its *right* of secession. Furthermore, other slave states might discern less expediency in remaining in the Union after several states with large slave populations had departed to form a proslavery confederacy.

The single-state secession strategy neatly countered Lincoln's supposed fusion strategy. Instead of the Union's president building a Republican party in southern buffer zones and drawing the Upper South away from slavery's Lower South base, secessionists would build a southern nation in the Lower South and drag the Upper South beyond Lincoln's patronage bribes. Or to use the modern metaphor, instead of slavery falling like the top row of a pile of dominoes, with the Border South and then the Middle South collapsing onto the Lower South, the Union would fall by secessionists' pulling out the lower row, with the Lower South and then the Middle South leaving the Border South no foundation for staying in the Union.

That was the secessionists' master plan, devised in private correspondence and carried out in public lockstep. On December 20, 1860, the secessionists' stronghold, South Carolina, withdrew its consent to Union. South Carolina's neighbor, Georgia, was wary of secession. But with its neighbor out, could Georgia stay in? After a brilliant internal debate, Georgia decided, narrowly, to join South Carolina. And so it went, neighbor following neighbor, throughout the Cotton South. By the time Lincoln was inaugurated on March 4, 1861, the seven Lower South states had left the Union. But the eight Upper South states, containing the majority of southern whites, still opposed secession.

The balance of power changed in mid-April after the Civil War started. Now the more northern South had to decide not on secession per se but on whether to join a northern or a southern army. In making that decision, the Middle South affirmed that each state had the American right to withdraw its consent to be governed. These southern men in the middle also reaffirmed that Yankee extremists were more hateful than secessionist extremists. The Garrisonian insult, encompassing all Southerners who would not unconditionally and immediately emancipate, had long infuriated most Southerners. The Republican insult, encompassing all Southerners who sought to dominate or depart the Union, was equally enraging. To protect their self-respect and honor, Southerners usually felt compelled to unite against taunting Yankees. That duty had so often drawn together a region otherwise partially disunited. In April 1861, when Lincoln sent reinforcements to federal troops in Charleston's harbor, the old tribal fury swept the Middle South. By May 1861, eleven angry southern states had departed the Union. In that fury, parallel to Republican rage over an allegedly anti-republican Slavepower, lies the solution to the largest apparent puzzle about secession: why 260,000 men, whatever their initial preference for Union, died for the Confederacy.

IX

THUS DID the secessionist minority of the no-longer-ruling southern minority escape the at-last-ruling northern majority. Thus did southern extremists move to abort the expected Republican attempt to rally a new Border South-northern national majority, with Lincoln's patronage supplying the organizational basis, with race removal providing the ideological basis, and with an ultimate constitutional amendment auguring the worst danger. But by moving outside a majoritarian Union's sway, the secessionist minority of the southern minority moved toward a more perilous rendezvous with majoritarianism's own requirement: the need to win men's minds and hearts. Considering the free-labor states' somewhat greater predominance of military power and considering northern determination to save majoritarian government from the southern minority, secession, to be effective, would have to sweep farther than the Middle South. Border Southerners would have to make common cause with secessionists rather than with Republicans.

Or to put the Confederacy's problem in the most revealing way, the secessionists, having secured a southern numerical majority, now had to rally a Calhoun-style concurrent majority: a concurrence of everyone. Now more than ever, the margin of error was thin for the only slaveholders in the New World who defied worldwide antislavery currents. The U.S. slavocracy, to prevail in its extraordinary Civil War gamble, had to control all Southerners, black and white. Several southern minorities could nullify the white majority in the eleven Confederate states, for the North was passionately united in its eighteen free-labor states. Let the four Border South states refuse to secede from the Union; let western Virginia nonslaveholders secede from Virginia; let eastern Tennessee nonslaveholders desert Tennessee; let the slaves depart from the slaveholders and . . .

The sequels would fill the rest. Slave runaways, having initiated the fugitive slave controversies that helped lead to civil war, would join northern armies and help secure an emancipating triumph. So too Border Southerners, whose possible fusion with Yankees had helped fuel disunion, would unite with Black Republicans on the battlefields. But though much is fittingly democratic about fugitive slaves doing in slaveholders and about the conditional antislavery Border South doing in the unconditional proslavery Lower South, democrats can hardly cheer the spectacle. The coming of the American Civil War is a case study in democracy's limitations.

Only an especially convulsive internal issue could expose those limits. As the American antebellum experience shows, a democratic system can survive a very large degree of divisiveness. Such national issues as nativism, temperance, national banks, protective tariffs, women's rights, and religious freedom were settled peaceably. Nor did some singular aspects of U.S. culture, peculiar among the world's republics to these North Americans, destroy this democracy. The unusually constant stream of U.S. localistic elections, for example, did not lead to more electioneering agitation than a stable governing system could handle. Those localistic elections usually focused on resolvable local issues. In contrast, national presidential campaigns, occurring only every four years, focused increasingly on the only unresolvable issue, slavery. Nor did America's unusually strong encouragement of individualistic eccentricity destroy nationalizing institutions. The national political parties found a peaceable common ground on every issue involving white individuals' opportunities except slavery—and for a long while on that issue too.

The point is that agitation over slavery ultimately superseded all other agitations and alone could expose a democratic system's most deep-seated, most universal limits. Despite its cult of majority rule, democracy is very susceptible to minority control. A minority that knows what it wants and knows how to manipulate the system will defeat a less determined majority every time. The impasse comes when a majority grows equally determined and the minority can not accept defeat. The problem is particularly explosive when the minority is a powerful ruling class and the dogma of government by consent permits imperious rulers to withdraw from the republic. In the United States, only the slavery issue called forth this sort of inflexible minority, determined to use every available power to rule supposedly barbaric blacks, assuredly infuriating outsiders, and uncertainly softhearted insiders. And in the New World, only the U.S. republican system swelled intransigent slaveholders with the illusion that they could command their own fate, whether by dominating or by departing a republic.

Lower South slaveholders exhausted all means of dominating before they departed. They tried ideological persuasion. That partly failing, they tried lynchings. That partly failing, they tried shaming dissenters into loyalty. Fearing verbal coercion would fail, they tried protective laws that might consolidate vulnerable outposts. When the northern majority finally found minority governance intolerable, the southern minority (or rather, initially, the secessionist minority of the southern minority) withdrew its consent to be ruled.

Two democratic imperatives clashed here: the majority's right to govern, Lincoln's favorite wartime slogan, and the minority's right to withdraw consent to be governed, Jefferson Davis's favorite patriotic emblem. The ideological clash would blur in the second half of the Civil War, after Lincoln's Union came to fight for slaves' right to withdraw their consent to be ruled by slaveholders. But in the first half of the Civil War, when Lincoln rejected black troops and repudiated his generals' emancipation initiatives, the issue was stark. Lincoln's Union initially fought to contain a minority that had controlled and now would revoke majority rule. The slaveholders fought to establish a Confederacy that would save a minority's consent to be governed and prevent the minority's property from becoming a discussable issue.

Latin American slavery controversies never carried the added burden of these showdowns over republicanism. And so in all the Americas after the Haitian slave revolt, only in the United States did the final fate of slavery hang on the verdict supposedly reserved for undemocratic governments: Whose regime can rally the largest and most sustained commitment on the battlefields?

6

"Freedom and Law Must Die Ere They Sever"
The North and the Coming of the Civil War

MARK WAHLGREN SUMMERS

God fight with ye, and overhead
Floats the dear banner of your dead.
They, and the glories of the Past,
The Future, dawning dim and vast,
And all the highest hopes of man
Are beaming triumph in your van!

—Bayard Taylor, 1861[1]

WHEN THE CALL for three-month volunteers went forth in mid-April, 1861, a nation awoke like a strong man rousing after sleep, or, rather, as orators and writers preferred to have it, after long and wasting sickness. How many volunteers were coming from Massachusetts, the first soldiers from the Bay State were asked, as they reached New York. "How *many*?" the answer came back. "We're *all* a-coming."[2] At times, that must have seemed a typical Yankee understatement. Lincoln asked for 75,000 men, but Indiana alone provided 30,000 instantly, and New York another 30,000. With a War Department overworked just divvying the swag, such a flood of men very nearly swamped the war effort. Soldiers drilled without guns, shoes, or uniforms. They arrived in camp to find no camp—just a stack of lumber, waiting to be turned into barracks. With no Congress in session to fund the fighting, every city of consequence, every state, even those of no consequence, had to raise money, and did so, in staggering amounts.[3]

The drama of those early days is the stuff of which good farce and bad romance is made. Within a week of the fall of Fort Sumter, 500 children were singing in a national allegory about "Disunion" at the Brooklyn Academy of Music.[4] Deaf-mutes at the Hartford asylum raised a company and outfitted them in gaudy Zouave uniforms. Unable to hear commands, they nonetheless were said to keep perfect step without music, and to move as rapidly as any general could wish.[5] New York's Empire City

Regiment included some of the most admired jailbirds in town. Its captain had just graduated from state prison, pending a new trial. Under him mustered champion wrestlers, and, an admiring observer noted, "every sporting and muscle man known to fame and the Police Courts for the last five years." Requirements for signing up were very strict. "Every recruit must prove that he has been in any number of 'plug musses' or a regular ring fight, or shot his man on sight, or showed his pluck in a historical barroom fuss, and, by George! [the commander] is getting men as fast as he can shake a stick at them."[6] Told that they would have to brave pro-Confederate mobs in Baltimore before they could get to the field, some of New York's recruited bruisers were so delighted at the prospect that they danced. "We can fix that Baltimore crowd!" they yelled. "Let 'em bring along their pavin' stones; we boys is sociable with pavin' stones!"[7]

For an historian of ironic pen, nothing could be easier than to limn the war as a three-month farce ushering in a four-year tragedy. The unpreparedness, the holiday spirit of so many soldiers makes it tempting to see them as embarked on a jaunt, rather than a serious business. Certainly not many of them had any notion of how long the fighting would last, though they worried lest it all end too soon.[8] A description of the Battle of Bull Run, with regiments in plumed caps and red kepis, banners emblazoned with Lone Stars, pelicans, and golden harps, and soldiers more interested in blackberry-picking than in pushing their advantage, would provoke disbelief.

From the vantage point of the slaughters yet to come, there certainly is something grotesque, if not poignant, in the spirit of carnival that so many Northerners displayed. Must war needs come? "Very well," a journalist wrote; "let's go it while we're young. We never had a civil war before, you know, . . . and now we've got one we're just going to show the world that we can beat it at that as well as every thing else."[9]

Beyond doubt, in this war, as in all others, recruits answered the summons for many reasons having little to do with high politics. Youths went to prove their manhood, Brahmins to reveal the hearts of oak that lay beneath fine linen. No recruiting sergeant could match the appeal of those on whose good opinion a man's reputation rested. Sweethearts and wives, fathers and sons, neighbors and business associates, all made enlistment something that it would have taken a special kind of courage to resist. One New York recruit's fiancée told him "she'd go if she were a man." As he remarked, a little ruefully, "Do you think I'd back out after that?"[10]

Yet the fervor was genuine, and quite emphatic. The setback at Bull Run dimmed the euphoria, but not the passion. Returning to Albany after jockeying for contracts in Washington, Thurlow Weed was astonished to find a major street turned into one long recruiting station. "Seven tents, with flags, stand in the middle of the street," he wrote Secretary of State William Seward. "All the citizens are Recruiting Sergeants."[11]

Why did they fight? Beyond the personal rewards of joining the fray, what did they think they were fighting for? From infantryman to ideologue, the spokesmen for the Union would have been clear: this was a fight for freedom around the world, against a little band of slaveholders, who, determined to rule in a hell of their own making rather than serve in a heaven no longer under their command, had broken sacred oaths and the public peace to set up a pretended and illegal government. The Slave Power did not speak for the white South, not even in those states it had bullied into severing ties with the Union. It could not even justify its actions on the tyrant's ground of necessity; slavery faced no immediate danger from the Republicans who carried the 1860 presidential election. Even members of the incoming administration were prepared to put themselves on record in favor of some new guarantee to slaveholders.

Against the usurpers stood common sense, the law of the land, the Lord Himself. Silent on secession though the Constitution was, its preamble proclaimed among its purposes the creation of "a more perfect Union." But the Articles of Confederation had already pronounced the Union perpetual. What sensible man could think a confederation dissoluble at the whim of any of its constituent parts an improvement?[12] Peaceable disunion was impossible, generations of Americans were warned. Rival countries would fight each other to the death; one secession would spawn a dozen more, till America seethed with nation-states as impotent and quarrelsome as the fly-speck kingdoms east of the Rhine. When the Great Republic perished, "croakers, prophets & despots of Europe" would rejoice, and not just over a chance of fresh pickings in North America. The United States, selected by the Lord as a model for government, would have become an object-lesson instead. To every democrat across the globe, the sundered Union would prove that free institutions failed today, just as they had when Caesars rode in triumph over the ruins of republican Rome.[13] Faced with that prospect, was it any wonder that like one Ohioan, the masses of the North would declare themselves ready to settle secession "at the point of the bayonet & at the mouth of the cannon?" As he wrote his congressman, "They say 'give *us & our posterity liberty* or *give us death*.' "[14]

Cherishing the Union did not require Republican credentials, or even the mild distaste for slavery that so many Northern Democrats felt. "There's no two ideas here about this war now," a newspaperman wrote from New York in early May. "Nobody ever loved the South better than I—nobody has fought longer or with a truer heart for their rights and interests in the Union, or would have continued to do so—and there are hundreds of thousands like me; but we can't go a broken Union or tearing out the stripes, or putting out the stars in the flag. We are too proud and vain of the 'greatest nation in all creation' to see it broken up and reduced to a series of petty and ever jarring republics or military despotisms."[15]

People fighting because they loved their country and hated the ingrates who would rend it asunder, boys raised to believe that liberty and Union must rise or fall together, churchgoers confirmed in their faith that the Lord had given the United States a sacred trust, one not yet fulfilled, Yankees contemptuous of everything that Southern society stood for, resolved to put the proud traitors in their place—all these reasons and more explain the willingness to fight and to die that Northerners felt. It is all perfectly obvious—to anyone, that is, who has read the historians who did the hard work of researching it, recreating it, and setting it forth.[16] But what on earth does that leave to be said here? Is there anything worth mentioning, beyond the obvious? I think so, and would like to dwell on two terms that many historians may even consider rather dirty words.

The first is *conservatism*. A dynamic society, positively fidgety with reform movements, *conservative*? Was not the Civil War rather our Second American Revolution? Freed from the shackles of Southern parochialism, the Congress put through an economic program unrivaled since Alexander Hamilton's day: a network of national banks strengthened by laws crushing out state rivals, a system of land-grant colleges, a homestead law to settle the West, transcontinental railroads subsidized from government coffers, and most of all, a protective tariff, the so-called War Tariff, which survived very nearly to the fiftieth anniversary of Gettysburg, and coddled "infant industries" well into dotage. "Old Hickory" himself could never have foreseen a presidency as potent as the Civil War made, nor Hamilton a Constitution as flexible. And who, apart from Democratic editorial-writers and a scattering of less dangerous lunatics, would have predicted that the breaking of the Union would mean not just the breaking of bonds twice as old, not just that slavery's shackles would be riven, never to be forged anew, but that the chains of racial caste would be loosened as well, and briefly seem as though they had been unfettered for good?[17]

No one could have foreseen it. That is just the point. From the rhetoric of 1861, the "new birth of freedom" might very nearly be assumed to be an unplanned pregnancy. One might even see that English liberals, in their sympathy for the Confederacy, were right on every point except the one that counted. The United States *was* waging a war against revolution, against change, and against what in those days passed for the popular will of half a dozen, possibly a dozen states. *

---

*If by Southerners we mean all adults of voting-age, then very likely a full turnout would have beaten secession everywhere. After all, few black slaves were inclined in the Confederacy's favor, and outside of the Gulf states, white Unionists, not to mention Cooperationists, abounded. But no one seriously suggested then that the popular will rested on a plebiscite of all inhabitants, those excluded for their race included.

But, the reader will protest, it had to be a war against slavery in some sense; after all, the Confederacy was making the war *for* slavery. Stolid Midwesterners like Ulysses S. Grant, far from abolitionists as they were, foresaw that any long fight would bring slavery to a quick end; and a year of fighting made more abolitionists than thirty years of *The Liberator*.[18] In any case, the war *became* a revolution. Does it really matter where we start, if we end where we should? I think it does, and as will be made clear, I am not sure the country did end in the right place.

That point about it being a war against slavery in some sense is not absolutely wrong–but it needs qualification. To understand why requires a refresher course on the political parties in the North. By 1861, to be sure, one could find the flotsam and jetsam of past political alternatives everywhere: Softs, Hards, South Americans, People's party men, and the fossil remains of the old Whig party, many of whom had rallied to the Constitutional Union ticket and John Bell in 1860. But only two names mattered: Republicans and Democrats. It was their political system, and in the sense that they would provide the recruits, the generals, and the terms of peace, it was their war.

If Northern Democrats had had their way, there would have been no war at all. Far from waging war on slavery or any other institution, they had been prepared from the start to make concessions to fix slavery into the Constitution for the first time: five unamendable amendments, to compromise the disputes between free and slave states, and transform the country's future, by freezing things pretty much as they were. The so-called Crittenden Compromise was in a sense, revolutionary, but it was a revolution to impose the status quo. It would mean Slavery and Union, now and forever, one and inoperable.[19]

Liberty and Union were both cherished American traditions. But so was compromise. It may bemuse us to see that the barter and dicker of principles can be raised to a high principle in its own right; but any Democrat, and quite a few old Whigs, could tell us that what we like to see as our healthy cynicism is naïveté of the most perilous sort. The willingness to sacrifice your own interests in part, that the country might live and prosper, is something no free government can do without. Inflexible politicians are as fatal to a republic as an inflexible Constitution would be to suppressing the Rebellion.[20] If Paris was worth a Mass, was not the one truly free country worth a concession?

So much for the Democrats, and they amounted to more than a handful in every Union state.[21] What of Republicans? Was not their party itself a declaration of war on slavery? So it was; and yet, as historians have pointed out, party spokesmen made their case in anything but revolutionary terms. Ask Salmon P. Chase, once known as the Attorney-General for runaway Negroes, and now Lincoln's Secretary of the Treasury, and he would tell you that the Constitution itself had been made by men who, slaveholders though they were, loved slavery itself too little to let the word go into the country's fundamental law. Republicans neither meant to improve upon nor subvert the Founders' will. They meant to realize desires beyond the power, but not beyond the hopes, of those who made the first Revolution. To the law of the land, they meant to restore the antislavery bias with which it had begun. Ask Abraham Lincoln, a Whig until there was very nearly no Whig party left, whether Republicanism meant a war on slavery, and he might admit that it did. But it was a defensive war. The real aggressor was Slavery, or rather, the masters of the South, given their power by a political system rigged to exaggerate the influence of slaveowners. It was that Slave Power that took every aggressive step: spurring invasions of European colonies, sparking wars with neighboring republics to spread slave territory, drilling private armies to topple lawful governments in the tropics or on the prairies, buying Northern politicians with offices and booty. No compromise was too sacred for it to break, no shakedown tactic too base for it to use to force the North into another retreat, no court too high for it to corrupt. The Republican party was revolutionary in the same way that the dikes of Holland are revolutionary in keeping the sea from going where it will.[22]

Now the fight had come, and it was reactive, not revolutionary. The real revolution was in that choice: five unamendable amendments or a sundered Union, slavery within or slavery without. If Northerners submitted to dictation or compulsory compromise now, they would be slaves ever after, compelled to purchase the Union over and over again, for new concessions to the lords of the lash. That day would come when, as Senator Robert Toombs of Georgia allegedly once boasted, he would call the roll of his slaves from Bunker Hill. This was not a war to make a more perfect Union, but to forestall a more perfect anarchy.[23] Not so long before, Mayor Fernando Wood of New York had spoken of turning his jurisdiction into a free city, ready to trade with North or South—which, as Lincoln remarked, was the first time he had ever heard of a front porch going into business for itself. But that was before the guns fired in Charleston Harbor. Within a week, Wood was standing before a crowd in Union Square reminding them of what the Confederate Secretary of War had vowed, that by the first of May, the Confederate ensign would fly over the Capitol, and soon after that, over Faneuil Hall in Boston. "My friends," Wood shouted, "before that banner can fly over Faneuil Hall in Boston, it must be carried over the dead body of every citizen of New York."[24]

It must also be carried over the dead body of quite a few more important Southerners, assuming they would stay dead. To be sure, patriots invoked generations yet unborn, when they spoke of the country's mission. But Edmund Burke would have appreciated the language of Union more than did Thomas Paine, for generations already passed away received a much more important role. Wood's mention of Faneuil Hall, the cradle of the Revolution, was no happenstance.[25] Never had the Revolutionary fathers received such a workout. When they were not being asked to frown down from Heaven or emerge from the crypt with a choice epithet, they were being inflicted with any number of tourists in need of patriotic refreshment. At least, that was what Nevada's governor had in mind when he wished that he had the power to take every secessionist in the land to the sacred sites of the past: to Lexington and Princeton, to Trenton and Valley Forge, where they might "commune with the ashes of the dead that lie there—fragrant yet to the nostrils of patriotism." Let them visit the tomb of Washington and the grave of Jackson, the upholder of the Union![26] And Lincoln's poor predecessor!

JAMES B-UCHANAN, may his tribe decrease! –
Awoke one night from a strange dream of peace,
And saw, within the curtain of his bed–
Making his t'other eye to squint with dread–
Old Jackson writing in a book of gold;
Exceeding rye had made Buchanan bold,
And to the stern ex-President he said:
"Wha- what writ'st thou?" The spirit shook his head,
The while he answered, with the voice of old,
"The names of those who ne'er their country sold!"
"And is mine one?" asked J. B. "Nary!" cried
The General, with a frown. Buchanan sighed,
And groaned, and turned himself upon his bed,
And took another 'nip' of 'rye', then said:
"Well, ere thou lay thy record on the shelf,
Write me at heart as one who sold himself
'Democs' and 'rye' so long my spirits were,
That when the 'Crisis' came–I wasn't there!"
The General wrote, and vanished. The next night
He came again, in more appalling plight,
And showed those names that all 'true men' detest–
And lo! Buchanan's name led all the rest![27]

If all Americans wanted to escape so dreadful a visitation, at least symbolically, the time had come for them to act. "When Providence puts together the 19th of April, 1776, when the first blood was shed at Lexington, and the 19th of April, 1861, when the first blood was shed at Baltimore, I tell you it means something," lawyer William Evarts told a war rally, as he stood before the image of the Father of his country. "When that statue of Washington sustains in its firm hands the flagstaff of Fort Sumter, I tell you it means something. There is but one question left, and that is, whether you mean something, too."[28]

> Defend from faction's wild commotion
> Our homes, our laws, our schools and spires,
> The names and graves of patriot sires,
> Till freedom reigns to farthest ocean.

> Ye loyal sons and true,
> Sons of the brave and free,
> Join hearts, join hands, to strike anew
> For God and liberty.[29]

Sons and *sires*: there is more in the language than a contrast of the insufficiently quick and the insufficiently dead. Denouncing the Confederates, it was natural for Alexander Dickson to call them "degenerate sons" of the Founders who made July Fourth so glorious, equally natural for the Chicago *Tribune* to brand the secessionists "parricides"; conservatism was built into the very imagery of the Union as a family or household, and into its connection to generations already passed away.[30]

From ancient glory to Old Glory is but the smallest of semantic steps, and very possibly one worth taking; for no sooner had the call for volunteers been issued than the nation's flag began to appear everywhere, even in Mayor Wood's speeches. Business-man George Templeton Strong saw first-hand what a difference a little bunting could make on April 17, when a crowd mustered before the offices of the southerly-inclined New York *Journal of Commerce* and started yelling. Perhaps remembering the mob that two days before had chased the *Herald*'s publisher James Gordon Bennett up Fulton Street and threatened to sack his printing office, the publishers hastily hung an American flag from the window. At that, there were cheers that "stirred one's blood a little, and the surface of the black mass was suddenly all in motion with waving hats. Then a line of policemen came down the street on a dog-trot, and the crowd thereupon moved promptly up Wall Street again, cheering lustily." Other editors of faltering Union sympathy were paid a call, too, and forced to show their colors—or, at any rate, their country's colors.[31]

That was just the beginning. By the following morning, as Strong noticed, the flag was everyplace, with "every cart horse decorated." As vestryman at the Trinity Church, Strong decided to have it flown from the steeple, not only as good in itself, as he explained in his diary, but as "a politic move." To his surprise, nobody objected, not even the old fogy of a rector. His worst problem was finding a banner within city limits. Flags were all sold out. At last, with a little help from a prominent merchant, Strong came up with one, and at half-past two on April 19, with the chimes playing "Hail Columbia," and two ship-riggers to arrange for the hoisting, it was raised the full 240 feet, while a crowd stretching down Broadway and Wall Street yelled with a spirit that took even Strong aback. "Are they really going to hoist the flag on the steeple, SIR?" one onlooker asked beforehand. "Well, now, *I* tell *you*, that's the *biggest thing* that's been done in New York in my time!"[32] Before a week was out, almost every important church in town had followed Trinity's example.

By now, New York positively raged in flags. The rustling of banners along Cortlandt Street was "like the noise of wings overhead."[33] With a massive rally scheduled for Saturday, April 20, there were very possibly more banners than recruits. "Broadway was almost hidden in a cloud of flaggery," a reporter wrote. "Nothing but red, white, and blue, red, white, and blue, greeted the eye, turn which way it would. Every window, every housetop, every awning, every stage, every railroad car, every hotel, every barroom, every liberty pole had its flag waving gayly, or rolled into graceful folds." As Strong threaded his way through the multitude, he found "every other man, woman, and child, bearing a flag or decorated with a cockade." Under the circumstances, perhaps the statue of George Washington would have had no choice but to carry one, too. In such a gathering, he would have looked underdressed any other way.[34]

If Strong was right in saying that the city seemed to have gone "suddenly wild and crazy," it went in quite a great company. In town after town, the departure of the local soldiers followed the same pattern: a rally in the square, with the show-stopper coming in the presentation of the Stars and Stripes, and the pledge of the boys in blue—or, in the case of New York's Seventh Regiment, in gray[35]—not to return until the banner waved in triumph and honor over all the land. Along the New York Central Railroad, flagmen stopped signaling with white rags, and adopted the red, white, and blue instead. In an age of hoop skirts, what could be more patriotic than the new fashion, a hoop of red, white, and blue? This, as one paper quipped, could be called the female war-(w)hoop; to which another editor responded, perhaps with more accuracy than felicity, that it was "one which our gallant troops would raise with much fervor."[36] "The Cross of Peter the Hermit fades before our Star-Spangled Banner," as one editor bragged.[37]

Showing the flag seems so natural that readers may wonder why anything need be made of it. It would have been far more awkward, say, for New York City's crowds to brandish little copies of the Declaration of Independence, much less issues of the *National Anti-slavery Standard*. Rallying round the national anthem would have been even harder: there was no national anthem. A group of respectable New Yorkers tried to get their countrymen to write a national hymn that summer, and when the entries were submitted, found themselves the nation's largest collectors of waste-paper. Four or five bales of made-to-order songs arrived in one afternoon; most of them could be described as the first wartime atrocities.[38] What else but the flag *was* there? And yet, to hear the rhetoric, the flag seems to have become not just a symbol for Liberty and Union, but a thing itself for which men would march and die.[39] Not talk of freedom and slavery, but of a banner "never yet tarnished," "the flag of my fathers," now "dishonored" or needing to be "avenged," got the biggest response from crowds. The crime of South Carolina in firing on Fort Sumter was its desecration, its insult "to the nation's flag."[40] "I ask you to look at those thirteen stripes, which wave in your midst," one soon-to-be general urged listeners. "They are the thirteen planks we are called upon this day to stand on, and God grant that it may be made an enduring platform, where we can all stand together."[41]

> O STAR SPANGLED BANNER! the Flag of our pride!
> Though trampled by traitors and basely defied,
> Fling out to the glad winds your Red, White, and Blue,
> For the heart of the North-land is beating for you!
> And her strong arm is nerving to strike with a will
> Till the foe and his boastings are humbled and still!
> Here's welcome to wounding and combat and scars
> And the glory of death—for the Stripes and the Stars![42]

Where, then, did that take the Union's will to go to war? To the simplest of shared common denominators, a love of country and of flag, as they had always been.

There is nothing wrong with this. But unless modified by a definition of what the flag *meant*—as a very few antislavery men did[43]—it is strongly and essentially conservative. As Reid Mitchell has argued, the Stars and Stripes need not stand even for so lofty an ideal as the nation itself. Those very rituals with which the banner was bestowed on departing regiments linked it most strongly to the community that soldiers left behind them, and to the wives, sweethearts, and children that only victory could render safe from treason's despoiling hand.[44] Defending the flag, finally, brings up words very old-fashioned, and very different from the language of reform or progress: honor, duty, heritage.

On that language of conservatism, one could go on forever, for it rang countless variations. John Pendleton Kennedy's appeal to Maryland was just one example. Throughout, a reader may find what might be described as the buzzwords of tradition and family: "brave ancestors," "cavalier blood," "your ancient flag," "your fathers," "duty," "honor." What had brought about secession? The folly of the people and popular politics. What was at stake in disunion? "Desertion of our duty, dishonor to our flag, voluntary disgrace cast upon the names of the heroes and sages who have made our country illustrious in human annals." And on the side of Union, "the blessed parent of our political life," were the finest of conservative values: "Is loyalty nothing? Submission to law nothing? Fidelity to duty nothing?"[45]

Roses do not grow from thistles, of course, and Kennedy, as a conservative Whig, could be expected to talk in conservative language. But so did just about everyone, outside of the abolitionists. Private letters are full of telling phrases: "the Union as our Fathers made it," "Her sons are true to the glorious old Union."[46] "*All* for the *Constitution* and *Laws*," another correspondent wrote.[47] This was no war to exterminate, nor subjugate, the New York *Herald* assured readers. It was simply sending out an oversized posse "for the recovery of certain United States custom houses, forts, arsenals, navy yards, mints, marine hospitals, courts of justice, post offices and post roads, and for the restoration of the 'supreme law of the land' in the revolted States."[48] The soldiers were, as one Massachusetts recruit described himself, "the *Police of the Nation*."[49]

Rare indeed was the Union soldier who would have seen his as a task of conquest, much less conversion. They were defenders, even in the narrowest sense. Standing picket on Virginia soil, one Vermonter saw himself not just as sentry for the Army of the Potomac, but as guardian for "our own homes and firesides." Staring across the Potomac at the Capitol some weeks later, he felt patriotism swell in him, higher "than the best peroration on the Union could have done. . . . Who would not fight, desperately if need be, rather than have this monument of our National greatness fall into the hands of an insurgent power?"[50]

This was a war to preserve, not to *realize*, the legacy of 1776. It was to uphold a system already essentially perfect.

> ALAS! TO THE South the Fourth is a mockery;
> Thank God! *to the North 'tis dearer than ever*;
> *To us*, 'tis the day, the bright day of Freedom,
> And Freedom and Law must *die* ere they sever.[51]

That Freedom and Law were as inseparable as Liberty and Union was a tremendously conservative force.[52] It meant that however far from the peacetime practice the government might go, its actions must keep the Constitution as a touchstone. The constitutional powers of the President, of Congress, of the military, might stretch like India rubber, but what got stretched had to be there to begin with.

Conservative thinking does not rule out radical change, and there were plenty of conservative Northerners who saw quite clearly from the first that before this war ended, slavery itself would be destroyed; what was more, they would have welcomed it. But the fault did not lie with them, nor even the crackbrained abolitionists. The slaveholders themselves had willed their own destruction; every white Southerner at the front was one less guard to keep the Negroes down. Not that Union men ruled out giving emancipation a helping hand, even the more conservative ones, if that was what it took to restore a government by law. Weeks before the war began, a New York reporter voiced sentiments that would grow increasingly popular in Republican ranks as necessity directed it. "I have never disguised my opinion that the South has had wrongs which patience might not pass," he conceded; ". . . but by the heaven above this earth of ours and the hell below it, this Union is worth more than all the niggers that ever trod the shore of Afric or made cotton below Mason and Dixon's line."[53] "Self preservation is the primal, highest law," an Illinois Republican argued, "and must be obeyed."[54] As the war went on, that readiness to allow radical change on the Union's behalf and the conservative strain of Unionism gained strength.

Granted, the slavery issue is pretty poor ground on which to base any argument about conservative views, and among radical Republicans, the hope that the war would renew, rather than restore the Union, never lay far from the surface. But the theme of restoration was played far more strongly at the beginning than the theme of rehabilitation, and for good reason: it is hard to make an argument that the good old Union is so sacred that the sooner the South comes back to a completely remodeled one, the better.

There was another reason why the language of Union would take on so conservative a coloring. It is bound tightly to the other term best defining the North's response to the call to arms. For the second word, let us look to John McPherson, a Pennsylvania boy, fighting mad, but not quite fighting age: "I am Union all over and should think it a disgrace to the name of McPherson if any one of that name should advocate any other doctrine," he wrote his uncle that spring. "If I was eighteen I would gladly volunteer, fight, and, if needs be, die for our glorious Union. In the ranks of the Sidney Volunteers are all classes and ages from eighteen to fifty three. Beardless boys, middle aged and aged men are to be seen, 'spoiling for a fight.' . . . Politics is all I or any other person can think about."[55]

Politics is all I or any other person can think about. That may be worth *our* thinking about. The war *was* politics, because politics never stopped. A letter sent to Senator John Sherman of Ohio one day after Lincoln's summons for volunteers was typical of dozens of others. The author was a patriot–of course he was. But after the obligatory remarks about flag, country, traitors, and "secret reptiles," he got down to the crying issue of the day, at least in his household. "I suppose the gravity of the crisis is such that little attention is paid to foreign appointments at this time," he wrote, but just in case, when the mission at Genoa opened up, the correspondent wanted it.[56] "We propose an appropriation of *one million dollars* to pay for the *scalps of rebels*," a member of the Ohio House wrote, the day after Fort Sumter surrendered. What could be more fitting for the hour? But what could be more fitting for the correspondent than his next sentence: "I rely on you and only you for a position under the Administration . . . Urge the heads of departments to send home the locofocos & Southern clerks &c. and *if possible* fill their places with Republicans and honest men."[57]

Generals got their places because they had prominent political backers or because they were well-placed politicians themselves. Regiments themselves were an extension of politics, in many cases. In New York, it might seem surprising that the colonel of a regiment would be a faro-dealer, with a record of having broken the heads of prominent fellow Democrats, having put one of them in bed for a fortnight. But all surprise vanished, when it was pointed out that he was the right-hand man of Mayor Fernando Wood, leader of the Mozart Hall faction of the Democratic party.[58] It was only natural, when the rival Tammany Hall had established its own corps, the "Jackson Guard," carefully picked and, as they boasted, "all substantial Democrats," headed by the fraternal society's Grand Sachem.[59]

Earning a quick immortality–and, since he died that spring, a timely one–Senator Stephen A. Douglas of Illinois had declared that only two parties remained: patriots and traitors. It made good copy, like so much else that Douglas said, but, like so much else that he said, was the triumph of imagination over observation. Even as the soldiers mustered, old-fashioned politics went on, full-blast.

There was, to be sure, much lip service about adjourning party warfare for the duration. Instead of playing capture the flag against each other, Democrat and Republican could rally together, join to elect congressmen and governors, and assemble one great Union party. In some states, a semblance of that actually occurred. Now and then a Republican congressman put in a good word for Democratic newspapers looking for government advertising.[60] The Union movement put an old Democrat into the governor's mansion at Columbus, and peopled the state house with men of like sentiments. Especially in the early days of the war, the very notion seemed attractive, and was talked threadbare.[61]

But there was more illusion to the Union movement than not. Democratic ranks wavered. Some places, they broke. But not for long, and in many states, not at all. "I take the Park co. Republican," one Indiana farmer wrote his congressman early that summer. "I take it to heare what is going on theare it is not that I wish to patternise the dambd Rotten Black Republican paper it is to get the nues of your town. . . . [After] I red the last paper from theare I throw it on the table and gumpt up and pased the Room and swore untill My wife said to me John Mankin you ar not in your rite mind[.]"[62]

Or witness the battle to replace Douglas himself. With Democrats nearly as numerous in Illinois as Republicans, and with the seat holding special symbolic importance, there were good reasons for Republican Governor Richard Yates to choose one of the Little Giant's Democratic followers. The Chicago *Tribune* suggested exactly that. But into the governor's office poured a host of letters in protest. What "impertinent & consummate *impudence*" in anyone to bestow the Senatorship outside of the party![63] Who won the election anyhow? Who would have won the Senate seat to begin with, if Democrats hadn't rigged the legislative districts to assure themselves a trusty majority of seats?[64] If no Republican was worthy, let the governor leave the chair vacant.[65] "As a nation, we recognize a God of providence," one pious Republican—alas, not the only one—argued. "In his wisdom he has removed Mr. Douglass. Have we not in this fact, as far as we are able to interpret His will, a plain indication of our duty?"[66] The governor had, at any rate: he chose a conservative Republican for the job.

Not only for Republicans did party loyalty get confused with duty—or for that matter, the will of the Lord. Many Democrats had mixed feelings about the war as a way of saving the Union.[67] For obvious reasons, they were far more sensitive to the way that the rhetoric of bipartisanship worked and, quite deliberately, to lay a stigma on thousands of voters who wanted to retrieve the Union by peaceful means, or at least ones of the strictest constitutional legitimacy, and who, by no coincidence, were all Democrats. Even the most belligerent partisans found it hard to watch unmoved as allies of a lifetime, many of them Union men to the core, were set upon with rotten eggs and dead cats by Republican cads and cadres, as presses long in faithful service were smashed and closed down, and as Democratic officeholders by the thousands lost their jobs to Republican supplicants. Kicking Democrats out the door while keeping a welcoming hand outstretched took skills of more than the ordinary gymnastic sort. "At no time since the foundation of the Government has party virulence so raged against Democrats as now," the Albany *Atlas and Argus* complained in July.[68]

What made it all the worse was that Democrats knew full well that they were the only true patriots. Union-saving had been their issue for a generation. Trained to think of Republicans as closet abolitionists, the so-called Peace Democrats were quick to scent hypocrisy in the flag-wavers who hitherto had saved their zeal for "niggerism": the cant of *"Bloodthirsty, war men, who have recently become so very patriotic, that they can't think of giving up those stars which they struck from their banners in 1856."*[69]

This meant that from the first the prosecution of a war was a tricky political business. Unless the administration was prepared to do the unthinkable—say, sharing the spoils, or putting more than a token Democrat into the cabinet—it would find it hard work keeping a bipartisan support for war. The more it talked about slavery, the more it would awaken all those suspicions so long entertained, that Republicans had actually wanted war rather than any compromise letting slavery linger yet awhile—that in their hearts, they preferred a Union of fewer, but better states, to the one that the Founders had created, where a white race's freedoms had been bought at the price of a black one's bondage.[70] There was only one way of keeping both parties together for this war, only one way of wresting the flag from Democrats' possession. The North's cause must be sold in terms that any conservative could accept: in effect, letting the Democrats play a big role in defining what a fight for the Union would mean, and not venturing far beyond that.

Lincoln's slowness to issue an emancipation proclamation, like his determination to see to it that, if war came, it would not be the Union that fired the first shot, is often explained away by his need to hold the Border South. As the abolitionist gibe went, "Mr. Lincoln would like to have God on his side, but he *must* have Kentucky." The point is a good one, and worth making. But having the Confederacy start the fight served another end, less noticed by historians, but pretty clear to contemporaries: it gave the administration the best possible chance of carrying along the Northern Democrats. He would need them, including those who steered clear of the Republican party from the first shot to the last. William Duncan, a conservative New York merchant, put it bluntest. It might be necessary to hang Lincoln and Seward and Greeley, he admitted, but that had to wait. "Our present duty is to sustain Government and Law, and give the South a lesson." "An insult to a nation's flag touches that nation on its sorest point," the New York *Herald* explained.[71]

One question still remains unanswered: So what? What matters it, how the Union went to war, if by the end it had undergone a radical change of mind and condition? After all, 1861 was not 1865. War's necessities would alter the Union, and the language justifying the destruction of secession. Slaves freeing themselves, soldiers confronting the reality of Southern society first-hand, the gropings for an explanation behind the apparently cruel will of the Lord all moved talk in a more radical direction. "He who wars against Radicalism simply wars against Almighty God," a North Carolina editor warned. "The churches, hoary with age, ... are trembling at its tread. Error, ignorance and superstition flee before it aghast, and all that they have supposed to be true disappears at its approach. Light and knowledge are its attendant angels, and hold their torches high for all the world of man to walk beneath them."[72] Even a few Democrats would come to accept the idea that there ought to be enough democracy to go around. For that matter, there would be fewer, though not necessarily better, Democrats—and that had to count as progress, of a sort.

Yet the war did not shift Northerners' thinking only in radical directions. Instead of breaking up the old parties, it rooted each one deeper; gone forever was the pattern that the North had known till now, of a general political smash-up once a generation. In their first conviction, that this had been a needless war made certain by selfish and fanatical Republicans, the Democrats never really changed. They enlisted; they waved the flag; many of them died, and some of them ended up worse than dead, as far as their party was concerned: they went Republican. But for those who lived to vote Democratic again, the grievance stayed with them, one lifelong scar: Republicans caused this war by standing in the way of a fair compromise between North and South—and, what was more, one with a good chance of being accepted among the reluctant secessionists and conditional Unionists who ran politics outside of the cotton belt. From start to end, Democrats protested every move away from the Union and Constitution as once it had been, from the games the President played with the writ of *habeas corpus* to the use of military commissions in Indiana.[73]

If in some respects, the public mind was more open to change—on race relations, for example—there may have been other ways in which the fighting confirmed the conservative strains in Northern thought. A few historians have glimpsed the changes in the intellectual elite.[74] Contemporaries saw it spread much more broadly than that. "I see much of good resulting from war in its effects upon the character of our people," a Bostonian wrote his friend Caleb Cushing. "It will teach them a love of order, it will teach them to obey, if it lasts, & it will

further teach them to reverence great men, a lesson long forgot-
ten."[75] The society to come would be one transfixed by demons
of subversion as never before in that century: not, as once had
been the case, of men in power determined to play Caesar or
Oliver Cromwell, but of common people. They might be Com-
munists or Confederate veterans, radicals, anarchists, or farmers.
They might be a threat to the public peace because they believed
in paper money, electing judges, or even the eight-hour day. But
they were everywhere. Once, politicians spoke of liberty as in
danger. Now, nobody talked that way—at least nobody respectable. Instead, the rhetoric was one so well practiced in wartime:
of threats to law and the public order, of a need to uphold the
government. A crusading zeal would drive on the great veterans'
organization, the Grand Army of the Republic, well into the
twentieth century. But a crusade for what? The GAR's triumphs
evoke the conservative language of '61: pensions for veterans'
families, the teaching of American history in the schools, a flag
in every classroom, and last, most lasting of all, the recitation of
the Pledge of Allegiance.

IN THE SPRING of 1866, Senator Ben Wade of Ohio took out time
from an argument over civil rights to congratulate himself. "I say
to you . . . that it will not be one month from to-day before any
man who claims that he is not a Radical here will wish to God he
had been," he told other members.[76] Laughter, presumably
friendly, greeted Wade's remarks, but in retrospect it has rather a
hollow ring. Though he knew it not, his career was about to
close, and so were those of a host of radical men. The generation
filling their places would be safer by far, and none more cautious, more safe, than those who once had worn the Union blue.
That fervent, exotic humanitarian radicalism that had given
politics before the war a sparkle, an effervescence, and only
added to slaveowners' fears of what Yankee rule would mean, was
fast running out. What replaced it would be nowhere near as
creative or inspiring.

A whimsical historian might well wonder: What if some of
those illustrious dead of Jefferson's day, who allegedly rose to

protest the creation of a Confederacy, were still around in 1866? What if they were actually sitting in the Senate gallery as Wade spoke? If they joined in the laughter, we can speculate, theirs would have been of the bitterest sort; for the republic that they had created had been saved at a tremendous expense, not yet fully paid. She was so well preserved, that they very well might not have recognized her.

7

Fort Sumter

At Last the War

CHARLES ROYSTER

AFTER THE FIRING on Fort Sumter and the early battles of the Civil War, many Americans went out of their way to put on record their disclaimers: They were going to fight the war, but no one should make the mistake of believing that they were responsible for it. In undertaking to discuss the start of the fighting and Americans' acceptance of combat, I must make some disclaimers of my own, in the hope that I will not be held responsible for subjects that are outside of my scope. I do not propose to analyze the crisis over Fort Sumter or to recount the mobilization of the armies or the battlefield expectations of the combatants. I will not try to assess the turn to belligerence by people in the Upper South states and by Democrats in the North. And I promise not to pile up examples of Northerners' and Southerners' inflicting bloodshed and devastation on each other. Instead, I want to explore one aspect of the public's embrace of war: the British military writer B. H. Liddell Hart called it "that vast human sigh of relief," and he remarked in 1929 that it was "one of the most recurrent phenomena in history, marking the outset of every great conflict, down to 1914."[1] I defer to the wisdom of others in judging the recurrence of this sigh of relief throughout history, but I do find evidence of it among Americans in the Civil War.

What was it? What did it mean? The only answers I can offer are speculative ones. One could hardly prove the spread among a vast populace of something so subtle and ambiguous as relief, let alone a sigh. Even if we can discern it with some confidence, we must still venture into the realm of conjecture when we try to understand its significance.

In the North, the months between secession in the Deep South and the start of fighting were filled with much talk and much suspense but not a widespread systematic preparation for war. In retrospect, after the outbreak of hostilities, this inaction struck many people as foolish, if not criminal. Once combat began, it seemed to have always been inevitable, and those who had not foreseen the necessity looked inexcusably lax. Like many others, the *New York Times* drew a contrast between "the apparent insensibility of the public" before April 12, 1861, and the subsequent outburst of enthusiasm for patriotic war. At last, unionists had shown they understood, in the words of the *Times*, that "war is a far less evil than degradation."[2] The North had escaped what Senator Salmon P. Chase called "the danger from compromise,"[3] and the notion that fighting might not occur—as well as a general disinclination to get ready for it—had been discredited. Now, after the firing on Fort Sumter, war could be seen in its true light, as the only way to vindicate the nation. Under those circumstances, the *Times* said, "it ceases to be an evil and becomes the source of actual and positive good. . . . we shall grow the stronger and the nobler by the very contest we are compelled to wage."[4] The often-described wave of patriotism and belligerence during the spring and summer of 1861 derived part of its vehemence from the contrast between anxious uncertainty before April and purposeful action thereafter. Many people in both sections could have said with Senator John Sherman: "Civil war is actually upon us & strange to say it brings a feeling of relief—the suspense is over."[5]

What, specifically, was wrong with the months or the years preceding the war? Looking back from the post-Sumter period, supporters of the war, even many who came to it reluctantly, said that they had left behind a squalid scene of moral corruption and confusion. Peace at any price had been all too tempting. Urging unity in defense of secession and slavery, James H. Thornwell told Southerners that they would not be responsible for the

blood shed in war; but if they quietly accepted the election of
Abraham Lincoln, they would thereby accept a moral condemnation of their social system, ending in their political subju-
gation to the North.[6] As soon as Southerners committed themselves to fighting in April 1861 they launched into what Mary
Tucker Magill later recalled as "the holiday times of the war"–
the early months before the costs grew clear. She could not fully
define the feeling, but she wrote: "There is something exhilarat-
ing in the bravery which will dare a great danger."[7] To risk
unknown, incalculable dangers was an essential element of
the exaltation.

Indeed, peacetime had seen too much calculation: too much
weighing of potential profits and losses, too many political
arrangements for the short term and for selfish ends. So argued
unionists and opponents of slavery who celebrated combat as a
reawakening of power, a reclaiming of control over the nation's
destiny. Reflecting on "the close of Mr. Buchanan's administration" from a distance of almost three years, the Reverend Henry
Clay Fish remembered that the North had been "subsiding into
the conviction that it was not worth while to try to interpose any
check to the ruinous course of events"–that is, Northerners
almost had accepted secession because politicians were corrupt
and citizens cared more for gain than for conscience.[8] But God
had given them war and, in doing so, had awakened the moral
sense and national pride almost lost in the secession winter's talk
of deal-making and commercial connections. And, lo, given a
war, the people proved equal to it and seemed to thrive on it,
these unionists boasted. There was a lesson in this experience,
drawn by the Reverend George Leon Walker in his 1861 Thanks-
giving sermon. Northerners had learned during the year "that
peace has its *horrors* as well as war. And that the horrors of peace
may sometimes find a blessed relief . . . in the welcome horrors
of war." Speaking of the early months of 1861, Walker used
images of darkness–a night of dishonor, a "blind nightmare," a
"slimy coil of serpents in a cave." War dispelled the darkness,
bringing light and day, so morally beneficial that "a perpetual
noon" of such light would be better than one more month of the

night that had preceded it.[9] The war seemed full of promise because its supporters expected it to bring a transformation they wanted, or at least vaguely imagined, but did not know how to attain by other means. Without knowing what course the war would take, they could welcome it as their salvation. Two days after the fall of Fort Sumter, Senator Sherman wrote: "I am for a war that will either establish or overthrow a Govt, and will purify the atmosphere of political life. We need such a war & we have it now."[10]

As we read the expressions of relief that war had begun, we might justifiably suspect that some speakers and writers overstated the likelihood that Northerners might have tolerated secession without a fight. The contrast between inaction and fervor was rhetorically effective, but of course the North's acceptance of combat had sources older than the secession winter. A leap into action was especially gratifying because war offered the opportunity to resolve conclusively the longstanding, much agitated, deeply embittered disputes between the North and the South. In fact, after the war, participants could see that one element of the relief they had felt was knowing that decades of cumulative sectional tension and irritation had at last come to a climax. A Confederate veteran and novelist, John Esten Cooke, likened the antebellum disagreements over slavery and states' rights to the mounting fires of a subterranean volcano, which grew beneath the surface of society for two generations. In 1850 men had tried to shut the opening crater, but in 1860 the lava had begun to flow. In Cooke's figurative wording the destructive burning lava was, of course, first the hostility, then the violence, of Northerners and Southerners. The metaphor of the volcano suggested that the hostility had to keep building up pressure and the violence had to break out. Though Americans before the war had thought themselves especially enlightened, religious, and peace-loving, they had learned through their own wartime enthusiasm, Cooke wrote, that "Man is a fierce and bloody animal under his broadcloth and spotless linen."[11] In other words, war came naturally to them when they met opposition. Why should they not plunge into violence?

The Federal veteran and novelist John William DeForest also saw in the sectional differences over "human bondage" and "political supremacy" an instigation to violence that could not have been prevented by any words or schemes of restraint. With the advantage of hindsight he portrayed the spring of 1861 as a time not of mental torpor but of the imminent breaking out of bloodletting born of prolonged frustrations. "As yet there was little bloodshed," he wrote, "the old respect for law and confidence in the processes of reason could not at once die, and men still endeavored to convince each other by argument while holding the pistol to each other's heads; but from the St. Lawrence to the Gulf there was a spiritual preparedness for slaughter which was to end in such murderous contests as should make ensanguined Europe rise from its thousand battlefields to stare in wonder." Far from being singularly peace-loving, DeForest suggested, Americans of 1861 were uncommonly war-minded. Their reasoning and arguing had failed. They were ready to put aside these inadequate means for resolving their conflicts and turn to means that promised to be conclusive. Then came what DeForest, with irony, called "that sublime summer of popular enthusiasm," during which the "few dead preceded like skirmishers the massive columns which for years should firmly follow them into the dark valley." Obviously, that enthusiasm pointed the way to the dark valley, but enthusiasm was what made that summer sublime. Just as George Leon Walker used an image of light and Mary Tucker Magill evoked the prospect of a holiday, DeForest repeated the word "summer" to convey a sense of brightness and happiness that had spread among large numbers of people when they knew that they would have a war.[12]

As the war grew longer and vaster, the power of hindsight, cast back on the secession winter and spring, revealed the obtuseness of those who had thought fighting might be avoided. Some Northern moralists sounded almost gleeful as they contrasted the peacetime delusions of a conceited people with the vulnerability exposed by war. Opponents of slavery, like the Reverend John Weiss, said that the conflict was "a witness against that unfaithfulness of the popular mind, which was willing to see the evils of the country grow to be so monstrous, that nothing but the sword could cure them." This was of course a tautology: Since the country had needed war to end slavery, slavery made war necessary. But who could justly dispute this proposition after seeing how war had humbled those who had mocked suffering black people while fancying themselves to be secure? Weiss imagined God saying to them: "Depart—into the fire of battle; become purged by fire!"[13] The notion that impenitent Americans might never have fought a war was thus not only foolish but also immoral.

A Federal veteran, Captain A. C. Little, speaking in 1868, condemned much more than slavery. To him antebellum American culture had become hollow materialism, "which pointed to its railroads and telegraphs, its mines of iron and of gold, its fields of coal and its granite warehouses, its dextrous agents dancing upon ropes above the thundering of Niagara, riding upon the wings of the wind, linking together continents by sub-marine cables, uniting oceans by isthmus canals, and said lo! this is my age, the age of material power." What vainglory this outlook had been became ever more apparent after war began. Captain Little described those days: "God reached forth his hand and tore aside the curtain, and discovered us to ourselves and to the world on the brink of disunion and f[r]atricidal strife. . . . Not until the demands of justice had been satisfied; not until we had offered up a bloody holocaust of half a million slain, did God roll back the over-arching cloud of lowering doom."[14] Though Little and others like him no doubt mourned these deaths, his moral standards for contrasting peacetime and wartime, as well as his tone of celebration over the humbling of the godless through bloodshed, left little doubt that the terrible war was gratifying. It had vindicated the prophets of punishment. And, they believed, it had brought to the United States a great reformation which the country's condition demanded but which its people had resisted until fortunately overcome by irresistible force.

One does not have to look very long among wartime and postwar writings to find the recurrent language of destiny. Even after Southerners had lost their fight for independence, they more often said that their struggle had been necessary than that it had been a mistake. Southerners who urged prompt reunion still honored the efforts of resistance before the final surrender. Northern unionists, as they urged on the fighting and as they commemorated their victory afterward, most often spoke of the war as a climactic conflict which God and the nation's history had brought about for the purpose of securing America's greatness. In both sections it was common to portray the combatants and the citizens as being in the hands of destiny. By implication, Americans had to welcome the fighting in 1861 because they were acting out a national history they could not direct into any other course.

Quite a while ago, destiny went out of fashion among historians as an explanatory system, though sometimes it can still be glimpsed, wearing a variety of new disguises, in modern histories. For a twentieth-century example of this old way of accounting for why people embraced war, I turn to Gertrude Stein. Early in the 1930s she wrote a quirky, provocative work titled *Four in America*, full of counterfactual playfulness and her trademark cryptic, gnomic utterances. One of her four Americans was Ulysses S. Grant, and the subjects of Grant and the Civil War, as well as the Great War of her own time, led her to write: "Everybody knows which side has won before there is a war, everybody knows it, but nobody likes to believe it, and then they make a war. . . . Everybody knows what most everybody knew, but now to show it they make a war and after the war is over they believe it. The real fighting has all always been done before the war commences but as everybody likes explanations everybody likes everything proved everybody likes a war so there has to be a war."[15] These observations are not history; they are not argument; they are hyperbole. They are Gertrude Stein's intuitive, psychological version of destiny at work in war. And she was writing not about God's will but about the people's minds, which, she suggested, needed–therefore wanted–a war to reach a conclusion that was easy to foresee, yet difficult to accept.

Obviously, I do not put forward Gertrude Stein as a competitor with scholarly analysts of the coming of the Civil War. This passage in her book nevertheless may resonate when we read comments on Americans' turn to civil war by contemporaries who said they had foreseen it, had wanted to avoid it, yet had undertaken it all the same. Many predictions during the early months of 1861, holding out the prospect of no war or a very short war, were qualified by the predictor's warning that, if fighting began, it would be continued. While still a Kentucky militia officer in March 1861, before he became a Confederate General, Simon Bolivar Buckner set great store by Northern conservatives' resistance to federal coercion of the South. At the same time, he said: "If the south should aggress it will unite public sentiment at the north against them and civil war will ensue."[16] The much-discussed peace-loving reluctance or materialistic passivity or moral torpor or political conservatism in the North were all present but were not the powerful bars to warmaking that they had seemed before the firing on Fort Sumter. And many people said that they had always known this.

Whether or not we fully believe the many people who claimed during and after the war that they long had seen the conflict coming, we may notice that such foresight soon became the sign of realism and wisdom. In the summer of 1864, Jefferson Davis said of the war: "I saw it coming, and for twelve years I worked night and day to prevent it, but I could not. The North was mad and blind."[17] In his accompanying comments, Davis showed less interest in contending that he or anyone could have prevented war than in offering his antebellum efforts as proof that he and the South bore no responsibility for the bloodshed. Rather than recall a suspenseful striving for peace, he presented himself as a far-sighted statesman, who had discerned the juggernaut while it was still in the distance.

In the North, Secretary of State William Henry Seward had made some much-quoted statements in 1861, predicting a short war and an easy victory for the union. Two years later, when he privately complained about Northerners' slowness in fully making up their minds to "fight out every obstacle to success," Henry W. Bellows reminded him that the expectation of a short war owed much to Seward's own cheerful promises at the start.

Seward replied: "I had to keep up the heart of the Nation, when my own was heaviest." He said that he had concluded in 1840 "that the South was slowly strengthening itself to do one of two things, to control the government in favor of the spread & sway of slavery, or to acquire such coherency & vigor as to break away & assert its separate independence."[18] He then had resolved to devote his life to resisting this Southern plot. In this version, Seward's heavy heart in 1861 resulted not so much from the start of bloodshed, which he had much reason to expect, but from concern over sustaining the Northern war effort until victory. Both Davis and Seward stressed in retrospect their prolonged antebellum resistance to the aggressiveness of the opposing section. Their expressions of regret that war finally had begun amounted to tacit self-congratulation for not having judged wrongly in expecting the other side to go all the way to bloodshed. It was a sad relief when the start of combat showed beyond a doubt that the Southern plan to rule or ruin—or the Northern intention to reduce the South—really had been at work all along and was not just a figment of agitators' rhetoric. The start of the war could thus be used to confirm the wisdom of those who led it and the necessity of fighting it.

To explain the persistence of Southerners' fighting, Seward turned away from their defense of slavery. The organized power of rebellion, he said, lived not so much in the strength of slavery "as in the pride & passion & self-commitment of the enemy."[19] Jefferson Davis said almost the same thing about Northerners in calling them mad and blind after they resorted to war. Fighting aroused new, or at least stronger, emotions. Those emotions supplanted inter-sectional political rivalries for control of the old union. In doing so, they took on a life of their own and became their own justification. The war must go on because it had begun; the outrages that had occurred since April 12, 1861, became incentives to persevere, which were as strong as or stronger than the antebellum reasons for going to war. For advocates of fighting, even those who lamented the coming of war, such passionate self-commitment could take the place of debates and second-guessing. Combatants and their supporters were doing what they had to do. They censured the folly of their enemies' determination to wage war, but they pleaded on their own behalf that they had no choice. Many people had argued that choice had still been possible until the firing on Fort Sumter. Afterward, people could more easily dismiss that notion—indeed, sometimes dismiss it retroactively for years or decades preceding the Civil War. The war provided a comforting sense of destiny for the losers no less than for the winners. I am concerned here not to contend that they were correct or incorrect but to suggest that they welcomed this guarantee of necessity. The path of action along which it pushed them might seem regrettable because so bloody, but they need not be ambivalent about following it. In this respect, the bitter emotions of combat simplified their lives, as many Northerners and Southerners said at the time.

The Southern historian E. Merton Coulter, writing more than fifty years ago, censured the Georgia politician Alexander H. Stephens for making gloomy remarks after states in the Deep South seceded. Though Stephens accepted the vice presidency of the Confederate States of America, he "was already a defeatist" before the war began, Coulter wrote. That word "already" resonates in this setting. A twentieth-century historian knew that there had come a point in the Confederacy's brief history when being a defeatist was unavoidably realistic. Eventually, a Southerner could hardly be anything else. Stephens's offense, in Coulter's eyes, was that he had "moaned" about impending ruin too early in the war. After the firing on Fort Sumter, Stephens said: "We shall be in one of the bloodiest civil wars that history has recorded."[20] Such predictions were not common then; however, I want to emphasize not Stephens's foresight but his fatalism, which he shared with President Jefferson Davis, who kept predicting Confederate victory until shortly before he was captured by Federal troops.

By fatalism I mean this shared conviction that the war had to be fought—and the acceptance of this conclusion not only by those who expected triumph but also by many who were bewildered or pessimistic. I do not know whether we can legitimately include such fatalism as an influence on the participants when we undertake to explain why Americans went to war. I do believe that it was an important element of Americans' willingness to let the war grow. James Dixon of Connecticut, a Republican United States senator who later switched to the Democratic party, did not welcome the prospect of war during the secession winter, and he knew that the Southern movement was not bluff but "the first appearings of a mighty revolution." He explained to a constituent that some politicians in Washington who wanted to "make an effort to extricate us from the danger" of war did not do so because they were "afraid of being called *timid—weak kneed—wanting in backbone.*" They saw, Dixon said, that the antislavery Senator Benjamin F. Wade won praise for his belligerence and was "jubilant . . . in the midst of the tempest."[21] The long-awaited, often-predicted showdown between North and South was at hand. Politicians in Washington could not prevent it partly because so many people wanted it, and partly because so many who did not want it had decided that the confrontation would occur, in which case resisting it seemed both futile and politically suicidal. Even Northerners who deplored the coming of the war and denounced the Northern war effort in 1862 and afterward largely remained quiet during the outburst of enthusiasm in 1861. The dominant images for the events of 1861 were tides and rivers and volcanoes and earthquakes and unstoppable rolling wheels and similar instances of movement that was inexorable.

Long after the Civil War, Oliver P. Temple, a Southerner, tried to recreate the secession winter and the days after the firing on Fort Sumter for readers who, he apparently suspected, might judge his conduct harshly. He had been a Tennessee slaveholder and had remained silent during the movement to secession—damning facts to one set of readers. Yet he also had thought secession and war a ruinous mistake for Southerners, and he became a prominent unionist. He wanted his readers to sympathize with the predicament of people caught in the momentum of events. He wrote: "In December 1860, the question was whether there was a sufficient cause for dissolving the Union. In February following, the question was, shall Tennessee secede? In

May, it was, what shall I, as an individual, do? Shall I go with my state into secession, or shall I remain true to the old government?" By the time this stark choice confronted Southerners, the gradations, the nuances, the moral complexities in the sectional conflict were no guides. One had to take a side as a whole–Republicans and Yankees and abolitionists or Southerners and secessionists and anti-democratic fire-eaters who were about to destroy slavery in a misguided effort to save it. Though choosing the latter looked "almost incredible" in retrospect, Temple said, many people had been led into it by events of the secession winter and spring.[22] While people believed themselves to be engaged in a series of decisions among many alternatives, they suddenly found that their only choice amounted to selecting which side they would take in a war. If we were to engage in Gertrude Stein's kind of speculation, we might say that the process of eliminating alternatives and narrowing the choices–a process extending over decades rather than just weeks–was made easier by the latent expectation that, if necessary, everything could eventually be resolved by a war.

Senator Dixon of Connecticut, caught in the dilemma that Oliver Temple later described, wrote from Washington: "We are fast drifting into disunion & civil war. Meanwhile the master minds of the nation seem paralysed. Some talk of concessions–some of coercion–but all seem bewildered by the magnitude of the great event approaching. . . . Many of our friends say let the consequences be what they may, nothing can be done to prevent the evil. Is this so? Can nothing be done?"[23] Dixon was encountering, in December 1860, the surrender to the momentum of war–and the relief experienced in that surrender–which showed itself so much more vividly after the firing on Fort Sumter. The answer to his questions–"Is this so? Can nothing be done?"–was "Yes," and he knew it.

Americans had come to this pass through a long train of expedient decisions and partial surrenders of the kind that no one could altogether escape. Robert Underwood Johnson's poem "The Vision of Gettysburg: 1863–1913" blamed the Founding Fathers for tolerating in their own era the perpetuation of slavery, which became the great problem for their descendants. He cried back to the founders, over the span of more than a century: *"On you, on you the blood of Gettysburg!"*[24] But why should people of the eighteenth century, who also dreaded dissolution and civil war in their time, bear not only their own burden but also that of people in the nineteenth century? The people who welcomed war after Fort Sumter was fired upon were the heirs of both a prolonged sectional confrontation and a repeated flight from responsibility.

I would like to close by quoting one more reflection on the First World War–another comment, like those of B. H. Liddell Hart and Gertrude Stein, on how war took possession of people. The speaker in 1924 was Newton D. Baker, who had served as Woodrow Wilson's Secretary of War during the great conflict. His audience was the Reserve Officers' Association of the United States, and he wanted to persuade them that they and he and a whole generation had made a terrible mistake, which must not be repeated. He said:

> I read not long ago a Greek play. I do not recommend you to read it, because it is so unutterably sad that you can only read three pages at a time, and then you have to stop. It is a play by Euripides, Iphigenia in Aulis. It is a story of the Greeks just as they were about to start off to the Trojan War. Agamemnon was the King. Calchas, the soothsayer, had been consulted as to what he had to say about it. He told King Agamemnon that the Greeks could not start off on this great international enterprise with hope of success unless they got Iphigenia, the daughter of Agamemnon, the most beautiful girl in Greece, and offered her as a sacrifice to the gods. Agamemnon sent off and got Iphigenia and his wife, the girl's own mother, Clytemnestra, brought her. And she only learned when she got her daughter there that she was to be slain on the altar of her own father, a sacrifice to national ambition. Then she ceased being the Queen and became all mother. National ambition became nothing to her. She wanted to grasp the girl and save her from that sacrifice. And it was too late.
>
> I have thought as I read that story, "Ah, the world has not changed very much. That is what we keep on doing all the

time." Instead of sacrificing a young girl, this generation has sacrificed ten million young men on the altars of national aspiration, simply because we did what Clytemnestra did—we waited until the time of sacrifice, when it is too late to rescue the youth.[25]

Newton D. Baker's rendering of Euripides was both a hope for future peace and a moral and psychological accounting for past war. He had seen—indeed, promoted—the great rush of wartime enthusiasm. He certainly did not repudiate it or the war. But he did regard them as tragic.

Notes

Introduction

1. The reconstruction of this episode of the final salute at Sumter is based on Abner Doubleday, *Reminiscences of Forts Sumter and Moultrie in 1860–61* (New York, 1876), 162, 171–72; and Samuel Wylie Crawford, *The Genesis of the Civil War: The Story of Fort Sumter, 1860—1861* (New York, 1887), 446, 470.

2. Arthur Link, ed., *The Papers of Woodrow Wilson*, vol. 4 (Princeton, 1973), 525.

3. Don E. Fehrenbacher, "The New Political History and the Coming of the Civil War," in *Lincoln in Text and Context: Collected Essays* (Stanford, 1987), 78. For a somewhat different view, see Michael Perman, *The Coming of the American Civil War*, 3rd ed. (Lexington, Mass., 1993), xv–xxi.

4. Roy P. Basler, ed., Marion Dolores Pratt and Lloyd A Dunlap, asst. eds., *The Collected Works of Abraham Lincoln*, 9 vols. (New Brunswick, 1953–55; *Supplements*, 1974, 1990, Christian Basler, co-ed.), 1:278; 394.

Chapter One. Lincoln and the Question of Individual Responsibility

Robert V. Bruce, my teacher, winner of the Pulitzer Prize for history, planted the seeds of this chapter in his 1989 Fortenbaugh Lecture at Gettysburg College, later published in my *Lincoln the War President: The Gettysburg Lectures* (Oxford University Press, 1992).

Discussing the subject with members of the 1992 Lincoln Seminar at Gettysburg College was one of the great pleasures of writing this chapter. I am indebted to Christina Ericson, Lisa Evans, Matt Graber, Will Keczkemethy, David Pike, Jeff Rogge, Bob Sandow, Ed Young, and Kathy Tallarico. Young people bright and beautiful, may the wind be often at your backs.

I wish to thank the institutions, too, that provided a platform to air the ideas in Chapter One. I presented parts of it, in addition to the Civil War Institute, at the Gettysburg College faculty seminar (with its free lunches to help soften criticism?); at the Lincoln Group of New York; as the Carl C. Rasmussen Lecture at the Lutheran Theological Seminary, Gettysburg; as the James Morton Callahan Lecture at West Virginia University; and as the Tenth Anniversary Lecture for the Lincoln Group of Florida, where one loyal member whispered that htis was the most controversial lecture in the Group's history. I would be remiss in failing to also acknowledge the kind invitation to speak at Lincoln Memorial University (founded by General Oliver Otis Howard of Gettysburg fame) as the Lloyd Ostendorf Lecturer in 1995. Preparing for the occasion afforded me the time to think over the issues for one final time. That a snowstorm canceled the lecture would surely have been taken by the ancients—and no doubt some today—as a divine message counseling silence.

I am grateful, too for comments on this chapter from Bob Bruce, Dan Crofts, Dick Current, Bill Freehling, Bill Gienapp, Howard Holzer, Lew Lehrman, Bruce Levine, Mark Neely, Charlie Royster, Mark Summers, and Ken Stampp. My lively sister, Judy, and my late brother, Adam, also took incisive looks at the chapter. Two colleagues at Gettysburg, Leslie Cahoon and Baird Tipson (now the president of Wittenberg University), saved me from crediting a quote from Shakespeare to the wrong character. Comments ranged all the way to ten typed pages; I think I managed to irritate one or two freinds.

Sometime after finishing the first draft, I had dinner with a group of historians in San Francisco, and the conversation turned to our most effective lectures in the classroom. I advanced as mine a discussion of medical care after battle. Unless one or two students, usually men, got ill and left to relieve themselves (I always hoped in the bathroom), I saw the lecture as a failure. Bruce Levine, who had just read this chapter, turned to me and said, "Now I understand your essay." I hope he also forgave me. I respect Lincoln deeply. I would be genuinely satisfied if future historians would show this chapter to be wrongheaded.

I am grateful to Sandy Skordrud and Daniel Boritt for reading proofs.

1. W. A. Swanberg, *First Blood* (New York: 1957), tells its tale well. Cf. Martin Abbott, "The First Shot at Fort Sumter," *Civil War History* 3 (1957): 41–45, and Robert Hendrickson, *Sumter: The First Day of the Civil War* (Chelsea, Mich., 1990), 179–88. Pryor is quoted from the *New York Tribune,* April 17, 1861, and Stephen D. Lee, "The First Step in the War," *Battles and Leaders of the Civil War* (New York, 1955 ed.), 1:76; Chesnut is quoted from C. Vann Woodward, *Mary Chesnut's Diary* (New Haven, 1981), 46. Historians disagree about Ruffin's exact role.

2. April 13, 1861.

3. Kenneth M. Stampp, *America in 1857: A Nation on the Brink* (New York, 1990), viii; Robert W. Johannsen, *Lincoln, the South and Slavery* (Baton Rouge, 1991), passim. The question of inevitability can be traced in the various anthologies mentioned in the bibliography.

4. Raymond Aron, *Introduction to the Philosophy of History, and Essay on the Limits of Historical Objectivity*, George J. Irwin, trans. (Boston, 1961), 178.

5. Ken Burns, "The Civil War," PBS, 1990; Roy P. Basler, ed., Marion Dolores Pratt and Lloyd A. Dunlap, asst. eds., 9 vols. (New Brunswick, 1953–55; *Supplements*, 1974, 1990, Christian Basler, co-ed.), 1:109.

6. Ibid., 108–15. Quotation is from p. 112.

7. Robert V. Bruce, "The Shadow of a Coming War," in Gabor S. Boritt, ed., *Lincoln, the War President: The Gettysburg Lectures* (New York, 1992), 1–28; Charles Royster, *The Destructive War: William Tecumseh Sherman, Stonewall Jackson, and the Americans* (New York, 1991).

8. David Potter, *The Impending Crisis, 1848–1861*, completed and edited by Don E. Fehrenbacher (New York, 1976), 49.

9. Basler, ed., *Collected Works of Lincoln*, 2:461.

10. Ibid., 318. For an excellent example of harsh language combined with utter rejection of the need for bullets, see 454. Don E. Fehrenbacher, *Prelude to Greatness: Lincoln in the 1850's* (Stanford, 1962), 89–92, dates Lincoln's above cited notes.

11. Rufus Choate to the Maine Whig Central Committee, August 9, 1856, in *Illinois Daily State Register*, August 21, 1856, as quoted in Albert J. Beveridge, *Abraham Lincoln, 1809–1858*, 2 vols. (Boston, 1928), 2:413; Basler, ed., *Collected Works of Lincoln*, 2:349–50; 3:21; cf. *Political Debates between Abraham Lincoln and Stephen Douglas* (Cleveland, 1895), 69.

12. *Congressional Globe*, 33:1, app. 323; 34:1, House, 220; 36:2, 796, 1332; 36:1, 572. The best works on the subject are David M. Potter, *Lincoln and His Party in the Secession Crisis* (New Haven, 1962 ed.); Kenneth M. Stampp, *And the War Came: The North and the Secession Crisis, 1860–61* (Chicago, 1964); and Daniel W. Crofts, *Reluctant Confederates: Upper South Unionists in the Secession Crisis* (Chapel Hill, 1989).

13. Basler, ed., *Collected Works of Lincoln*, 3:502.

14. Ibid., 5:537; 2:321, 272; 3:481. I have been at work on a study of Lincoln's understanding of history for many years now.

15. Ibid., 2:271; 3:553.

16. Ibid., 4:13.

17. Ibid., 3:550; 2:355, 454; 3:316. These, like the earlier quotations, are merely examples. As the Georgia state legislature debated disunion in 1861, Henry Benning used Lincoln's exact words: "there will be no war." Benning reflected the views of many militant secessionists. William W.

Freehling and Craig Simpson, eds., *Secession Debated: Georgia's Showdown in 1860* (New York, 1993), 131.

18. Quoted in Arthur M. Schlesinger, Jr., "War and the Constitution: Abraham Lincoln and Franklin D. Roosevelt," in Boritt, ed., *Lincoln, the War President*, 160.

19. Edmund Wilson, *Patriotic Gore: Studies in the Literature of the American Civil War* (New York, 1962), 130.

20. Bruce, "The Shadow of a Coming War," 24.

21. Basler, ed., *Collected Works of Lincoln*, 1:439; 4:259. In the context of the Civil War Lincoln chose to ignore the War of Independence which, as he said repeatedly, achieved much.

22. Ibid., 5:49.

23. Ibid., 2:355; 3:454.

24. Ibid., 4:132. The same language seemed to be also favored by those on the other side who saw the issue of slavery in the territories as "a humbug and a nuisance." *Richmond Whig*, March 2, 1861.

25. Ibid., 4:95; 5:1; John Hay to J. G. Nicolay, Aug. 7, 1863, in Tyler Dennett, ed., *Lincoln and the Civil War in the Diaries and Letters of John Hay* (New York, 1939), 77.

26. Basler, ed., *Collected Works of Lincoln*, 7:512; (cf. 4:438–39); 4:160.

27. Alexander H. Stephens, *A Constitutional View of the Late War Between the States*, 2 vols. (Philadelphia, 1868–70), 2:448; Basler, ed., *Collected Works of Lincoln*, 2:385; 4:236.

28. Ibid., 4:269.

29. Charles Francis Adams, Jr., *Charles Francis Adams, 1835–1915: An Autobiography*, (Boston, 1900), 69.

30. Potter and Fehrenbacher, *The Impending Crisis*, 431.

31. Basler, ed., *Collected Works of Lincoln*, 4:124.

32. Bruce, "The Shadow of a Coming War," 18.

33. This paragraph relies on my "The Voyage to the Colony of Linconia," *Historian* 37 (1975): 619–32. The classic statement on avoidance comes from Anna Freud, "The Ego and the Mechanism of Defense," *The Writings of Anna Freud*, vol. 2, Cecil Baines, trans. (New York, 1966), 69–70. See also the standard psychiatric literature.

34. Basler, ed., *Collected Works of Lincoln*, 7:281; 1:75; 3:315; 7:23. David Potter, "Why the Republicans Rejected Both Compromise and Secession," in George Harmon Knoles, ed., *The Crisis of the Union, 1860–1861* (Baton Rouge, 1965), 105.

35. Basler, ed., *Collected Works of Lincoln*, 4:150; Charles M. Segel, ed., *Conversations with Lincoln* (New York, 1961), 43.

36. Donn Piatt, *Memories of the Men Who Saved the Union* (New York, 1887), 33–4, 30. Piatt can be untrustworthy, but the above rings true and has been credited by Bruce, Fehrenbacher, and Potter, among others.

37. See Potter and Stampp in note 12. Incidentally, Douglass also believed firmly even as 1860 came to an end that there would be no war. Philip Foner, ed., *The Life and Writings of Frederick Douglass*, 4 vols. (New York, 1952), 2:528–29.

38. William M. French, *Life, Speeches, State Papers and Public Services of Gov. Oliver P. Morton* (Indianapolis, n.d.), 130; Basler, ed., *Collected Works of Lincoln*, 4:195.

39. Ibid., 4:172.

40. Ibid., 4:211.

41. Leroy P. Graf and Ralph H. Haskins, eds., *The Papers of Andrew Johnson*, vol. 4, 1860–61 (Knoxville, 1967), 310–11.

42. Corwin to Lincoln, Jan. 18, 1861, Abraham Lincoln Papers, 14:6284; Basler, ed., *Collected Works of Lincoln*, 4:190, 243, 240–41.

43. James M. McPherson, *Ordeal by Fire: The Civil War and Reconstruction* (New York, 1992), 143; Basler, ed., *Collected Works of Lincoln*, 4:271; Piatt, *Memories*, 34.

44. Basler, ed. *Collected Works of Lincoln*, 4:237; Albert Mordell, ed., *Selected Essays by Gideon Welles: Civil War and Reconstruction* (New York, 1959) 40; John G. Nicolay and John Hay, *Abraham Lincoln: A History*, 10 vols. (New York, 1890), 3:394–95.

45. Samuel Ward to S. L. M. Barlow, March 31, 1861, S. L. M. Barlow Papers, Huntington Library, San Marino, Calif.; Earl Schenck Miers, William E. Baringer, and C. Percy Powell, eds., *Lincoln Day by Day: A Chronology*, 3 vols. (Washington, 1960), 3:30–32; Basler, ed., *Collected Works of Lincoln*, 3:316. See also Current, *Lincoln and the First Shot*, 78–86; and Crofts, *Reluctant Confederates*, 297.

46. The above simplifies matters. Potter moved in the direction of Stampp and Current in his later work. The most recent important contribution, Crofts, *Reluctant Confederates*, leans toward Stampp and Current over the Sumter question, but toward Potter in its understanding of the secession crisis. For the historiography of Fort Sumter see the bibliography and also Richard N. Current, *Lincoln and the First Shot* (Philadelphia, 1963), 182–208, and Potter, *Lincoln and His Party*, "Preface to the 1962 Edition," xi–xxxii. The words quoted are from Current, *Lincoln and the First Shot*, 193, a book that represents well this last view, together with Stampp, *And the War Came*, 262–86. For Potter's original position, see *Lincoln and His Party*, 336–75.

47. Basler, ed., *Collected Works of Lincoln*, 4:245.

48. Ibid., 237; Crofts, *Reluctant Confederates*, 375; Stampp, "The United States and National Self-determination," in Boritt, ed., *Lincoln, the War President*, 133.

49. Basler, *Collected Works of Lincoln*, 8:332–33; Theodore C. Pease and James G. Randall, eds., *The Diary of Orville Hickman Browning*, 2 vols.

(Springfield, Ill., 1927), 1:453; William Tecumseh Sherman, *Memoirs of General W. T. Sherman*, Charles Royster, ed. (New York, 1990), 185–86; *Congressional Globe*, 36:2, 312; Stephens quoted in *Autobiography of Col. Richard Malcolm Johnston*, 2nd ed. (Washington, 1901), 152, based on Johnston's diary.

50. Basler, ed., *Collected Works of Lincoln*, 3:19.

51. Ibid., 4:271; 5:478; 7:282, 535; 8:333; Katherine Helm, *The True Story of Mary, Wife of Lincoln. . . .* (New York, 1928), 233.

52. Ibid., 8:332.

53. Ibid., 8:333.

Chapter Two. *"Little Women" Who Helped Make This Great War*

The author wishes to thank Dee Andrews, Robin Einhorn, Eli Leon, Karen Sawislak, and Beverly Voloshin for their prompt, generous, and very helpful attention to this essay. She also wants to make clear that not all of the above are equally persuaded by the argument.

1. See Clement Eaton, *The Freedom-of-Thought Struggle in the Old South* (New York, 1964).

2. Glenna Matthews, *The Rise of Public Woman: Woman's Power and Woman's Place in the United States, 1630–1970* (New York, 1992).

3. On women's participation in public rituals in the nineteenth century see Mary Ryan, *Women in Public: Between Banners and Ballots* (Baltimore, 1990).

4. Elizabeth Regine Varon, " 'We mean to be counted': White Women and Politics in Antebellum Virginia" (Ph.D. Dissertation, Yale University, 1993), 290; Victoria E. Bynam, *Unruly Women: The Politics of Social and Sexual Control in the Old South* (Chapel Hill, 1992), 54.

5. See Glenna Matthews, *"Just a Housewife": The Rise and Fall of Domesticity in America* (New York, 1987); see also Paula Baker, "The Domestication of Politics: Women and American Political Society, 1780–1920," *American Historical Review* 89 (June 1984): 620–47.

6. On women's impact on American publishing see Mary P. Ryan, *The Empire of the Mother: American Writing about Domesticity 1830–1860* (New York, 1982).

7. As quoted in Matthews, *"Just a Housewife,"* 50.

8. As quoted in Jeanne Boydston, Mary Kelley, and Anne Margolis, *The Limits of Sisterhood: The Beecher Sisters on Women's Rights and Woman's Sphere* (Chapel Hill, 1988), 182.

9. Lydia Maria Child, "The Kansas Emigrants," in *Autumnal Leaves: Tales and Sketches in Prose and Rhyme* (New York, 1857), 343f.

10. Carolyn L. Karcher, "From Pacifism to Armed Struggle: L. M. Child's 'The Kansas Emigrants' and Antislavery Ideology in the 1850s," *Emerson Society Quarterly* 34 (3d Quarter 1988): 141–58, 142.

11. See Carolyn L. Karcher, "Lydia Maria Child and the Example of John Brown," *Race Traitor* 1 (Winter 1993): 21–44.

12. Harriet A. Jacobs, *Incidents in the Life of a Slave Girl*, L. Maria Child, ed., introduction by Jean Fagan Yellin (Cambridge, Mass., 1987), xix.

13. As quoted in the *Liberator*, Jan. 4, 1856.

14. Dorothy Sterling, *Ahead of Her Time: Abby Kelley and the Politics of Antislavery* (New York, 1991), 14.

15. George C. Rable, *Civil Wars: Women and the Crisis of Southern Nationalism* (Urbana, Ill., 1989), 18.

16. Elizabeth Fox-Genovese, *Within the Plantation Household: Black and White Women of the Old South* (Chapel Hill, 1988), 244.

17. Elizabeth Moss, *Domestic Novelists in the Old South: Defenders of Southern Culture* (Baton Rouge, 1992), 105.

18. Varon, " 'We mean to be counted,' " 201.

19. Ibid., 418.

20. As quoted in Pat Ferrero, Elaine Hedges, and Julie Silber, *Hearts and Hands: The Influence of Women and Quilts on American Society* (San Francisco, 1987), 72.

21. Paul Finkelman, "Women Abolitionists and the Law," paper given at the annual meeting of the Pacific Coast Branch of the American Historical Association, Corvallis, Oregon, August 1992.

22. Matthews, *The Rise of Public Woman*, 126.

23. See Wendy Hamand, "The Women's National Loyal League: Feminist Abolitionists and the Civil War," *Civil War History* 35 (March 1989): 39–58.

24. See Reid Mitchell, "The Northern Soldier and His Community," in Maris A. Vinovskis, ed., *Toward a Social History of the American Civil War: Exploratory Essays* (Cambridge, Eng., 1990), for a discussion of the correspondence between women and their soldier husbands. See also Mitchell, "The Perseverance of the Soldiers," in Gabor S. Boritt, ed., *Why the Confederacy Lost* (New York, 1992).

25. See Moss, *Domestic Novelists of the Old South*, chap. 5, for an account of the unusual correspondence between the novelist Augusta Jane Evans and the Confederate general P. G. T. Beauregard, for example. Evans was one of the very few Southern women able to gain the attention of politicians and military leaders during the course of the war.

26. Drew Gilpin Faust, "Altars of Sacrifice: Confederate Women and the Narratives of War," *Journal of American History* 76 (March 1990): 1228.

27. Bellows to Jane Hoge and Mary Livermore, Oct. 29, 1863, USSC Documents, 2:63, Huntington Library, San Marino, Calif.

Chapter Three. African-Americans and the Coming of the Civil War

1. Benjamin Quarles, *The Negro in the Civil War* (Boston, 1953), ix.

2. On the notion of the Civil War as a "Second American Revolution" in recent scholarship see, for example, James M. McPherson, *Abraham Lincoln and the Second American Revolution* (New York, 1991); Eric Foner, *Reconstruction: America's Unfinished Revolution, 1863–1877* (New York, 1988); and Bruce Levine, *Half Slave and Half Free: The Roots of Civil War* (New York, 1992). Kenneth M. Stampp, "The Irrepressible Conflict," in *The Imperiled Union: Essays on the Background of the Civil War* (New York, 1980), 191. On the debate over emancipation as both seized and given, see James M. McPherson, "Who Freed the Slaves?," and Ira Berlin, "Emancipation and Its Meaning in American Life," in *Reconstruction* 2, no. 3 (1994): 35–44.

3. *Douglass Monthly*, July, April 1861.

4. Maria Stewart, a speech in Boston's Franklin Hall, Sept. 21, 1832, quoted in Dorothy Sterling, ed., *We Are Your Sisters: Black Women in the Nineteenth Century* (New York, 1984), 154.

5. *Report on the Proceedings of the Colored National Convention, Held at Cleveland, Ohio, on Wednesday, September 6, 1848* (Rochester, 1848), 19, quoted in C. Peter Ripley et al., eds., *The Black Abolitionist Papers*, 5 vols., (1985–92), 3:24. On "two abolitionisms," see Jane H. Pease and William H. Pease, *They Who Would Be Free: Blacks' Search for Freedom 1830–61* (New York, 1974), 3–16.

6. Eric Foner, "Politics, Ideology, and the Origins of the Civil War," in George M. Fredrickson, ed., *Nation Divided: Problems and Issues of the Civil War and Reconstruction* (Minneapolis, 1975), reprinted in Michael Perman, ed., *The Coming of the American Civil War*, 3d ed. (Lexington, Mass, 1993), 186.

7. *Frederick Douglass' Paper*, March 4, 1853, Aug. 15, 1856.

8. Samuel Ringgold Ward, *Autobiography of a Fugitive Negro* (1855; rpt. New York, 1968), 77; Abraham Lincoln, "Annual Message to Congress," Dec. 1, 1862, in Roy P. Basler, ed., Marion Dolores Pratt and Lloyd A. Dunlap, asst. eds., *The Collected Works of Abraham Lincoln*, 9 vols. (New Brunswick, N.J., 1953), 5:537.

9. Leon F. Litwack, *North of Slavery: The Negro in the Free States, 1790–1860* (Chicago, 1961), 248–250.

10. See Larry Gara, *Liberty Line: The Legend of the Underground Railroad* (Lexington, Ky., 1961). On Vigilance Committees, see Pease and Pease, *They Who Would Be Free*, 207–12.

11. Bibb in *Liberator*, April 12, 1850; Providence meeting quoted in Pease and Pease, *They Who Would Be Free*, 217; Philadelphia resolutions in C. Peter Ripley, ed., *Witness for Freedom: African-American Voices on Race, Slavery, and Emancipation* (Chapel Hill, 1993), 182; Powell, in *Liberator*, Oct. 11, 1850.

12. Pease and Pease, *They Who Would Be Free*, 219–32. Three of the fugitives who fought off their pursuers at Christiana fled to Canada via Frederick Douglass's home in Rochester, New York. After having been fed and sheltered by Douglass, and then taken by carriage to the Genessee River where they departed for Canada, one of the fugitives gave the abolitionist a revolver as a token of gratitude. See David W. Blight, *Frederick Douglass' Civil War: Keeping Faith in Jubilee* (Baton Rouge, 1989), 94.

13. *Liberator*, July 7, 1854. On Burns and his rescue, see Ripley, ed., *Black Abolitionist Papers*, 4:395–97. In February 1855, members of the black Twelfth Baptist Church in Boston, of which Burns had been a member, purchased his freedom. A Boston woman sponsored Burns's education at Oberlin College through 1857. He eventually settled in St. Catherines, Canada West, where he died in 1862.

14. Ruggles, in Ripley, ed., *Black Abolitionist Papers*, 3:172; Mary Armstead to William Still, Aug. 26, 1855, and John H. Hill to William Still, Oct. 30, 1853, in Carter G. Woodson, ed., *The Mind of the Negro as Reflected in Letters Written During the Crisis, 1800–1860* (Washington, 1926), 566, 583.

15. Benjamin Quarles, "The Revolutionary War as a Black Declaration of Independence," in Quarles, *Black Mosaic: Essays in Afro-American History and Historiography* (Amherst, 1988), 57. See the resolutions of a Philadelphia meeting in October 1850 in Ripley, ed., *Witness for Freedom*, 179–83.

16. *Frederick Douglass' Paper*, July 21, 1851, in Philip S. Foner, ed., *The Life and Writings of Frederick Douglass* (New York, 1950), 5:192–93.

17. Quoted in Don E. Fehrenbacher, *The Dred Scott Case: Its Significance in American Law and Politics* (New York, 1978), 347.

18. *Provincial Freeman*, April 25, 1857, quoted in Ripley, ed., *Black Abolitionist Papers*, 4:362; Shadd Cary quote in Quarles, *Black Abolitionists*, 231; speech by Purvis, in City Assembly Room, New York, May 12, 1857, in Ripley, ed., *Black Abolitionist Papers*, 4:363–64; and Frances Ellen Watkins Harper, speech printed in *National Antislavery Standard*, May 23, 1857, quoted in Sterling, ed., *We Are Your Sisters*, 162. Watkins Harper married in 1860. I have used her married name because that is how she is best known, especially during her later literary career.

19. Quarles, *Black Abolitionists*, 235; Rock, address in Faneuil Hall, Boston, *Liberator*, March 12, 1858, reprinted in Thomas R. Frazier, ed., *Afro-American History: Primary Sources*, shorter ed. (New York, 1971), 73–74; *Douglass Monthly*, Jan. 1859.

20. Martin R. Delany, *The Condition, Elevation, Emigration, and Destiny of the Colored People of the United States* (1852; rpt. New York, 1968), 199; Nell Irvin Painter, "Martin R. Delany: Elitism and Black Nationalism," in Leon Litwack and August Meier, eds., *Black Leaders of the Nineteenth Century* (Urbana, 1988), 149–71.

21. Jason H. Silverman, "Mary Ann Shadd and the Search for Equality," in Litwack and Meier, eds., *Black Leaders*, 87–100; and Sterling, ed., *We Are Your Sisters*, 165–75.

22. Floyd J. Miller, *The Search for a Black Nationality: Black Emigration and Colonization* (Urbana, 1975), 192–93, 228–31, 232–49.

23. *Proceedings of the First Convention of the Colored Citizens of the State of Illinois, Convened at the City of Chicago, October 6–8, 1853*, in Philip S. Foner and George E. Walker, eds., *Proceedings of the Black State Conventions, 1840–1865* (Philadelphia, 1980), 60–62. Pease and Pease, *They Who Would Be Free*, 267–72.

24. Eugene D. Genovese, *From Rebellion to Revolution: Afro-American Slave Revolts in the Making of the New World* (Baton Rouge, 1979), 106–17. I take my use of the term abolition "emissaries" (constantly used by white Southerners in the late 1850s) from Steven A. Channing, *Crisis of Fear: Secession in South Carolina* (New York, 1970), 38–57; and Clarence L. Mohr, *On the Threshold of Freedom: Masters and Slaves in Civil War Georgia* (Athens: University of Georgia Press, 1986), 8, 28.

25. McDowell quoted Genovese, *From Rebellion to Revolution*, 116. Withers quoted from Charleston *Courier*, Jan. 30, 1859, in Channing, *Crisis of Fear*, 39n. 38.

26. Channing, *Crisis of Fear*, 50.

27. Kenneth M. Stampp, *America in 1857: A Nation on the Brink* (New York, 1990), 35–36; Genovese, *From Rebellion to Revolution*, 128–29.

28. New Orleans *Picayune*, Jan. 2, 1857, quoted in Stampp, *America in 1857*, 36; Sarah Fitzpatrick, interviewed in 1938, quoted in John W. Blassingame, ed., *Slave Testimony: Two Centuries of Letters, Speeches, Interviews, and Autobiographies* (Baton Rouge, 1977), 640.

29. Mohr, *On the Threshold of Freedom*, 3–40, "mob psychosis" quotation on 35. Donald E. Reynolds, *Editors Make War: Southern Newspapers in the Secession Crisis* (Nashville, 1970), 97–117.

30. Rome and Macon, Georgia, quotations in Mohr, *On the Threshold of Freedom*, 36–37.

31. Solomon Northrup, *Twelve Years a Slave* (1852), quoted in Blassingame, ed., *Slave Testimony*, lxiv.

32. William L. Andrews, *To Tell a Free Story: The First Century of Afro-American Autobiography, 1760–1865* (Urbana, 1986), 172; Frederick Douglass, *My Bondage and My Freedom* (1855; rpt. New York, 1969), 272.

33. Lawrence W. Levine, *Black Culture and Black Consciousness: Afro-American Folk Thought from Slavery to Freedom* (New York, 1977), xi; William H. Seward, "The Irrepressible Conflict," speech in Rochester, New York, Oct. 25, 1858, reprinted in Edwin C. Rozwenc, ed., *The Causes of the American Civil War* (Boston, 1961), 11.

34. Stowe, quoted in Eugene D. Genovese, *Roll Jordan Roll: The World the Slaves Made* (New York, 1972), 249; Albert J. Raboteau, *Slave Religion: The Invisible Institution in the Antebellum South* (New York, 1978), 312.

35. Nathan Irvin Huggins, *Black Odyssey: The African-American Ordeal in Slavery* (1977; rpt. New York, 1990), 182. On slave expectations of emancipation, see Ira Berlin et al., eds., *Freedom: A Documentary History of Emancipation, 1861–1867*, series I, vol. III, *The Wartime Genesis of Free Labor* (New York, 1990), 7–9. Ball quoted in Raboteau, *Slave Religion*, 291. "N.L.J." to William Still, April 16, 1859, in Woodson, ed., *The Mind of the Negro*, 563.

36. Channing, *Crisis of Fear*, 17–57; Mohr, *On the Threshold of Freedom*, 3–67. Frederick Douglass, *The Life and Times of Frederick Douglass* (1881; rpt. New York, 1962), 332.

37. Smith, in *Weekly Anglo-African*, Aug. 24, 1861, in James M. McPherson, ed., *The Negro's Civil War: How American Negroes Felt and Acted During the War for the Union* (New York, 1965), 31; *Douglass Monthly*, May 1861, in Foner, ed., *Life and Writings of Frederick Douglass*, 3:98–99.

Chapter Four. The Political System and the Coming of the Civil War

I have not attempted in these notes to indicate the sources of many of the ideas contained in this essay. The accompanying bibliographical essay reveals more fully the many scholars whose work has influenced my thinking about the origins of the Civil War.

1. Kenneth M. Stampp, "The Irrepressible Conflict," *The Imperiled Union: Essays on the Background of the Civil War* (New York, 1980), 223–31.

2. Thomas B. Alexander, "The Civil War as Institutional Fulfillment," *Journal of Southern History* 47 (Feb. 1981): 3–32, explores some of the Constitution's provisions that exacerbated the sectional conflict. Don E. Fehrenbacher notes, however, that other aspects of the Constitution ignored by Alexander, including a two-house Congress, the three-fifths clause, and the difficulty of adopting an amendment, had the opposite effect. "The New Political History and the Coming of the Civil War," *Pacific Historical Review* 54 (May 1985): 128–29. Fehrenbacher's point is well taken, but I agree with Alexander that on balance the Constitution was an important and often ignored factor in the war's origins.

3. Quoted in Allan Nevins, *The Emergence of Lincoln* (New York, 1950), 2:331. Of course, as Fehrenbacher points out, had it been easier to amend the Constitution, such fears would have been stronger and may have reached a climax even earlier. "New Political History and the Coming of the Civil War," 128–29.

4. Roy P. Basler, ed., Marion Dolores Pratt and Lloyd A. Dunlap, asst. eds., *The Collected Works of Abraham Lincoln*, 9 vols. (New Brunswick, 1953–55), 4:264. Cf. Kenneth M. Stampp, "The Concept of a Perpetual Union," *Journal of American History* 65 (June 1978): 5–33.

5. Lincoln polled 1,839,000 votes in the free states, compared with 1,573,000 for his three opponents. Yet he received 180 of the North's 183 electoral votes. By way of contrast, he won only 26,000 votes (out of 1,300,000 cast) in the slave states.

6. Alexander, "Civil War as Institutional Fulfillment," 22–30, presents a very careful analysis of these points.

7. Quoted in John R. Howe, *The Changing Political Thought of John Adams* (Princeton, 1966), 213.

8. In a different context, Michael F. Holt emphasizes the importance of this feature of nineteenth-century politics in "Some Paradoxes of American Politics in Past Perspective," paper delivered at a conference on American political history at UCLA in May, 1990 (in the author's possession).

9. Edward Everett to Sir Henry Holland, June 25, 1854, Copy, Edward Everett Papers, Massachusetts Historical Society, Boston.

10. Richard Brown, "The Missouri Crisis, Slavery, and the Politics of Jacksonianism," *South Atlantic Quarterly* 65 (1966):55–72.

11. The discussion that follows draws heavily on my book, *The Origins of the Republican Party, 1852–1856* (New York, 1987), where extensive documentation is provided to substantiate these points.

12. Albany *Argus*, Oct. 30, 1855.

13. Don E. Fehrenbacher, "The Republican Decision at Chicago," in Norman Graebner, ed., *Politics and the Crisis of 1860* (Urbana, 1961), 33.

14. The fullest explication of this point is in P. Orman Ray, *The Repeal of the Missouri Compromise* (Cleveland, 1909).

15. J. H. Clay Mudd to Alexander H. Stephens, May 22, 1860, quoted in Nevins, *Emergence of Lincoln*, 2:224n.

16. James M. Banner, "The Problem of South Carolina," in Stanley Elkins and Eric McKitrick, eds., *The Hofstadter Aegis: A Memorial* (New York, 1974), 60–93; William W. Freehling, *The Road to Disunion: Secessionists at Bay, 1776–1854* (New York, 1990), 213–86.

17. Michael F. Holt, *The Political Crisis of the 1850s* (New York, 1978), 230–37.

18. Holt, "Some Paradoxes of American Politics," 21–24.

19. It is worth pointing out that historians who criticize the new political history and insist that the realignment of the 1850s was entirely attributable to the action of party leaders in passing the Kansas-Nebraska Act generally deny that these leaders' subsequent actions had a determinative effect on the outbreak of war. How politicians so quickly lost the power to control public events begs explanation. Moreover, if meaningful politi-

cal alternatives no longer existed, it is difficult to see how these historians can avoid the conclusion that the war was inevitable. In actuality, both political leaders *and* voters played a crucial role in the coming of the war.

20. Had Clay been elected, Texas might still have been annexed but without a fraudulent southern boundary; the war with Mexico would not have occurred; and the Wilmot Proviso would not have been introduced in Congress.

21. The fullest development of this point is in Holt, *Political Crisis of the 1850s*.

22. William J. Cooper, *The South and the Politics of Slavery, 1828–1856* (Baton Rouge, 1978), analyzes this development in southern politics, although unfortunately his treatment is limited to national elections.

23. William E. Gienapp, "The Republican Party and the Slave Power," in Robert Abzug and Stephen E. Maizlish, eds., *New Perspectives on Race and Slavery in America* (Lexington, 1986), 51–78; J. G. de Roulhac Hamilton, "Lincoln's Election an Immediate Menace to Slavery in the States," *American Historical Review* 37 (July 1932): 700–711. A number of historians have stressed Lincoln's moderation and argued that since it was pledged not to interfere with slavery in the states, the Republican party posed no threat to the South. While this characterization of Lincoln is accurate, pronouncements by the radical antislavery wing of the Republican party make it easy to see why Southerners were not reassured.

24. Southern Unionists resorted to similar tactics to defeat secession, particularly in the border states. The Unionist governor of Maryland, for example, refused to call the legislature into session, thus blocking any popular convention, while in Kentucky the legislature declined to authorize a convention, thus denying voters the chance to decide the issue.

25. For the effect of state boundaries on the secession movement, see Alexander, "Civil War as Institutional Fulfillment," 28–29.

Chapter Five. The Divided South

1. The most important published secondary sources for this essay are discussed in the bibliography below. To avoid repetition, these notes will be restricted to sources of quotations, statistics, etc., to occasional comments on primary sources, and to acknowledgment of unpublished insights of fellow historians.

2. A point forcefully made in Seymour Drescher, "The Long Goodby: Dutch Capitalism and Antislavery," forthcoming. I am grateful to Professor Drescher for allowing me to read his unpublished paper.

3. All U.S. demographic statistics in this essay are drawn from *The Statistics of the Population of the United States*, Francis A. Walker, comp.

(Washington, 1872), 11–74, and from U.S. Bureau of the Census, *A Century of Population Growth: From the First Census of the United States to the Twelfth, 1790–1900* (Washington, 1909).

4. For the Brazilian/Cuban figures, see Robert Conrad, *The Destruction of Brazilian Slavery, 1850–1888* (Berkeley, 1972), 283, and Rebecca J. Scott, *Slave Emancipation in Cuba: The Transition to Free Labor, 1860–1899* (Princeton, 1985), 7.

5. David Brion Davis, *Slavery and Human Progress* (New York, 1984), 291.

6. Conrad, *Destruction of Brazilian Slavery*, 301.

7. *The Writings of Thomas Jefferson*, Alfred A. Lipscomb, ed., 20 vols. (Washington, 1903), 2:192.

8. For the only Latin American parallel I know of to this singular and crucial U.S. phenomenon, see Seymour Drescher, "Brazilian Slavery in Comparative Perspective," in *The Abolition of Slavery and the Aftermath of Emancipation in Brazil*, Rebecca J. Scott et al., eds. (Durham, N.C., 1988), 49 n.72.

9. Claudia Dale Golden, "The Economics of Emancipation," *Journal of Economic History* 33 (1973): 70.

10. See Dew's "Review of the Debate in the Virginia Legislature," in *The Pro-slavery Argument* (Philadelphia, 1853), esp. 482–84.

11. I am grateful to David Brion Davis for first suggesting to me the eccentricity of Garrisonian polemics in the perspective of Latin American dialectics. Garrison was most unusual not so much for his doctrine of immediate abolition, which was rarer in Latin America but omnipresent in Brazil in 1880–88, as for his insulting and contemptuous tone about the slaveholders, which few abolitionists south of the border displayed.

12. Some fellow specialists will think I overemphasize Republicans' fear for white men's republicanism. They instead emphasize that a moral outrage about black slavery or an economic lust for free laborers' capitalistic opportunity lay more at the heart of the Republican persuasion. But after reading the massive collection of Republican newspapers and pamphlets in the American Antiquarian Society, I am convinced that those other themes were emphasized less often—and the abolition theme in a very vague way. This is not to deny, however, that economic drives and, less often, humanitarian concern for blacks lent further zeal to a Republican persuasion which needed all the passion it could muster, in order to secure victory in 1860.

The difference between my reading of this evidence and some other scholars' view of these Republican sources, I am convinced, has nothing to do with the amount of time, skill, or care spent reading the documents or with the amount of space devoted to anti-Slavepower rhetoric in the sources. Instead, the differing perceptual lens of the researching historians yields different reading of the evidence. My assumptions about the historical process are perhaps too catholic, for I do not believe that any one factor necessarily causes historical events. I am therefore impressed when one factor, in this case the Slavepower's impact on the republican political process, is emphasized in the Republican sources more often than any other. But were I to believe that economic fears, hopes, or ideologies govern the historical process, I would more emphasize the Republicans' free labor ideology. Similarly, were I to think that the Declaration of Independence relentlessly drove white men toward color-blind egalitarianism, I would more emphasize Republican rhetoric on the moral disaster of enslaving blacks and on the need to secure slavery's ultimate extinction. But since I am convinced that defense of a cherished political system can be as important to the human species as defense of a cherished economic system, and since I consistently find that the acceptance of other multicultural minorities into the white male political system, in keeping with an indisputable implication of the Declaration, was a weaker impulse to antebellum white males than their crasser pursuits, both in Lincoln's era and in Jefferson's, I believe the sources when they emphasize the Slavepower's threat to the white male political system more than slaveholders' threats to white male economic opportunity.

Fellow specialists will see the parallel in my way of reading the proslavery literature. U.S. slaveholders defended *racial* slavery, for blacks only, more often than color-blind slavery, for all lower classes. If I believed that economics always lies at the foundation of worldview, I would more emphasize the theme less emphasized in the sources: the defense of slavery per se, regardless of race. But since I conceive that people's worldviews can be founded on racial identities not less than on class identities, I again am influenced by the predominant theme in the sources, when choosing what to emphasize.

13. Just as I think Abraham Lincoln was looking for ways to build a *National* Republican party early in his presidency, so Michael Holt and Kenneth Stampp think that Lincoln sought to nationalize the Republicans' base of support in 1864–65. See Michael F. Holt, *Political Parties and American Political Development from the Age of Jackson to the Age of Lincoln* (Baton Rouge, 1992), 323–53; Kenneth M. Stampp, *The Era of Reconstruction, 1865–1877* (New York, 1965), 24–49.

Chapter Six. *"Freedom and Law Must Die Ere They Sever"*

1. Bayard Taylor, "To the American People," *Independent*, May 9, 1861.

2. Allan Nevins, *The War for the Union: The Improvised War, 1861–1862* (New York, 1959), 88.

3. Nevins, *The War for the Union: The Improvised War*, 88–90, 171–79; Philadelphia *Daily News*, July 5, 1861.

4. *Independent*, April 18, 1861.

5. Albany *Atlas and Argus*, July 12, 1861.

6. "Ching Foo," Sacramento *Union*, May 28, 1861.

7. Allan Nevins and Milton Halsey Thomas, eds., *The Diary of George Templeton Strong*, 4 vols. (New York, 1952), 3:132.

8. But not all believed the war would be a short one. See Chicago *Tribune*, April 16, 1861; "Ching Foo."

9. "Ching Foo."

10. Thurlow Weed to William Henry Seward, May 4, 1861, Seward Mss., University of Rochester; New York *Herald*, April 21, 1861; see also a similar incident in Milwaukee, *Independent*, May 2, 1861.

11. Thurlow Weed to William H. Seward, July 27, 1861, Seward Mss.; long before that, Central Park and the Battery had turned into vast, crowded military encampments. See *Independent*, May 2, 1861.

12. For the origins of the doctrine of a perpetual Union, see Kenneth M. Stampp, *The Imperiled Union: Essays on the Background of the Civil War* (New York, 1980), 3–36.

13. Robert L. Stanton, *The Church and the Rebellion: A Consideration of the Rebellion Against the Government of the United States* (New York, 1864), 32–33; Speech of Robert J. Walker, New York *Herald*, April 21, 1861; C. Collins to Horatio King, Nov. 25, 1860, Horatio King Mss., Library of Congress (hereafter cited as LC). For fears that disunion would breed dictatorships, see John G. Winter to Andrew Johnson, Feb. 28, 1861, in Leroy P. Graf and Ralph W. Haskins, eds., *The Papers of Andrew Johnson*, vol. 4, *1860–61* (Knoxville, 1976), 346.

14. A. Denny to John Sherman, Jan. 23, 1861, John Sherman Mss., LC.

15. "Ching Foo"; like sentiments appear in Alfred Minus to John Sherman, Jan. 26, 1861, Sherman Mss.; Courtlandt Palmer to Thomas Ewing, Jan. 15, 1861, Ewing Family Mss., LC.

16. Notably, in Bell Irvin Wiley, *The Life of Billy Yank: The Common Soldier of the Union* (Baton Rouge, 1952), 38–44; Reid Mitchell, *Civil War Soldiers* (New York, 1988), 11–18; Kenneth M. Stampp, *And the War Came: The North and the Secession Crisis, 1860–61* (Baton Rouge, 1950), 239–62.

17. Leonard P. Curry, *Blueprint for Modern America: Non-Military Legislation of the First Civil War Congress* (Nashville, 1968); James M. McPherson, *Abraham Lincoln and the Second American Revolution* (New York, 1991), 3–22.

18. For predictions of slavery's injury, if not demise, see *Douglass' Monthly* (May 1861): 450, 451; Jeptha Fowlkes to Andrew Johnson, March 10, 1861, in Graf and Haskins, eds., *Papers of Andrew Johnson*, 4:379; New York *Herald*, April 24, 1861; Thomas Ewing, Jr. to Ellen Ewing, April 21,

1861, Hugh Ewing to Thomas Ewing, Sr., Jan. 9, 1861, Ewing Family Mss.; A. W. Spies to William Henry Seward, Nov. 17, 1861, Seward Mss.

19. See Stampp, *And the War Came*, 123–78; Hyman, *A More Perfect Union*, 40–47; Henry Ward Beecher's sermon in *Independent*, April 18, 1861.

20. On the tradition and justification for compromise, see Peter B. Knupfer, *The Union as It Is: Constitutional Unionism and Sectional Compromise, 1787–1861* (Chapel Hill, 1991). For contemporary expressions of the sacredness of compromise, see George W. Moore to John G. Davis, Jan. 27, 1861, John G. Davis Mss., Indiana Historical Society.

21. Silbey, *A Respectable Minority*, 144–57. Across the North, indeed, Democrats could expect to carry 45 percent of the vote, and, with two exceptions, in no state did they get less than 40 percent on a regular basis.

22. Eric Foner, *Free Soil, Free Labor, Free Men: The Ideology of the Republican Party Before the Civil War* (New York, 1970), 40–102; *Independent*, April 18, 1861.

23. Henry Ward Beecher, *Freedom and War: Discourses on Topics Suggested by the Times* (Boston: Ticknor & Fields, 1863), 126–27; *Independent*, April 18, 1861; speech of Wendell Phillips, in ibid., May 2, 1861; Chicago *Tribune*, April 15, 16, 1861. For Toombs's boast, see, for example, *Douglass' Monthly* (May 1861): 453.

24. *New York Herald*, April 21, 1861; for the original boast, see Chicago *Tribune*, April 19, 1861. Northerners, indeed, came to believe that a separate country had been the traitors' fall-back position. Their original aim was to seize Washington, D.C., and proclaim themselves the true rulers of the United States. See Stanton, *The Church and the Rebellion*, 28–32.

25. Nor was he the only one to dwell on the Hall's new significance. See "J.A.W.," Chicago *Tribune*, April 22, 1861.

26. Philadelphia *Daily News*, July 5, 1861; Sacramento *Union*, July 3, 1861. The legendary role that Washington played is treated with special care in Paul C. Nagel, *One Nation Indivisible: The Union in American Thought, 1776–1861* (New York, 1964), 177–94; indeed, for any study of the contradictions, ambiguities, and varieties in the creed of the Union, Nagel is indispensable.

27. Sacramento *Union*, April 10, 1861.

28. *New York Herald*, April 21, 1861. One might add that when Evarts got the year of the battle of Lexington wrong, that, too, doubtless meant something.

Another perfect example of past speaking to the present might be found in the Baltimore *Clipper*'s contrasts on April 18, 1861: "The Star Spangled Banner is the flag of Washington, Jefferson, Adams, Henry, Lafayette, Pulaski, Gates, Putnam, Jackson, Scott, Decatur, Perry, Clay and Taylor. The Southern banner is the flag of Davis, Rhett, Yancey, Pickens, Twiggs and Toombs. Under which, oh Patriots of Maryland, will ye rally?" See also

Chicago *Tribune*, April 18, 1861; sermon of the Rev. Henry Ward Beecher, "The National Flag," *Independent*, May 2, 1861.

29. From a hymn written by the Reverend Dr. Thompson of the Tabernacle Church at 34th Street in New York for the occasion. New York *Herald*, April 22, 1861. For similar poetry, see "The Great Bell Roland," by Theodore Tilton, *Independent*, April 18, 1861.

30. Nagel, *One Nation Indivisible*, 177–94; Chicago *Tribune*, April 16, 1861; see also John Campbell to Andrew Johnson, June 24, 1861, in Graf and Haskins, eds., *Papers of Andrew Johnson*, 4:508. Let me hasten to add that I am attempting no Oedipal, nor psycho-history of disunion by this argument; both sides, in fact, did their best to get right with the Fathers, rather than replace or kill them–to imitate their example, rather than surpass it. See Mitchell, *Civil War Soldiers*, 20–23.

31. Allan Nevins and Milton Halsey Thomas, eds., *Diary of George Templeton Strong* (New York, 1952), 3:123. Bennett learned his lesson instantly, and with the typical *Herald* excess, hung out *two* flags. See Douglas Fermer, *James Gordon Bennett and the New York Herald: A Study of Editorial Opinion in the Civil War Era, 1854–1867* (New York, 1986), 187–98. For the similar treatment meted out to Philadelphia newspapers, see William Dusinberre, *Civil War Issues in Philadelphia, 1856–1863* (Philadelphia, 1965), 117–18. The Chicago *National Demokrat* received a like fate. See Chicago *Tribune*, April 19, 1861.

32. Nevins and Thomas, eds., *Diary of George Templeton Strong*, 3:124–26; for the height, see *New York Herald*, April 21, 1861.

33. *Independent*, May 2, 1861.

34. *New York Herald*, April 21, 1861; Nevins and Thomas, eds., *Diary of George Templeton Strong*, 3:127.

35. The same was true of Chicago's troops, outfitted by A. D. Titsworth & Co. in spiffy uniforms of "cadet grey." Chicago *Tribune*, April 23, 1861.

36. Chicago *Tribune*, April 19, 1861; Wiley, *Life of Billy Yank*, 28–30; *Independent*, May 2, 1861; Baltimore *Clipper*, May 1, 1861; Albany *Atlas and Argus*, July 12, 1861.

37. *New York Herald*, April 22, 1861.

38. Nevins and Thomas, eds., *Diary of George Templeton Strong*, 3:161–62. The "Star-Spangled Banner," however, was probably the most popular song extant. Within days of the firing on Fort Sumter, it was being republished and sold widely at forty cents per hundred, or three dollars per thousand. *Independent*, May 2, 1861.

39. *New York Herald*, April 21, 1861; for recruiting advertisements, inviting enlistments "for the protection of the Stars and Stripes," see Chicago *Tribune*, April 22, 1861; for other rationales of the same basis, see dispatch from Fulton County, Chicago *Tribune*, April 23, 1861; see also Graf and Haskins, eds., *Papers of Andrew Johnson*, 4:496.

40. *New York Herald*, April 17, 18, 21, 1861. For an identical editorial response, see "Our Country's Flag," Baltimore *Clipper*, April 18, 1861.

41. *New York Herald*, April 21, 1861.

42. Edna Dean Proctor, "The Stripes and the Stars," *Independent*, April 25, 1861. See also Chicago *Tribune*, April 19, 1861.

43. Notably the Rev. Henry Ward Beecher, who, in his sermon to departing soldiers, stressed that the flag had a meaning beyond nationhood. "It is not a painted rag," he told his audience. "It is a whole national history. It is the Constitution. It is the Government." So far, so good, as far as conservatives were concerned. But from there, he went on to its fullest significance: it stood for the highest principle of America, *"Divine right of liberty in man."* And that liberty, he made quite clear, was one from which the nation's banner had been too long estranged, a liberty that knew no place for slavery. Now the war rededicated it, made it a banner worth defending. Wendell Phillips would say much the same at the Music Hall in Boston. See *Independent*, May 2, 1861; also *Douglass' Monthly* (May 1861): 451.

44. Mitchell, *Civil War Soldiers*, 19–20.

45. Frank Freidel, ed., *Union Pamphlets of the Civil War, 1861–1865* (Cambridge, Mass., 1967), 1:86–102.

46. H. D. Brigham to Richard Yates, April 24, 1861; T. H. Cavanaugh to Yates, April 24, 1861, Richard Yates Mss., Illinois State Historical Society, Springfield.

47. D. P. Hyffe to Richard Yates, April 20, 1861, Yates Mss.

48. *New York Herald*, April 24, 1861.

49. George M. Fredrickson, *The Inner Civil War: Northern Intellectuals and the Crisis of the Union* (New York, 1965), 73.

50. Emil and Ruth Rosenblatt, eds., *Hard Marching Every Day: The Civil War Letters of Private Wilbur Fisk, 1861–1865* (Lawrence, 1992), 7, 16.

51. Philadelphia *Daily News*, July 4, 1861.

52. It was also one that even the antislavery Rev. Henry Ward Beecher endorsed in his oration, "The National Flag": "Every color means liberty; every thread means liberty; every form of star and beam or stripe of light means liberty; not lawlessness, not license; but organized, institutional liberty—liberty through Law, and laws for Liberty!" *Independent*, May 2, 1861.

53. "Ching Foo," Sacramento *Union*, Feb. 13, 1861.

54. Anson S. Miller to Elihu Washburne, Dec. 9, 1861, Elihu Washburne Mss., LC; see also Rosenblatt, ed., *Hard Marching Every Day*, 34.

55. John B. McPherson to Edward McPherson, April 17, 1861, Edward McPherson Mss., Library of Congress. John got his wish. By September, he was in the ranks as a quarter-sergeant.

56. George C. Baker to John Sherman, April 16, 1861, Sherman Mss.

57. Samuel E. Browne to John Sherman, April 14, 1861, Sherman Mss.

58. "Ching Foo," Sacramento *Union*, May 28, 1861. It was not enough to save Wood, who lost the mayoralty later that year. See Jerome Mushkat, *Fernando Wood: A Political Biography* (Kent, Ohio, 1990), 116–24.

59. Albany *Atlas and Argus*, July 15, 1861.

60. As, say, with Schuyler Colfax to James A. Cravens, Oct. 7, 1861, James A. Cravens Mss. Indiana Historical Society.

61. Christopher Dell, *Lincoln and the War Democrats: The Grand Erosion of Conservative Tradition* (Rutherford, N.J., 1975), 51–66, 102–23; John Abbott to Richard Yates, June 10, 1861, Yates Mss.

62. John Mankins to John G. Davis, June 28, 1861, Davis Mss. See also Philadelphia *Daily News*, July 4, 1861, for a Republican denunciation of bipartisan sentiments.

63. E. Pickering to Richard Yates, June 10, 1861, Yates Mss.

64. C. S. Pitkin to Richard Yates, June 10, 1861. See also A. W. Cavarly to Yates, June 10, 1861, Yates Mss.

65. J. M. Allen to Richard Yates, June 11, 1861, see also E. Pickering to Yates, June 10, 1861, Yates Mss.

66. C. S. Pitkin to Richard Yates, June 10, 1861, see also R. W. Smith to Yates, June 6, 1861, E. Pickering to Yates, June 10, 1861, Yates Mss.

67. See, for example, John Adair to Joseph Lane, July 19, 1861, Benjamin Stark to Lane, May 19, Aug. 20, 1861, Joseph Lane Mss., Lilly Library, Indiana University; G. Wright to Richard yates, April 25, 1861, S. Hester to Yates, April 23, 1861, T. M. Seawell to Yates, April 23, 1861, Yates Mss.; J. A. Trimble to ——, July 29, 1861, Trimble Mss., Ohio Historical Society.

68. D. A. Farley to John G. Davis, Jan. 16, 1862, Davis Mss.; John Campbell to Andrew Johnson, June 24, 1861, in Graf and Haskins, eds., *Papers of Andrew Johnson*, 4:508; Albany *Atlas and Argus*, July 13, 1861.

69. S. G. Arnold to Manton Marble, April 15, 1861, Manton Marble Mss., LC; Thomas J. Whittemore to Caleb Cushing, Sept. 19, 1861, Caleb Cushing Mss., LC; L. G. Burton and others to John G. Davis, June 21, 1861, James B. Ryan to Davis, Dec. 25, 1861, Davis Mss.

70. See, for example, William S. Holman to Allen Hamilton, Jan. 11, 1861, Allen Hamilton Mss., Indiana Historical Society; James Ferguson to John G. Davis, Feb. 3, 1861, Davis Mss.; J. W. Merriam to Horatio King, April 21, 1861, King Mss.; John A. Trimble to Stephen A. Douglas, Jan. 2, 1861, Trimble Mss.

71. Nathaniel P. Tallmadge to William Henry Seward, Oct. 20, 1861, Seward Mss.; Nevins and Thomas, eds., *Diary of George Templeton Strong*, 3:120–21; New York *Herald*, April 18, 1861; in a similar vein, see Dusinberre, *Civil War Issues in Philadelphia*, 122–23.

72. Raleigh *North Carolina Standard*, Aug. 17, 1868.

73. The resilience of the Democrats is well analyzed in Joel H. Silbey, *A Respectable Minority: The Democratic Party in the Civil War Era, 1860–1868* (New York, 1977), 30–88; the resentments can be found in E. M. Benson to John G. Davis, Jan. 13, 1861, D. A. Farley to Davis, Jan. 15, 1862, G. W. Hughes to Davis, Jan. 29, 1862, Davis Mss.; Frederick Grimke to Alexander S. Boys, April 20, 1861, Alexander S. Boys Mss., Ohio Historical Society.

74. Most notably, Fredrickson, *Inner Civil War*, 130–50, 183–216.

75. Thomas Dwight to Caleb Cushing, Nov. 11, 1861, Cushing Mss.

76. Cincinnati *Commercial*, March 5, 1866.

Chapter Seven. Fort Sumter: At Last the War

1. B. H. Liddell Hart, *Sherman: Soldier, Realist, American* (New York, 1929), 75. See also Wood Gray, *The Hidden Civil War: The Story of the Copperheads* (New York, 1942), 50.

2. *New York Times*, April 16, 1861.

3. S. P. Chase to J. W. Grimes, Jan. 14, 1861, Salmon P. Chase Papers, Historical Society of Pennsylvania, Philadelphia.

4. *New York Times*, April 16, 1861.

5. John Sherman to W. T. Sherman, April 12, 1861, William Tecumseh Sherman Papers, Library of Congress, Washington, D.C.

6. J. H. Thornwell, *The State of Our Country* (Columbia, S.C., 1861), 9, 22–25, 31–32. See also J. H. Thornwell to R. L. Dabney, Nov. 24, 1860, R. L. Dabney Papers, Union Theological Seminary in Virginia, Richmond.

7. Mary Tucker Magill, *Women, or Chronicles of the Late War* (Baltimore, 1871), 5.

8. Henry Clay Fish, *The Valley of Achor a Door of Hope; or, the Grand Issues of the War* (New York, 1863), 10–13.

9. George Leon Walker, *What the Year Has Done for Us. A Sermon Preached . . . November 21, 1861* (Portland, Me., 1861), 6–7.

10. John Sherman to W. T. Sherman, April 14, 1861, Sherman Papers.

11. [John Esten Cooke], "Introductory," 1–16, John Esten Cooke Papers, #38-599-A, Alderman Library, University of Virginia, Charlottesville.

12. John William DeForest, *Miss Ravenel's Conversion from Secession to Loyalty*, Gordon S. Haight, ed. (1867; New York, 1960), 58, 69–70.

13. John Weiss, *Northern Strength and Weakness. An Address . . . April 30, 1863* (Boston, 1863), 12, 15.

14. Frank Moore, comp., *Memorial Ceremonies at the Graves of Our Soldiers* (Washington, D.C., 1869), 371–72.

15. Gertrude Stein, *Four in America* (New Haven, Conn., 1947), 26. Reprinted by permission of Yale University Press.

16. S. B. Buckner to B[eriah] Magoffin, March 8, 1861, Simon Bolivar Buckner Letters, Illinois State Historical Library, Springfield.

17. [James P. Gilmore], *Down in Tennessee, and Back by Way of Richmond* (New York, 1864), 272.

18. H. W. B[ellows] to wife, April 23, 1863, Henry W. Bellows Papers, Massachusetts Historical Society, Boston.

19. Ibid.

20. E. Merton Coulter, *The Confederate States of America: 1861–1865* (Baton Rouge, La., 1950), 5–6.

21. James Dixon to Leonard Bacon, Dec. 26, 1860, Bacon Family Correspondence, Series I, Box 7, Sterling Library, Yale University, New Haven, Connecticut.

22. Oliver P. Temple, *East Tennessee and the Civil War* (1899; Freeport, N.Y., 1971), 134–137.

23. James Dixon to Leonard Bacon, Dec. 12, 1860, Bacon Family Correspondence.

24. Robert Underwood Johnson, *Poems of Fifty Years: 1880–1930* (New York, 1931), 356–361, quoted at 360.

25. Newton D. Baker, "Pacifism," *Field Artillery Journal* 15 (April–June 1925): 159–60. The printed text of the speech erroneously reads "Taurus" for "Aulis."

For Further Reading
A Bibliography

Chapter One. "And the War Came"?
Abraham Lincoln and the Question of Individual Responsibility,
by Gabor S. Boritt

The bibliographical notes for the other chapters of this book thoroughly cover the historical literature on the coming of the Civil War. Especially relevant to Chapter One are the works noted in Chapters Three, on slavery, and Four, on politics. The notes here, therefore, focus only on general historiographical introductions and on Lincoln.

Useful anthologies include Kenneth M. Stampp, ed., *The Causes of the Civil War,* 3rd ed. (1959, 1965; New York, 1991); Norton Garfinkle, ed., *Lincoln and the Coming of the Civil War* (Boston, 1959); Edwin C. Rozwenc, *The Causes of the American Civil War,* 2nd ed. (1961; Lexington, Mass., 1972); third edition by Michael Perman, *The Coming of the American Civil War* (Lexington, Mass., 1993); Rozwenc, *Slavery as a Cause of the Civil War,* 2nd ed. (Boston, 1963); Hans L. Trefousse, *The Causes of the Civil War: Institutional Failure or Human Blunder?* (Hinsdale, Ill., 1971). Garfinkle, Perman, Rozwenc, and Trefousse illustrate the views of historians. Stampp's collection includes both primary documents and a selection of historians' writings. Rozwenc's earlier editions also presented some primary sources.

The only book-length historiographic treatment, going as far as the immediate post-World War II period, came from Thomas J. Pressly: *Americans Interpret Their Civil War* (Princeton, 1954). Briefer looks are in Howard K. Beale, "What Historians Have Said About the Causes of the Civil War," *Social Science Research Council Bulletin* 54 (1946): 55–102; Arthur Schlesinger, Jr., "The Causes of the Civil War: A Note on Historical Sentimentalism," *Partisan Review* 16 (1949): 969–81; and Pieter Geyl, "The American Civil War and the Problem of Inevitability," *New England Quarterly* 24 (1951): 147–68. The three most recent surveys are Eric Foner, "The Causes of the American Civil War: Recent Interpretations and New Directions," in *Politics and Ideology in the Age of the Civil War* (New York, 1980), 15–33; Kenneth M. Stampp, "The Irrepressible Conflict," in *The Imperiled Union: Essays on the Background of the Civil War* (New York, 1980), 191–245; and Don E. Fehrenbacher, "The New Political History and the Coming of the Civil War," in *Lincoln in Text and Context: Collected Essays* (Stanford, Calif., 1987), 72–92. John Niven, *The Coming of the Civil War, 1837–1861* (Arlington Heights, Ill., 1990), 144–73, provides a good bibliographical discussion.

For Lincoln the indispensable source remains Roy P. Basler, ed., Marion Dolores Pratt and Lloyd Dunlap, assistant eds., *The Collected Works of Abraham Lincoln,* 9 vols. (New Brunswick, N.J., 1953–55, and *Supplements,* 1974, 1990). This needs to be complemented with Harold Holzer, ed., *Lincoln-Douglas Debates: The First Complete and Unexpurgated Text* (New York, 1993). The Lincoln of the 1850s is ripe for new scholarship, though some excellent work exists. Most important is Don E. Fehrenbacher, *Prelude to Greatness: Lincoln in the 1850's* (Stanford, 1962). Harry V. Jaffa, *The Crisis of the House Divided: An Interpretation of the Issues in the Lincoln-Douglas Debates* (New York, 1959), and Robert W. Johannsen, *Lincoln, the South, and Slavery: The Political Dimension* (Baton Rouge, 1991), are both thought-provoking. Books still deserving to be consulted include: Albert J. Beveridge, *Abraham Lincoln, 1809–1858,* 2 vols. (Boston, 1928); J. G. Randall, *Lincoln the President,* 4 vols. (New York, 1945–55); and Allan Nevins, *The Emergence of Lincoln,* 2 vols. (New York, 1950).

The charge that Lincoln deliberately provoked the war at Sumter, first made in the Confederate spring of 1861, received a long lease after the war from the writing of the dead republic's former president and vice president. Its most scholarly statement came from Charles W. Ramsdell, "Lincoln and Fort Sumter," *Journal of Southern History* 3 (1937): 259–88, and its longest and most absurd from John S. Tilley, *Lincoln Takes Command* (Chapel Hill, 1941). J. G. Randall's response should have put an end to the matter: "To say that Lincoln meant that the first shot would be fired by the other side *if a first shot was fired,* is by no means the equivalent of saying that he deliberately maneuvered to have the shot fired." "When War Came in 1861," *Abraham Lincoln Quarterly* 1 (1940): 41; see also Randall's "Lincoln's Sumter Dilemma," in *Lincoln the Liberal Statesman* (New York, 1947). However, popular fascination with intrigue and conspiracy, and the pedagogical value of discussing the issue, continue the circulation of the false charges. See for example Eugene H. Berwanger, *The Civil War Era: Historical Viewpoints* (Fort Worth, 1994), 70–84.

The politics of the road to secession and war are ably analyzed in the following books: David Potter, *Lincoln and His Party in the Secession Crisis* (1942, but use the forthcoming Baton Rouge, 1995, ed.); Kenneth M. Stampp, *And the War Came: The North in the Secession Crisis, 1860–61* (Baton Rouge, 1950); Richard N. Current, *The Lincoln Nobody Knows* (New York, 1958), 104–130; and *Lincoln and the First Shot* (Philadelphia, 1963). See also Potter, "Why the Republicans Rejected Both Compromise and Secession," and Stampp's "Comment" on the above in George Harmon Knoles, ed., *The Crisis of the Union, 1861–1865* (Baton Rouge, 1965), 90–113; Stampp, "Lincoln and the Secession Crisis," in *The Imperiled Union: Essays on the Background of the Civil War* (New York, 1980), 163–88; and Current, "Who Started the War, Abraham Lincoln or Jefferson Davis?" in *Arguing With Historians: Essays on the Historical and the Unhistorical* (Middletown, CT, 1988), 31–51. John Niven, *Gideon*

Welles: Linclon's Secretary of Navy (New York, 1973), and Daniel W. Crofts, *Reluctant Confederates: Upper South Unionists in the Secession Crisis* (Chapel Hill, 1989), title notwithstanding, shed important light on Lincoln.

I think there is broad agreement among historians that David Potter and Don E. Fehrenbacher, *The Impending Crisis, 1848–1861* (New York, 1976), which pays ample attention to Lincoln, is the best work on the coming of the Civil War.

By the time this book appears, the standard popular biography of Lincoln will be David Herbert Donald, *Lincoln* (New York, 1995). The best brief overview is Mark E. Neely, Jr., *The Last Best Hope of Earth: Abraham Lincoln and the Promise of America* (Cambridge, Mass., 1993). William Hanchett, *Out of the Wilderness: The Life of Abraham Lincoln* (Urbana, Ill., 1994) is a quick introduction for beginners.

Chapter Two. "Little Women" Who Helped Make This Great War, by Glenna Matthews

Standard works on antebellum women or on women and reform include the following. On Southern women consult Anne Firor Scott, *The Southern Lady: From Pedestal to Politics, 1830–1930* (Chicago, 1970), and Catherine Clinton, *The Plantation Mistress: Woman's World in the Old South* (New York, 1982). On abolitionist women consult Eleanor Flexner, *Century of Struggle: The Woman's Rights Movement in the United States* (Cambridge, 1959); Louis Filler, *The Crusade Against Slavery, 1830–1860* (New York, 1960); Aileen S. Kraditor, *Means and Ends in American Abolitionism: Garrison and His Critics on Strategy and Tactics, 1834–1850* (New York, 1969); and Blanche Glassman Hersh, *The Slavery of Sex: Feminist-Abolitionists in America* (Urbana, 1978).

Written within the last ten years or so have been these works. On the South, see Elizabeth Fox-Genovese, *Within the Plantation Household: Black and White Women of the Old South* (Chapel Hill, 1988). See also Victoria E. Bynum, *Unruly Women: The politics of Social and Sexual Control in the Old South* (Chapel Hill: University of North Carolina Press, 1992); Jean Friedman, *The Enclosed Garden: Women and Community in the Evangelical South, 1830–1900* (Chapel Hill: University of North Carolina Press, 1985); and Jane H. Pease and William H. Pease, *Ladies, Women, and Wenches: Choice and Constraint in Antebellum Charleston and Boston* (Chapel Hill, 1990). For reform see Nancy Hewitt, *Women's Activism and Social Change, Rochester, New York, 1822–1872* (Ithaca, 1984); Lori D. Ginzberg, *Women and the Work of Benevolence: Morality, Politics, and Class in the Nineteenth-Century United States* (New Haven, 1990); Wendy Hamand Venet, *Neither Ballots nor Bullets: Women Abolitionists and the Civil War* (Charlottesville, 1991); and Shirley J. Yee, *Black Women Abolitionists: A Study in Activism, 1828–1860* (Knoxville, 1992). Jean Fagan Yellin's *Women and Sisters: The Antislavery*

Activists in American Culture (New Haven, 1989) is an interdisciplinary study of iconography.

A pioneering article dealing with antebellum women's political culture was Paula Baker's "The Domestication of Politics: Women and American Political Society, 1780–1920," *American Historical Review* 89 (June 1984): 620–47. See also Suzanne Lebsock, *The Free Women of Petersburg: Status and Culture in a Southern Town, 1784–1860* (New York, 1984), and Glenna Matthews, *The Rise of Public Woman: Woman's Power and Woman's Place in the United States, 1630–1970* (New York, 1992). On women's voluntarism see Anne Firor Scott, *Natural Allies: Women's Associations in American History* (Urbana, 1991). On women in public life see Mary P. Ryan, *Women in Public: Between Banners and Ballots, 1825–1880* (Baltimore, 1990).

An important category of books dealing with women and the coming of the Civil War consists of biographies of individual reformers. A classic study is Gerda Lerner's *The Grimké Sisters from South Carolina: Pioneers for Woman's Rights and Abolition* (New York, 1971). Newer works include Celia Morris, *Fanny Wright: Rebel in America* (Urbana, 1992); Elizabeth Cazden, *Antoinette Brown Blackwell: A Biography* (Old Westbury, 1983); Deborah Pickman Clifford, *Crusader for Freedom: A Life of Lydia Maria Child* (Boston, 1992); Dorothy Sterling, *Ahead of Her Time: Abby Kelley and the Politics of Antislavery* (New York, 1991); Joan Hedrick, *Harriet Beecher Stowe: A Life* (New York, 1994); and Carolyn Karcher, *The First Woman in the Republic: A Cultural Biography of Lydia Maria Child* (Durham, N.C., 1995). Three biographies of Sojourner Truth are in the works, two by the historians Nell Painter and Margaret Washington.

There is now a rich body of work on women's literary culture in the nineteenth century. The major works include the following. See Nina Baym, *Woman's Fiction: A Guide to Novels by and about Women in America, 1820–1870* (Ithaca, 1978); Mary Kelley, *Private Woman, Public Stage: Literary Domesticity in Nineteenth-Century America* (New York, 1984); Glenna Matthews, *"Just a Housewife": The Rise and Fall of Domesticity in America* (New York, 1987); Jeanne Boydston, Mary Kelley, and Anne Margolis, *The Limits of Sisterhood: The Beecher Sisters on Women's Rights and Woman's Sphere* (Chapel Hill, 1988); Hazel Carby, *Reconstructing Womanhood: The Emergence of the Afro-American Woman Novelist* (New York, 1987); Jane Tompkins, *Sensational Designs: The Cultural Work of American Fiction, 1790–1860* (New York, 1985); and Elizabeth Moss, *Domestic Novelists in the Old South: Defenders of Southern Culture* (Baton Rouge, 1992). See also Deborah E. McDowell and Arnold Rampersad, eds., *Slavery and the Literary Imagination* (Baltimore, 1989).

There is now beginning to be a social history of the Civil War. See Maris Vinovskis, ed., *Toward a Social History of the American Civil War: Exploratory Essays* (Cambridge, 1990); George C. Rable, *Civil Wars: Women and the Crisis of Southern Nationalism* (Urbana, 1989); Catherine Clinton and Nina Silber, eds., *Divided Houses: Gender and the Civil War* (New York, 1992); Anne C. Rose, *Victorian America and the Civil War* (Cambridge, 1992); and Reid Mitchell, *The Vacant Chair: The Northern Soldier Leaves Home* (New York, 1993).

Chapter Three. They Knew What Time It Was: African-Americans and the Coming of the Civil War, by David W. Blight

Numerous published collections of primary sources contain a great depth of material on the African-American experience and the coming of the Civil War. The largest collections of documents are C. Peter Ripley et al., eds., *The Black Abolitionist Papers*, 5 vols. (Chapel Hill, 1985–92), and Ira Berlin et al., eds., *Freedom: A Documentary History of Emancipation, 1861–67*, 4 vols. to date (New York, 1982–). Frederick Douglass's writings have been collected and annotated in John W. Blassingame et al., eds., *The Frederick Douglass Papers*, 4 vols. to date (New Haven, 1979–), and Philip S. Foner, ed., *The Life and Writings of Frederick Douglass*, 5 vols. (New York, 1950–75). Carter G. Woodson pioneered the early collection of black abolitionist documents in his *Negro Orators and Their Orations* (New York, 1925) and *The Mind of the Negro as Reflected in Letters Written During the Crisis, 1800–1860* (New York, 1925, 1926). The most extensive collection of interviews with ex-slaves is George Rawick, ed., *The American Slave: A Composite Autobiography*, 41 vols. (Westport, Conn., 1972–79). The Rawick collection has a useful guide in Donald M. Jacobs, ed., *Index to "The American Slave"* (Westport, Conn., 1981). Other collections of significant value are Charles L. Perdue, Jr., Thomas E. Barden, and Robert K. Phillips, eds., *Weevils in the Wheat: Interviews with Virginia Ex-Slaves* (Bloomington, 1980); Howard H. Bell, ed., *Minutes of the Proceedings of the National Negro Conventions, 1830–1864* (New York, 1969); John W. Blassingame, ed., *Slave Testimony: Two Centuries of Letters, Speeches, Interviews, and Autobiographies* (Baton Rouge, 1977); James M. McPherson, ed., *The Negro's Civil War: How American Negroes Felt and Acted During the War for the Union* (New York, 1965); and Dorothy Sterling, ed., *We Are Your Sisters: Black Women in the Nineteenth Century* (New York, 1985).

Many editions of slave narratives and other antebellum free black autobiographies are currently in print, including the landmark works of Frederick Douglass and Harriet Jacobs. For recent editions that place these narratives within their historical context of the 1840s and 1850s, see David W. Blight, ed., *Narrative of the Life of Frederick Douglass, an American Slave* (1845; rpt. Boston, 1993); and Jean Fagan Yellin, ed., *Incidents in the Life of a Slave Girl, Written by Herself* (1860; rpt. Cambridge, Mass., 1987). Among many works on the slave narratives in literary studies, two of the most useful are William L. Andrews, *To Tell a Free Story: The First Century of Afro-American Autobiography, 1760–1865* (Urbana, 1986), and Charles T. Davis and Henry Louis Gates, Jr., eds., *The Slave's Narrative* (New York,

1985). A valuable work on all forms of black writing in the nineteenth century is Vernon Loggins, *The Negro Author: His Development in America to 1900* (Port Washington, N.Y., 1931). Any consideration of black abolitionism should include a reading of David Walker, *Appeal to the Coloured Citizens of the World, But in Particular, and Very Expressly, to Those of The United States of America,* Charles M. Wiltse, ed. (1829; rpt. New York, 1965), and of the works included in Sterling Stuckey, ed., *The Ideological Origins of Black Nationalism* (Boston, 1972).

Black abolitionism is still best surveyed in Benjamin Quarles, *Black Abolitionists* (New York, 1969). An excellent overview of the stages in the development of black abolitionism, as well as the impact of the self-improvement formula, is in C. Peter Ripley et al., eds., *The Black Abolitionist Papers,* 3:3–69. The most thorough treatments of antebellum black communities and leadership strategies are Jane H. Pease and William H. Pease, *They Who Would Be Free: Blacks' Search for Freedom, 1830–61* (New York, 1974), and Leon F. Litwack, *North of Slavery: The Negro in the Free States, 1790–1860* (Chicago, 1961). On the free black experience generally, see the essays in James Oliver Horton, *Free People of Color: Inside the African American Community* (Washington, D.C., 1993). On antebellum black urban life, see James Oliver Horton and Lois E. Horton, *Black Bostonians: Family Life and Community Struggle in the Antebellum North* (New York, 1979); Leonard P. Curry, *The Free Black in Urban America, 1800–1850: The Shadow of a Dream* (Chicago, 1981); and Julie Winch, *Philadelphia's Black Elite: Activism, Accommodation, and the Struggle for Autonomy, 1787–1848* (Philadelphia, 1988). The lives of several black abolitionists are illuminated in the international context in which many worked in R. J. M. Blackett, *Beating Against the Barriers: Biographical Essays in Nineteenth Century Afro-American History* (Baton Rouge, 1986). On the careers of some nine pre–Civil War leaders, see Leon F. Litwack and August Meier, eds., *Black Leaders of the Nineteenth Century* (Urbana, 1988). The role of black women in the abolition movement is developed in Shirley J. Yee, *Black Women Abolitionists: A Study in Activism, 1828–1860* (Knoxville, 1992). The theme of black independence in the antislavery movement is analyzed in Sterling Stuckey, *Slave Culture: Nationalist Theory and the Foundation of Black America* (New York, 1987). Black emigration before the Civil War is thoroughly examined in Floyd J. Miller, *The Search for a Black Nationality: Black Emigration and Colonization* (Urbana, 1975). Among many useful surveys of the antislavery movement is James B. Stewart, *Holy Warriors: The Abolitionists and American Slavery* (New York, 1976). On the Fugitive Slave Act and resistance to it, see Stanley W. Campbell, *The Slave Catchers: Enforcement of the Fugitive Slave Law, 1850–1860* (Chapel Hill, 1968), and Thomas P. Slaughter, *Bloody Dawn: The Christiana Riot and Racial Violence in the Antebellum North* (New York, 1991). The most important works on antislavery politics, and on the antislavery interpretation of the Constitution, are Eric Foner, *Free Soil, Free Labor, Free Men: The Ideology of the Republican Party Before the Civil War* (New York, 1970); Richard H. Sewell, *Ballots for Freedom: Antislavery Politics in the United States, 1837–1861* (New York, 1976); and William E. Gienapp, *The Origins of the Republican Party, 1852–1856* (New York, 1987).

The most useful guide into the massive literature on slavery is Peter J. Parrish, *Slavery: History and the Historians* (New York, 1989). A good single-volume, interpretive history of slavery is Peter Kolchin, *American Slavery, 1619–1877* (New York, 1993). The theme of cultural resistance and expectation among slaves, especially in their religion and folk life, is well developed in Eugene D. Genovese, *Roll, Jordan, Roll: The World the Slaves Made* (New York, 1974); Albert J. Raboteau, *Slave Religion: The Invisible Institution in the Antebellum South* (New York, 1978); Lawrence W. Levine, *Black Culture and Black Consciousness: Afro-American Folk Thought from Slavery to Freedom* (New York, 1977); John W. Blassingame, *The Slave Community: Plantation Life in the Antebellum South* (1971; rev. ed., New York, 1979); and Charles Joyner, *Down by the Riverside: A South Carolina Slave Community* (Urbana, 1984). Nathan I. Huggins, *Black Odyssey: The African-American Ordeal in Slavery* (1977; rpt. New York, 1990), is an imaginative treatment of the entire experience of slaves from West African origins to the Civil War. Two important essays that augment as well as counter the cultural resistance school of slavery historiography are Ira Berlin, "Time, Space and the Evolution of Afro-American Society on British Mainland North America," *American Historical Review* 85 (1980): 44–78, and Peter Kolchin, "Reevaluating the Antebellum Slave Community: A Comparative Perspective," *Journal of American History* 70 (1983): 579–601. A good example of growing literature on the social history of emancipation, covering the questions of insurrection panics and black expectations on the eve of the war, is Clarence L. Mohr, *On the Threshold of Freedom: Masters and Slaves in Civil War Georgia* (Athens, Ga., 1986), and Lynda Morgan, *Emancipation in Virginia's Tobacco Belt, 1850–1870* (Athens, Ga., 1992). Benjamin Quarles, *Allies for Freedom: Blacks and John Brown* (New York, 1974), covers African-American associations and the Harper's Ferry raid.

Among general works about race, slavery, black leadership, and the Civil War era, the most important are W. E. B. DuBois, *Black Reconstruction in America, 1860–1880* (New York, 1935); Benjamin Quarles, *The Negro in the Civil War* (Boston, 1953); James M. McPherson, *The Struggle for Equality: Abolitionists and the Negro in the Civil War and Reconstruction* (Princeton, 1964); Wilson J. Moses, *The Golden Age of Black Nationalism,* (Hamden, Conn., 1978); Leon F. Litwack, *Been in the Storm So Long: The Aftermath of Slavery* (New York, 1979); David Brion Davis, *Slavery and Human Progress* (New York, 1984); and David W. Blight, *Frederick Douglass' Civil War: Keeping*

Faith in Jubilee (Baton Rouge, 1989). Among recent general works on the coming of the Civil War that treat the black experience extensively is Bruce Levine, *Half Slave, Half Free: The Roots of the Civil War* (New York, 1992).

Chapter Four. The Crisis of American Democracy: The Political System and the Coming of the War, by William E. Gienapp

The literature on the coming of the Civil War is vast and complex. The broad general historiography is surveyed in the notes to Chapter One. For this chapter two important recent surveys of interpretations of the war's origins are Kenneth M. Stampp, "The Irrepressible Conflict," in *The Imperiled Union: Essays on the Background of the Civil War* (New York, 1980), 191–245, and Eric Foner, "The Causes of the American Civil War: Recent Interpretations and New Directions," in *Politics and Ideology in the Age of the Civil War* (New York, 1980), 15–33. A useful discussion with many historiographic references is John Niven, *The Coming of the Civil War, 1837–1861* (Arlington Heights, Ill., 1990). The fullest historiographic treatment can be found in Thomas J. Pressly, *Americans Interpret Their Civil War* (Princeton, 1954), which unfortunately is now badly out of date.

Thomas B. Alexander, "The Civil War as Institutional Fulfillment," *Journal of Southern History* 47 (Feb. 1981): 3–32, presents an imaginative and stimulating discussion of political institutions and the war's origins. Other treatments of this theme are offered by Roy F. Nichols, *The Disruption of American Democracy* (New York, 1948); David Donald, "An Excess of Democracy: The American Civil War and the Social Process," in *Lincoln Reconsidered: Essays on the Civil War Era*, 2nd ed. (New York, 1961), 209–35; and Lee Benson, *Toward the Scientific Study of History: Selected Essays* (Philadelphia, 1972), 225–340. In an unpublished paper, "Some Paradoxes of American Politics in Past Perspective" (1990), Michael F. Holt calls attention to additional relevant points in a different context. Don E. Fehrenbacher notes certain qualifications concerning Alexander's argument in "The New Political History and the Coming of the Civil War," *Pacific Historical Review* 54 (May 1985): 117–42. While not concerned with the origins of the Civil War, Joel H. Silbey's excellent *The American Political Nation, 1838–1893* (Stanford, 1991) provides a thorough and useful discussion of the parameters of the nineteenth-century political system. Also see his useful *The Partisan Imperative: The Dynamics of American Politics Before the Civil War* (New York, 1985), which more explicitly examines antebellum political culture and the war's origins. For a discussion of the growing partisan focus on the presidency and its impact on electoral procedures, see Richard P. McCormick, *The Presidential Game: The Origins of American Presidential Politics* (New York, 1982). Kenneth M. Stampp analyzes the Constitution's fundamental ambiguity concerning secession in "The Concept of a Perpetual Union," *Journal of American History* 65 (June 1978): 5–33.

The fullest discussion of the sectional conflicts is Allan Nevins, *Ordeal of the Union*, 2 vols. (New York, 1947), and *The Emergence of Lincoln*, 2 vols. (New York, 1950). Nevins's account is gracefully written, but it is melodramatic and contradictory in its interpretation. The best analysis of this period is David M. Potter's *The Impending Crisis, 1848–1861* (New York, 1976), which demonstrates the author's deep understanding of the subject. Good shorter treatments can be found in James M. McPherson, *Ordeal by Fire: The Civil War and Reconstruction* (New York, 1982), and Richard H. Sewell, *A House Divided: Sectionalism and Civil War, 1848–1865* (Baltimore, 1988).

The best survey of politics in the 1840s is William R. Brock, *Parties and Political Conscience: American Dilemmas, 1840–1850* (1979). For American expansionism and its impact on the party system, see Frederick Merk, *Manifest Destiny and Mission in American History* (New York, 1963); Robert J. Morgan, *Whig Embattled: The Presidency under John Tyler* (Lincoln, Nebr., 1954); James C. N. Paul, *Rift in the Democracy* (Philadelphia, 1961); Frederick Merk, *Slavery and the Annexation of Texas* (New York, 1972); and Charles Sellers, *James K. Polk, Continentalist, 1843–1846* (Princeton, 1966). The controversy over the Wilmot Proviso is detailed in Chaplain Morrison, *Democratic Politics and Sectionalism: The Wilmot Proviso Controversy* (Chapel Hill, 1967). Holman Hamilton, *Prologue to Conflict: The Crisis and Compromise of 1850* (Lexington, 1964), is excellent on the last great sectional compromise. Potter's *Impending Crisis* has a supurb chapter on the Compromise of 1850 as well.

The fullest history of Southern politics in this period is William W. Freehling, *The Road to Disunion: Secessionists at Bay, 1776–1854* (New York, 1990). Also important, though unfortunately limited only to national elections, is William J. Cooper, *The South and the Politics of Slavery, 1828–1856* (Baton Rouge, 1978). For John C. Calhoun's career, see John Niven, *John C. Calhoun and the Price of Union* (Baton Rouge, 1988), and Gerald M. Capers, *John C. Calhoun, Opportunist: A Reappraisal* (Gainesville, Fla., 1960). Good discussions of the depth of Calhoun's alienation from the new democratic political system are William W. Freehling, "Spoilsmen and Interests in the Thought of John C. Calhoun," *Journal of American History* 52 (1965): 25–42, and J. William Harris, "Last of the Classical Republicans: An Interpretation of John C. Calhoun," *Civil War History* 30 (1984): 255–67. Ernest M. Lander, Jr., *Reluctant Imperialists: Calhoun, the South Carolinians, and the Mexican War* (Baton Rouge, 1980), and Robert Barnwell, *Love of Order: South Carolina's First Secession Crisis* (Chapel Hill, 1982), analyze the erratic political course of Calhoun and South Carolina leaders in this decade.

The party realignment of the 1850s is discussed in numerous histories of the sectional conflict. Particularly stimulating on this and many other topics is Michael F. Holt, *The Political Crisis of the 1850s* (New York, 1978). The fullest analysis appears in William E. Gienapp, *The Origins of the*

Republican Party, 1852–1856 (New York, 1987). There are striking insights scattered throughout the essays in Michael F. Holt, *Political Parties and American Political Development from the Age of Jackson to the Age of Lincoln* (Baton Rouge, 1992). Robert W. Fogel, *Without Consent of Contract: The Rise and Fall of American Slavery* (New York, 1989), 281–337, offers another analysis with particular attention to economic issues. For theoretical discussions of the process of party realignment in American history, see Walter Dean Burnham, *Critical Elections and the Mainsprings of American Politics* (New York, 1970); James L. Sundquist, *Dynamics of the Party System: Alignment and Realignment of Political Parties in the United States,* rev. ed. (Washington, 1983); and Jerome M. Clubb, William H. Flanigan, and Nancy H. Zingale, *Partisan Realignment: Voters, Parties, and Government in American History* (Beverly Hills, 1980). Paul Kleppner examines long-term voting patterns in *The Third Electoral System, 1853–1892: Parties, Voters, and Political Cultures* (Chapel Hill, 1979).

Richard H. Sewell ably discusses the Liberty and Free Soil parties in *Ballots for Freedom: Antislavery Politics in the United States, 1837–1860* (New York, 1976), 43–253. Also useful are Vernon L. Volpe, *Forlorn Hope of Freedom: The Liberty Party in the Old Northwest, 1838–1848* (Kent, 1990), and Frederick Blue, *The Free Soilers: Third Party Politics, 1848–54* (Urbana, 1973). For the drafting and passage of the Kansas-Nebraska Act, see Roy F. Nichols, "The Kansas-Nebraska Act: A Century of Historiography," *Mississippi Valley Historical Review* 43 (Sept. 1956): 187–212; Potter, *Impending Crisis,* 145–76; and Robert W. Johannsen, *Stephen A. Douglas* (New York, 1973), 401–34. Larry Gara, *The Presidency of Franklin Pierce* (Lawrence, 1991), succinctly covers Pierce's ill-fated term in office. Holt's *Political Crisis of the 1850s* contains the best analysis of the Know Nothing party. Tyler Anbinder, *Nativism and Slavery: The Northern Know Nothings and the Politics of the 1850's* (New York, 1992), distorts fundamentally the nature of this crucial party and is of little value.

The most successful third party, of course, was the Republican party. The most extensive coverage of the party's early history is presented in my *Origins of the Republican Party.* Differing views of the ideology of the Republican party are advanced in Eric Foner, *Free Soil, Free Labor, Free Men: The Ideology of the Republican Party Before the Civil War* (New York, 1970); Eugene H. Berwanger, *The Frontier Against Slavery: Western Anti-Negro Prejudice and the Slave Extension Controversy* (Urbana, 1967); William E. Gienapp, "The Republican Party and the Slave Power," Robert Abzug and Stephen E. Maizlish, eds., *New Perspectives on Race and Slavery in America* (Lexington, 1986), 51–78; and Holt, *Political Crisis of the 1850s.* The best study of affairs in Kansas, which were so critical to the Republican party's success, is James A. Rawley, *Race and Politics: "Bleeding Kansas" and the Coming of the Civil War* (Philadelphia, 1969). Richard J. Carwardine, *Evangelicals and Politics in*

Antebellum America (New York, 1993), ably treats a strangely neglected topic and greatly adds to our understanding of the early Republican party.

The events of 1857 and their catastrophic impact on the party system are skillfully recounted in Kenneth M. Stampp, *America in 1857: A Nation on the Brink* (New York, 1990). Specialized treatments can be found in Don E. Fehrenbacher, *The Dred Scott Case: Its Significance in Law and Politics* (New York, 1978); James L. Huston, *The Panic of 1857 and the Coming of the Civil War* (Baton Rouge, 1987); and Richard Carwardine, "The Religious Revival of 1857-8 in the United States," *Studies in Church History* 15 (1978): 393-406. The best histories of the Lecompton struggle are Nichols, *Disruption of American Democracy*, 104-225, and Stampp, *America in 1857*, 144-81, 266-332. Don E. Fehrenbacher offers a sure-handed analysis in *The South and Three Sectional Crises* (Baton Rouge, 1980), 45-65. For John Brown's troubled life and the impact of his raid on Harpers Ferry, see Stephen B. Oates, *To Purge This Land with Blood: A Biography of John Brown* (New York, 1970), a good but somewhat apologetic account. For an overview of Buchanan's fateful four years in the White House, see Elbert B. Smith, *The Presidency of James Buchanan* (Lawrence, 1975). The qualities of Buchanan's leadership are analyzed in William E. Gienapp, " 'No Bed of Roses': James Buchanan, Abraham Lincoln, and Political Leadership in the Civil War Era," in Michael J. Birkner, ed., *James Buchanan and the Political Crisis of the 1850s* (forthcoming). Mark Summers places Buchanan's sorry record on corruption in a larger context in *The Plundering Generation: Corruption and the Crisis of the Union, 1849-1861* (New York, 1987).

For the development of the Republicans' electoral majority in the North, see William E. Gienapp, "Nativism and the Creation of a Republican Majority in the North Before the Civil War," *Journal of American History* 72 (Dec. 1985): 529-59, and Gienapp, "Who Voted for Lincoln?," in John L. Thomas, ed., *Abraham Lincoln and the American Political Tradition* (Amherst, 1986), 50-97.

Southern politics in this decade have not received as much attention as the subject warrants, but two good overviews are Freehling, *Road to Disunion*, and Cooper, *Politics of Slavery*. Also see Cooper's *Liberty and Power: Southern Politics to 1860* (New York, 1983). When completed, Freehling's wide-ranging study will be the fullest account we have of Southern politics from the beginning of the democratic revolution to secession. James M. Banner, "The Problem of South Carolina," in Stanley Elkins and Eric McKitrick, eds., *The Hofstadter Aegis: A Memorial* (New York, 1974), 60-93, analyzes the unique political experience of that state. Southern nationalism is elegantly covered in John McCardell, *The Idea of a Southern Nation: Southern Nationalists and Southern Nationalism, 1830-1860* (New York, 1979). Eric Walther, *The Fire-Eaters* (Baton Rouge, 1992), offers biographical sketches of some leading Southern radicals but inadequately addresses the difficult question of their influence in making secession a reality. For the secession movement in various states, see William L. Barney, *The Secessionist Impulse: Alabama and Mississippi in 1860* (Princeton, 1974); Lacy J. Ford, Jr., *Origins of Southern Radicalism: The South Carolina Upcountry, 1800–1860* (New York, 1988); J. Mills Thornton III, *Politics and Power in a Slave Society: Alabama, 1800–1860* (Baton Rouge, 1978); Stephen Channing, *Crisis of Fear: Secession in South Carolina* (New York, 1974); Marc W. Kruman, *Parties and Politics in North Carolina, 1836–1865* (Baton Rouge, 1983); and Daniel W. Crofts, *Reluctant Confederates: Upper South Unionists in the Secession Crisis* (Chapel Hill, 1989).

The best analysis of Northern opinion during the secession crisis is Kenneth M. Stampp, *And the War Came: The North and the Secession Crisis, 1860–1861* (Baton Rouge, 1950). One should also see David M. Potter, *Lincoln and His Party in the Secession Crisis* (New Haven, 1942). In *Lincoln and the First Shot* (Philadelphia, 1963), Richard Current offers a sound analysis of the beginning of the war that discusses the decisions and actions of both governments in this final crisis.

Chapter Five. The Divided South, Democracy's Limitations, and the Causes of the Peculiarly North American Civil War, by William W. Freehling

The best overall comparative treatments of emancipation in the Americas are David Brion Davis, *Slavery and Human Progress* (New York, 1984), and C. Duncan Rice, *The Rise and Fall of Black Slavery* (New York, 1975). Seymour Drescher, "Brazilian Abolition in Comparative Perspective," in *The Abolition of Slavery and the Aftermath of Emancipation in Brazil*, Rebecca J. Scott et al., eds. (Durham, N.C., 1988), is a particularly suggestive essay. Other useful accounts of Brazilian emancipation include Robert E. Conrad, *The Destruction of Brazilian Slavery, 1850–1888* (Berkeley, 1972), best on the early phase of free-womb emancipation; Robert Brent Toplin, *The Abolition of Slavery in Brazil* (New York, 1972), best on the later phase of immediatist emancipation; and Carl Degler, *Neither Black nor White: Slavery and Race Relations in Brazil and the United States* (Madison, Wis., 1986), best on racial/sexual differences between the two countries but weaker on democratic/political differences. Fine localistic studies of Brazilian slavery and its collapse include Stuart B. Schwartz, *Sugar Plantations in the Formation of Brazilian Society: Bahia, 1550–1835* (Cambridge, Eng., 1985); Mary C. Karasch, *Slave Life in Rio de Janeiro, 1808–1850* (Princeton, 1987); and Stanley Stein, *Vassouras: A Brazilian Coffee Country, 1850–1900: The Roles of Planter and Slaves in a Plantation Society* (Princeton, 1985).

For studies of emancipation in Cuba, second in importance only to Brazil for U.S. comparisons, the excellent literature includes Rebecca J. Scott, *Slave Emancipation in Cuba: The Transition to Free Labor, 1860–1899*

(Princeton, 1985); Franklin W. Knight, *Slave Society in Cuba During the Nineteenth Century* (Madison, Wis., 1970); Arthur F. Corwin, *Spain and the Abolition of Slavery in Cuba, 1817–1886* (Austin, Tex., 1967); and Robert L. Paquette, *Sugar Is Made with Blood: The Conspiracy of LaEscalera and the Conflict Between Empires over Slavery in Cuba* (Middletown, Conn., 1988). Among the helpful books on other Latin American countries are Peter Blanchard, *Slavery and Abolition in Early Republican Peru* (Wilmington, Del., 1992); C. L. R. James, *The Black Jacobins: Touissant L'Overture and the San Domingo Revolution* (New York, 1963); John V. Lombardi, *The Decline and Abolition of Negro Slavery in Venezuela, 1820–1854* (Westport, Conn., 1971); and Francisco A. Scarano, *Sugar and Slavery in Puerto Rico: The Plantation Economy of Ponce, 1800–1850* (Madison, Wis., 1984).

This essay is being published more or less simultaneously in William W. Freehling, *The Reintegration of American History: Slavery and the Civil War* (New York, 1994), where several other essays expand on the themes here presented. The latest survey of Slave South politics is William W. Freehling, *The Road to Disunion*, vol. 1, *Secessionists at Bay, 1776–1854* (New York, 1990). The latest and best books on post-nati emancipation in the North include Gary B. Nash and Jean Soderlund, *Freedom by Degrees: Emancipation in Pennsylvania and Its Aftermath* (New York, 1991), and Shane White, *Somewhat More Independent: The End of Slavery in New York City, 1770–1810* (Athens, Ga., 1991). The best book on the erosion of slavery in the Border South is Barbara J. Fields, *Slavery and Freedom on the Middle Ground: Maryland During the Nineteenth Century* (New Haven, Conn., 1985). The best book on Thomas Jefferson Randolph and the Virginia Antislavery Debate is Alison Goodyear Freehling, *Drift Toward Dissolution: The Virginia Slavery Debate of 1831–32* (Baton Rouge, 1982). Racial proslavery thought is brilliantly illuminated in William Stanton, *The Leopard Spots: Scientific Attitudes Toward Race in America, 1815–59* (Chicago, 1960). Of Eugene D. Genovese's books on a non-racial proslavery thought, the best is *The Slaveholders' Dilemma: Freedom and Progress in Southern Conservative Thought, 1820–1860* (Columbia, S.C., 1992). The Nullification Crisis is discussed in William W. Freehling, *Prelude to Civil War: The Nullification Controversy in South Carolina, 1816–1836* (New York, 1966), and in Richard E. Ellis, *The Union at Risk: Jacksonian Democracy, States' Rights, and the Nullification Crisis* (New York, 1987). William J. Cooper, *The South and the Politics of Slavery, 1828–1856* (Baton Rouge, 1978), expertly underlines the importance of Southern loyalty politics. Bertram Wyatt-Brown, *Southern Honor: Ethics and Behavior in the Old South* (New York, 1982), illuminates honor as a source of loyalty politics. The constraints on discussion of slavery in the South are well discussed in Stanley M. Elkins, *Slavery: A Problem in American Institutional and Intellectual Life* (Chicago, 1959). The Gag Rule and Texas Annexation Crises are discussed and documented at length in

Freehling, *Road to Disunion*. On the fugitive slave law, see Stanley W. Campbell, *The Slave Catchers: Enforcement of the Fugitive Slave Law, 1850–1860* (Chapel Hill, 1968). On the Kansas-Nebraska Act, compare Robert W. Johannsen, *Stephen A. Douglas* (New York, 1973), with Roy F. Nichols, "The Kansas-Nebraska Act: A Century of Historiography," *Mississippi Valley Historical Review* 43 (1956): 187–212. The latest account of the Kansas aftermath is in Kenneth M. Stampp, *America in 1857: A Nation on the Brink* (New York, 1990). Don E. Fehrenbacher, *The Dred Scott Case: Its Significance in American Law and Politics* (New York, 1978), is a model monograph. Ronald T. Takaki, *A Pro-slavery Crusade: The Agitation to Reopen the African Slave Trade* (New York, 1971), and Robert E. May, *The Southern Dream of Caribbean Empire, 1854–1862* (Baton Rouge, La., 1973), are best on their respective subjects.

Pending the needed new synthesis of the late antebellum South's course to secession, the subject is best approached through local or state studies. Among the best are J. William Harris, *Plain Folk and Gentry in a Slave Society: White Labor and Black Slavery in Augusta's Hinterlands* (Middletown, Conn., 1986); J. Mills Thornton, *Politics and Power in a Slave Society: Alabama, 1800–1860* (Baton Rouge, 1978); Paul D. Escott, *Many Excellent People: Power and Privilege in North Carolina, 1850–1900* (Chapel Hill, 1985); Lacy K. Ford, Jr., *Origins of South Carolina Radicalism: The South Carolina Upcountry, 1800–1860* (New York, 1988); Michael P. Johnson, *Toward a Patriarchal Republic: The Secession of Georgia* (Baton Rouge, 1977); William L. Barney, *The Secessionist Impulse: Alabama and Mississippi in 1860* (Princeton, 1974); and Daniel W. Crofts, *Reluctant Confederates: Upper South Unionists in the Secession Crisis* (Chapel Hill, 1989). The best Southern debate on secession can be followed in *Secession Debated: Georgia's Showdown in 1860,* William W. Freehling and Craig Simpson, eds. (New York, 1993).

The shrewdest analyses of the Northern side of the coming of the Civil War emphasize Northerners' distinction between white men's freedom from the Slavepower and black men's freedom from slavery. Pride of place belongs to Michael Holt, *The Political Crisis of the 1850s* (New York, 1978); Larry Gara, "Slavery and the Slave Power: A Crucial Distinction," *Civil War History* 15 (1969): 5–18; and William E. Gienapp, "The Republican Party and the Slave Power," in *New Perspectives on Race and Slavery in America,* Robert H. Abzug and Stephen E. Maizlish, eds. (Lexington, Ky., 1986), 51–78. For countervailing emphases on antislavery and on economics, see Richard H. Sewell, *Ballots for Freedom: Antislavery Politics in the United States, 1837–1860* (New York, 1976), and Robert W. Fogel, *Without Consent or Contract: The Rise and Fall of American Slavery* (New York, 1989). The best synthesis of the Republicans' worldview, even if it stresses a little heavily the economic side of the mentality, is Eric Foner, *Free Soil, Free Labor, Free Men: The Ideology of the Republican Party Before the Civil War*

(New York, 1970). The best synthesis of the whole period, North and South, remains David M. Potter, *The Impending Crisis, 1848–1861* (New York, 1976).

Chapter Six. *"Freedom and Law Must Die Ere They Sever: The North and the Coming of the Civil War,"* by Mark W. Summers

The rallying of the Union under arms has been done very nearly to death. Still unsurpassed for the transformation and ambivalence of Northern sentiments during the secession crisis is Kenneth M. Stampp, *And the War Came: The North and the Secession Crisis* (Baton Rouge, 1950). For the reaction of those enlisting, no two books can match those of Reid Mitchell, *Civil War Soldiers* (New York, 1988), and Bell Wiley, *The Life of Billy Yank: The Common Soldier of the Union* (Baton Rouge, 1952). The most impressive study of Northern society, cultural, economic, and ideological, is Philip Shaw Paludan's *"A People's Contest": The Union and Civil War, 1861–1865* (New York, 1988). Few state studies can match the latter, except that of John Niven, *Connecticut for the Union* (New Haven, 1965). For the rallying of Union men outside of the free states, one book affords a suggestive beginning for future research: Carl Degler's *The Other South: Southern Dissenters in the Nineteenth Century* (New York, 1974).

The war's impact on ideology matters just as much as ideology's impact on war sentiment. Here the best starting place would be with a rather small segment of the intellectual elite, handled with his usual ability by George Fredrickson in *The Inner Civil War: Northern Intellectuals and the Crisis of Disunion* (New York, 1965). For the larger issues of Union and nationalism from 1789 to 1861, the authoritative airing can be found in Paul Nagel's *One Nation Indivisible: The Union in American Thought, 1776–1861* (New York, 1964). How war affected legal thinking and jurisprudence, in both conservative and radical ways, is explored in magnificent depth in Harold Hyman, *A More Perfect Union* (New York, 1973).

As for the role that partisan politics played, the best place to begin is with Eric Foner, *Free Soil, Free Labor, Free Men: The Ideology of the Republican Party Before the Civil War* (New York, 1970), which evaluates Republican thought and the issue of the Slavepower conspiracy up to 1861. Until recently, the Democratic maneuvers and mindset were neglected. Now they have been ably covered for the Civil War years in Joel Silbey, *A Respectable Minority: The Democratic Party in the Civil War Era* (New York, 1977); Christopher Dell, *Lincoln and the War Democrats: The Grand Erosion of Conservative Tradition* (Rutherford, N.J., 1975); and Jean Baker, *Affairs of Party: The Political Culture of Northern Democrats in the Mid-Nineteenth Century* (Ithaca, 1983).

Contributors

David W. Blight, Associate Professor of History and Black Studies at Amherst College, is author of *Frederick Douglass' Civil War: Keeping Faith in Jubilee* (1989), and editor of *When This Cruel War Is Over: The Civil War Letters of Charles Harvey Brewster* (1992) and *Narrative of the Life of Frederick Douglass, an American Slave* (1993).

William W. Freehling, Singletary Professor of the Humanities at the University of Kentucky, won the Nevins Prize and the Bancroft Prize for *Prelude to Civil War* (1965), and the Owsley Prize for *The Road to Disunion*, vol. 1, *Secessionists at Bay, 1776–1854* (1990). His most recent book is *The Reintegration of American History: Slavery and the Civil War* (1994).

William E. Gienapp, Professor of History at Harvard University, won the Craven Award for *The Origins of the Republican Party, 1852–1865* (1987). He co-authored the textbook *Nation of Nations: A Narrative History of the American Republic* (1990).

Glenna Matthews most recently served as Visiting Associate Professor of History at the University of California, at Los Angeles and at Berkeley. Her books include *The Rise of Public Woman: Woman's Power and Woman's Place in the United States, 1630–1970* (1992). She is the co-author of *Running as a Woman: Gender and Power in American Politics* (1994).

Charles Royster, Boyd Professor of History at Louisiana State University, received the Parkman Prize for *A Revolutionary People at War: The Continental Army and American Character, 1775–1783* (1979). His most recent book, *The Destructive War: William Tecumseh Sherman, Stonewall Jackson, and the Americans* (1991), received the Bancroft Prize, the Sydnor Award, and the Lincoln Prize.

Mark Summers is Professor of History at the University of Kentucky. His books include *Railroads, Reconstruction and the Gospel of Prosperity* (1984), *The Plundering Generation* (1988), *The Era of Good Stealings* (1993), and *The Press Gang* (1994).

Gabor S. Boritt, Director of the Civil War Institute and Fluhrer Professor at Gettysburg College, is author of *Lincoln and the Economics of the American Dream* (1978, 1994). His most recent books include *Lincoln's Generals* (1994) and *War Comes Again: Comparative Vistas on the Civil War and World War II* (1995).

Printed in the United Kingdom
by Lightning Source UK Ltd.
135405UK00001B/6/P